D0064493

INTRODUCTION

This Snapshot guide, excerpted from my guidebook *Rick Steves' Eastern Europe*, introduces you a trio of grand Polish cities: historic Kraków, thriving Warsaw, and gorgeous Gdańsk. Covering the best of Poland, this book offers an enjoyable cross-section of this proud nation.

Poland's historical capital, Kraków, clusters around one of Europe's biggest and most inviting market squares. Explore Kraków's picture-perfect Old Town—filled with museums, restaurants, university life, and Old World charm—and head to the Kazimierz neighborhood to learn about Poland's Jewish story. Side-trip to the world's most powerful memorial to the victims of the Holocaust at Auschwitz-Birkenau concentration camp.

For a look at today's Poland, visit Warsaw—leveled in World War II, rebuilt soon after, and now rapidly gentrifying. Stroll through Warsaw's reconstructed Old Town, promenade along newly spiffed-up boulevards, gape up at the communist-style Palace of Culture and Science, and dip into engaging museums on WWII history, native son Fryderyk Chopin, Polish painters, and much more.

On the Baltic Coast, Gdańsk offers a vibrantly colorful main drag fronted by opulent old Hanseatic facades, plus inspiring tales from the toppling of communism at the shipyard where the Solidarity trade union was born. Nearby in Pomerania is a pair of medieval red-brick sights: the imposing Gothic headquarters of the Teutonic Knights, Malbork Castle; and the appealing, gingerbread-scented town of Toruń.

To help you have the best trip possible, I've included the following topics in this book:

- **Planning Your Time,** with advice on how to make the most of your limited time

- **Orientation,** including tourist information (abbreviated as TI), tips on public transportation, local tour options, and helpful hints
- **Sights** with ratings:
  - ▲▲▲—Don't miss
  - ▲▲—Try hard to see
  - ▲—Worthwhile if you can make it
  - No rating—Worth knowing about
- **Sleeping** and **Eating,** with good-value recommendations in every price range
- **Connections,** with tips on trains, buses, and boats

Practicalities, near the end of this book, has information on money, phoning, making hotel reservations, eating, transportation, and more, plus Polish survival phrases.

To travel smartly, read this little book in its entirety before you go. It's my hope that this guide will make your trip more meaningful and rewarding. Traveling like a temporary local, you'll get the absolute most out of every mile, minute, and dollar.

Szczęśliwej podróży—happy travels!

Rick Steves

POLAND

POLAND

Polska

Americans who think of Poland as run-down—full of rusting factories, smoggy cities, and gloomy natives—are speechless when they step into Kraków's vibrant main square, Gdańsk's colorful pedestrian drag, or Warsaw's lively Old Town. While parts of the country are still cleaning up the industrial mess left by the Soviets, Poland also has some breathtaking medieval cities that show off its kind-hearted people, dynamic history, and unique cultural fabric.

The Poles are a proud people—as moved by their spectacular failures as by their successes. Their quiet elegance has been tempered by generations of abuse by foreign powers. The Poles place a lot of importance on honor, and you'll find fewer scams and con artists here than in other Eastern European countries.

In a way, there are two Polands: lively, cosmopolitan urban centers, and countless tiny farm villages in the countryside. City-dwellers often talk about the "simple people" of Poland—those descended from generations of farmers, working the same plots for centuries and living an uncomplicated, agrarian lifestyle. This large contingent of salt-of-the-earth folks—who like things the way they are—is a major reason why Poland was so hesitant to join the European Union, and remains fiercely "Euroskeptic."

Poland is arguably Europe's most devoutly Catholic country. Catholicism has long defined these people, holding them together through times when they had little else. Squeezed between Protestant Germany (originally Prussia) and Eastern Orthodox Russia, Poland wasn't even a country for generations (1795-1918). Its Catholicism helped keep its spirit alive. In the last century, while "under communism" (as that age is referred to), Poles once again found their religion a source of strength as well as rebellion—they could express dissent against the athe-

istic regime by going to church. Some of Poland's best sights are churches, usually filled with locals praying silently. While these church interiors are worth a visit, be especially careful to show the proper respect (maintain silence, keep a low profile, and if you want to snap pictures, do so discreetly).

Visitors are sometimes surprised at how much of Poland's story is a Jewish story. Before World War II, 80 percent of Europe's Jews lived in Poland. Warsaw was the world's second-largest Jewish city (after New York) with 380,000 Jews (out of a total population of 1.2 million). Poland was a magnet for Jews because of its relatively welcoming policies. Still, Jews were forbidden from owning land; that's why they settled mostly in the cities. But the Holocaust (and a later Soviet policy of sending "troublemaking" Jews to Israel) decimated the Jewish population. This tragic chapter, combined with postwar border shifts and population movements, made Poland one of Europe's most ethnically homogeneous countries. Today, virtually everyone in the country is an ethnic Pole, and only a few thousand Polish Jews remain. (For simplicity, in this book I've used the term "Pole" to describe someone who's ethnically Polish as opposed to Jewish—though many Jews were "Polish" in that they were citizens of Poland.)

Poland has long been extremely pro-America. Of course, their big neighbors (Russia and Germany) have been their historic enemies. And when Hitler invaded in 1939, the Poles felt let down by their supposed European friends (France and Britain), who declared war on Germany but provided virtually no military support to the Polish resistance. America, meanwhile, has been regarded as the big ally from across the ocean—and the home of about 10 million Polish Americans. In 1989, when Poland finally

POLAND

Poland Almanac

Official Name: Rzeczpospolita Polska (Republic of Poland), or Polska for short.

Snapshot History: This thousand-year-old country has been dominated by foreigners for much of the last two centuries, finally achieving true independence (from the Soviet Union) in 1989.

Population: Nearly 38.5 million people, slightly more than California. About 97 percent are ethnic Poles who speak Polish (though English is also widely spoken). Three out of every four Poles are practicing Catholics. The population is younger than most European countries, with an average age of 39 (Germany's is 42).

Latitude and Longitude: 52°N and 20°E (similar latitude to Berlin, London, and Edmonton, Alberta).

Area: 122,000 square miles, the same as New Mexico (or Illinois and Iowa put together).

Geography: Because of its overall flatness, Poland has been a corridor for invading armies since its infancy. The Vistula River (650 miles) runs south-to-north up the middle of the country, passing through Kraków and Warsaw, and emptying into the Baltic Sea at Gdańsk. Poland's climate is generally cool and rainy—40,000 storks love it.

Biggest Cities: Warsaw (the capital, 1.7 million), Kraków (757,000), and Łódź (747,000).

Economy: The Gross Domestic Product is $815 billion, with a GDP per capita of $20,900. The 1990s saw an aggressive and successful transition from state-run socialism to privately owned capitalism. Still, Poland's traditional potato-and-pig-farming society is behind the times, with 16 percent of the country's workers producing less than 3 percent of its GDP. About one in ten Poles is unemployed, and nearly one in five lives in poverty. And yet, perhaps because its economy is so primitive, Poland fared especially well through the recent economic downturn.

Currency: 1 złoty (zł, or PLN) = 100 groszy (gr) = about 30 cents; 3 zł = about $1.

won its freedom, many Poles only half-joked that they should apply to become the 51st state of the US.

Over the last few years, Poland beefed up its infrastructure to prepare for the Euro Cup soccer championship, which it co-hosted with Ukraine in June of 2012. For Europeans, this is just one step down from hosting the Olympics. Cities hosting matches (Warsaw, Gdańsk, Poznań, and Wrocław), as well as the rest of the country, enjoyed a wave of new construction and refurbishment, leaving dingy old quarters refreshed and re-energized. Poland used

Real Estate: A typical one-bedroom apartment in Warsaw (250 square feet) rents for roughly $600 a month.

Government: Poland's mostly figurehead president selects the prime minister and cabinet, with legislators' approval. They govern along with a two-house legislature (Sejm and Senat) of 560 seats. Prime Minister Donald Tusk, leader of the centrist Civic Platform, was re-elected in 2011. President Bronisław Komorowski, also of the Civic Platform, won a five-year term following Lech Kaczyński's death in 2010. (For more on Polish politics, see page 14.)

Flag: The upper half is white, and the lower half is red—the traditional colors of Poland. Poetic Poles claim the white represents honor, and the red represents the enormous amounts of blood spilled by the Poles to honor their nation. The flag sometimes includes a coat of arms with a crowned eagle (representing Polish sovereignty). Under Poland's many oppressors (including the Soviets), the crown was removed from the emblem, and its talons were trimmed. On regaining its independence, Poland coronated its eagle once more.

The Average Pole: In spite of its tumultuous history, Poland is a relatively upbeat nation: 74 percent of all Poles report they are "quite happy." Half use the Internet, and the average Pole will live to about age 76. The average Polish woman gets married at age 24 and will have 1.3 children.

Not-so-Average Poles: Despite the many "Polack jokes" you've heard (and maybe repeated), you likely know of many famous Polish intellectuals—you just don't realize they're Polish. The "Dumb Polack" Hall of Fame includes Karol Wojtyła **(Pope John Paul II),** Mikołaj Kopernik **(Nicolas Copernicus),** composer **Fryderyk Chopin,** scientist **Marie Curie** (née Skłodowska), writer Teodor Józef Korzeniowski (better known as **Joseph Conrad,** author of *Heart of Darkness*), filmmaker **Roman Polański** (*Chinatown, The Pianist*), politician **Lech Wałęsa, Daniel Libeskind** (the master architect for redeveloping the 9/11 site in New York City)...and one of this book's co-authors.

the Euro Cup as an excuse to improve its rail system, creating a network of high-speed trains to more quickly and smoothly link together its major cities.

On my first visit to Poland, I had a poor impression of Poles, who seemed brusque and often elbowed ahead of me in line. I've since learned that all it takes is a smile and a cheerful greeting—preferably in Polish—to break through the thick skin that helped these kind people survive the difficult communist times. With a friendly hello *(Dzień dobry!),* you'll turn any grouch into an ally. It may help to know that, because of the distinct cadence of Polish, Poles speaking English sometimes sound more impatient, gruff, or irritated than they actually are. Part of the Poles' charm is that they're not as slick and self-assured as many Europeans: They're kind, soft-spoken, and quite shy. On a recent train trip in Poland, I offered my Polish seatmate a snack—and spent the rest of trip enjoying a delightful conversation with a new friend.

Helpful Hints

Restroom Signage: To confuse tourists, the Poles have devised a secret way of marking their WCs. You'll see doors marked with *męska* (men) and *damska* (women)—but even more often, you'll simply see a triangle (for men) or a circle (for women). A sign with a triangle, a circle, and an arrow is directing you to the closest WCs.

Pay to Pee: Many Polish bathrooms charge a small fee. You may even be charged at a restaurant where you're paying to dine. Don't let this minor inconvenience interfere with your enjoyment of your trip. Yes, it's an annoying hassle—but at least it's cheap (usually around 1 zł).

Train Station Lingo: "PKP" is the abbreviation for Polish National Railways ("PKS" is for buses). In larger towns with several train stations, you'll normally use the one called Główny (meaning "Main"—except in Warsaw, where it's Centralna). *Dworzec główny* means "main train station." Underneath most larger stations are mazes of walkways—lined with market stalls—that lead to platforms *(peron)* and exits *(wyjście)*. Most stations have several platforms, each of which has two tracks *(tor)*. Departures are generally listed by the *peron*, so keep your eye on both tracks for your train. Arrivals are *przyjazdy*, and departures are *odjazdy*. Left-luggage counters or lockers are marked *przechowalnia bagażu*. *Kasy* are ticket windows. These can be marked (sometimes only in Polish) for specific needs—domestic tickets, international tickets, and so on; ask fellow travelers to be sure you select the right line. Ticket and "information" windows are more often than not staffed by monolingual grouches. Smile sweetly, write down your destination and time, and hang onto your patience. The line you choose will invariably be the slowest one—leave plenty of time to buy your ticket before your train departs (or, if you're running out of time, buy it on board for 10 zł extra). For longer and/or express journeys, you'll likely be given two separate tickets: one for the trip itself, and the other for your seat assignment. On arriving at a station, to get into town, follow signs for *wyjście do centrum* or *wyjście do miasta*. Ongoing construction to improve Poland's rail lines may make some of your train journeys take much longer than normal, and delays are common.

Museum Tips: Virtually every museum in Poland is closed

Top 10 Dates That Changed Poland

A.D. 966—The Polish king, Mieszko I, is baptized a Christian, symbolically uniting the Polish people and founding the nation.

1385—The Polish queen (called a "king" by sexist aristocrats of the time) marries a Lithuanian duke, starting the two-century reign of the Jagiełło family.

1410—Poland defeats the Teutonic Knights at the Battle of Grunwald, part of a Golden Age of territorial expansion and cultural achievement.

1572—The last Jagiellonian king dies, soon replaced by bickering nobles and foreign kings. Poland declines.

1795—In the last of three Partitions, the country is divvied up by its more-powerful neighbors: Russia, Prussia, and Austria.

1918—Following World War I, Poland gets back its land and sovereignty.

1939—The Free City of Gdańsk (then called Danzig) is invaded by Nazi Germany, starting World War II. At war's end, the country is "liberated" (i.e., occupied) by the Soviet Union.

1980—Lech Wałęsa leads a successful strike, demanding more freedom from the communist regime.

1989—Poland gains independence under its first president—Lech Wałęsa. Fifteen years later, Poland joins the European Union.

2010—President Lech Kaczyński and 95 other high-level government officials are killed in a plane crash in Russia.

on Monday. The ticket window for any museum typically closes a half-hour before the museum's closing time, and this last-entry deadline is strictly enforced. Poland's museums are notorious for tweaking their opening times—try to confirm hours locally if you have your heart set on a particular place.

Polish Artists: Though Poland has produced world-renowned scientists, musicians, and writers, the country isn't known for its artists. Polish museums greet foreign visitors with fine artwork by unfamiliar names. If you're planning to visit any museums in Poland, two artists in particular are worth remembering: **Jan Matejko,** a 19th-century positivist who painted grand historical epics; and one of his students, **Stanisław Wyspiański,** a painter and playwright who led the charge of the Młoda Polska movement—the Polish answer to Art Nouveau—in the early 1900s.

Telephones: Remember these Polish prefixes: 800 is toll-free, and 70 is expensive (like phone sex). Many Poles use mobile phones (which come with the prefix 50, 51, 53, 60, 66, 69, 72, 78, 79, or 88).

Polish History

Poland is flat. Take a look at a topographical map of Europe, and you'll immediately appreciate the Poles' historical dilemma:

The path of least resistance from northern Europe to Russia leads right through Poland. Over the years, many invaders—from Genghis Khan to Napoleon to Hitler—have taken advantage of Poland's strategic location. The country is nicknamed "God's playground" for the many wars that have rumbled through its territory. Poland has been invaded by Soviets, Nazis, French, Austrians, Russians, Prussians, Swedes, Teutonic Knights, Tatars, Bohemians, Magyars—and, about 1,300 years ago, Poles.

Medieval Greatness

The first Poles were a tribe called the Polonians ("people of the plains"), a Slavic band that showed up in these parts in the eighth century. In 966, Mieszko I, Duke of the Polonian tribe, adopted Christianity and founded the Piast dynasty (which would last for more than 400 years). Centuries before Germany, Italy, or Spain first united, Poland was born.

Poland struggled against two different invaders in the 13th century: the Tatars (Mongols who ravaged the south) and the Teutonic Knights (Germans who conquered the north). But despite these challenges, Poland persevered. The last king of the Piast dynasty was also the greatest: Kazimierz the Great, who famously "found a Poland made of wood and left one made of brick and stone"—bringing Poland (and its capital, Kraków) to international prominence. The progressive Kazimierz also invited Europe's much-persecuted Jews to settle here, establishing Poland as a haven for the Jewish people—which it would remain until the Nazis arrived.

Kazimierz the Great died at the end of the 14th century without a male heir. His grand-niece, Princess Jadwiga, became "king" (the Poles weren't ready for a "queen") and married Lithuanian Prince Władysław Jagiełło, uniting their countries against a common enemy, the Teutonic Knights. Their marriage marked the beginning of the Jagiellonian dynasty and set the stage for Poland's Golden Age. During this time, the Polish nobility began to acquire more political might, Italy's Renaissance (and its architectural styles) became popular, and the Toruń-born astronomer Nicholas Copernicus shook up the scientific world with his bold new heliocentric theory. Up on the Baltic coast, the port city of

Gdańsk took advantage of its Hanseatic League trading partnership to become one of Europe's most prosperous cities.

Foreign Kings and Partitions

When the Jagiellonians died out in 1572, political power shifted to the nobility. Poland became a republic of nobles governed by its wealthiest 10 percent—the *szlachta*, who elected a series of foreign kings. In the 16th and 17th centuries—with its territory spanning from the Baltic Sea to the Black Sea—the Polish-Lithuanian Commonwealth was the largest state in Europe.

But over time, many of the elected kings made poor diplomatic decisions and squandered the country's resources. To make matters worse, the nobles' parliament (Sejm) introduced the concept of *liberum veto* (literally "I freely forbid"), whereby any measure could be vetoed by a single member of parliament. This policy—which effectively demanded unanimous approval for any law to be passed—paralyzed the Sejm's waning power. Sensing the Commonwealth's weakness, in the mid-17th century forces from Sweden rampaged through Polish and Lithuanian lands—devastating the landscape in the so-called "Swedish Deluge." While Poland eventually reclaimed its territory, a third of its population was dead. The Commonwealth continued to import self-serving foreign kings, including Saxony's Augustus the Strong and his son, who drained Polish wealth to finance vanity projects in their hometown of Dresden.

By the late 18th century, Poland was floundering—and surrounded by three land-hungry empires (Russia, Prussia, and Austria). The Poles were unaware that these neighbors had entered into an agreement now dubbed the "Alliance of the Three Black Eagles" (since all three of those countries, coincidentally, used that bird as their symbol); they began to circle Poland's white eagle like vultures. Stanisław August Poniatowski, elected king with Russian support in 1764, would prove to be Poland's last.

Over the course of less than 25 years, Russia, Prussia, and Austria divided Poland's territory among themselves in a series of three Partitions. In 1772 and again in 1790, Poland was forced into ceding large chunks of its territory to its neighbors. Desperate to reform their government, Poles enacted Europe's first democratic constitution (and the world's second, after the US Constitution) on May 3, 1791—still celebrated as a national holiday. This visionary document protected the peasants, dispensed with both *liberum veto* and the election of the king, and set up something resembling a modern nation. But the constitution alarmed Poland's neighbors, who swept in soon after with the third and final Partition in 1795. "Poland" disappeared from Europe's maps, not to return until 1918.

Even though Poland was gone, the Poles wouldn't go quietly. As the Partitions were taking place, Polish soldier Tadeusz Kościuszko (also a hero of the American Revolution) returned home to lead an unsuccessful military resistance against the Russians in 1794.

Napoleon offered a brief glimmer of hope to the Poles in the early 19th century, when he marched eastward through Europe and set up the semi-independent "Duchy of Warsaw" in Polish lands. But that fleeting taste of freedom lasted only eight years; with Napoleon's defeat, Polish hopes were dashed. The Congress of Vienna, which redistributed Polish territory to Prussia, Russia, and Austria, is sometimes called (by Poles) the "Fourth Partition." In a classic case of "my enemy's enemy is my friend," the Poles still have great affection for Napoleon for how fiercely he fought against their mutual foes.

The Napoleonic connection also established France as a safe haven for refugee Poles. After another failed uprising against Russia in 1830, many of Poland's top artists and writers fled to Paris—including pianist Fryderyk Chopin and Romantic poet Adam Mickiewicz (whose statue adorns Kraków's main square and Warsaw's Royal Way). These Polish artists tried to preserve the nation's spirit with music and words; those who remained in Poland continued to fight with swords and fists. By the end of the 19th century, the image of the Pole as a tireless, idealistic insurgent emerged. During this time, some Romantics—with typically melodramatic flair—dubbed Poland "the Christ of nations" for the way it was misunderstood and persecuted by the world, despite its inherent nobility.

As the map of Europe was redrawn following World War I, Poland emerged as a reborn nation, under the war hero-turned-head of state, Marshal Józef Piłsudski. The newly reformed "Second Polish Republic," which patched together the bits and pieces of territory that had been under foreign rule for decades, enjoyed a diverse ethnic mix—including Germans, Russians, Ukrainians, Lithuanians, and an enormous Jewish minority. A third of Poland spoke no Polish. The historic Baltic port city of Gdańsk—which was bicultural (German and Polish)—had been given a special "free city" status to avoid dealing with the prickly issue of whether to assign it to Germany or Poland. But the peace was not to last.

World War II

On September 1, 1939, Adolf Hitler began World War II by attacking Gdańsk to bring it into the German fold. Before the month was out, Hitler's forces had overrun Poland, and the Soviets had taken over a swath of eastern Poland (today still part of Ukraine,

Belarus, and Lithuania).

The Nazis considered the Poles *slawische Untermenschen,* "Slavic sub-humans" who were useful only for manual labor. Remember that Poland was also home to a huge population of another group the Nazis hated, Jews. Nazi Germany annexed Polish regions that it claimed historic ties to, while the rest (including "Warschau" and "Krakau") became a puppet state ruled by the *Generalgouvernement* and Hitler's handpicked governor, Hans Frank. The Nazis considered this area *Lebensraum*—"living space" that wasn't nice enough to actually incorporate into Germany, but served perfectly as extra territory for building things that Germans didn't want in their backyards...such as Auschwitz-Birkenau, the notorious death camp that functioned like a factory for the mass-production of murder.

The Poles anxiously awaited the promised military aid of France and Britain; when help failed to arrive, they took matters into their own hands, forming a ragtag "Polish Home Army" and staging incredibly courageous but lopsided battles against their powerful German overlords (such as the Warsaw Uprising). With six million deaths over six years—including both Polish Jews and ethnic Poles—Poland suffered the worst per-capita WWII losses of any nation. By the war's end, one out of every five Polish citizens was dead—and 90 percent of those killed were civilians.

Throughout the spring of 1945, as the Nazis retreated from their failed invasion of the Soviet Union, the Red Army gradually "liberated" Poland from Nazi oppression, guaranteeing it another four decades of oppression under another regime. At the war's end, the victorious Allies shifted Poland's borders significantly westward—folding historically German areas into Polish territory, and appropriating previously Polish areas for the USSR. This prompted a massive movement of populations—which today we'd decry as "ethnic cleansing"—as Germans were forcibly removed from western Poland, and Poles from newly "Soviet" territory were transplanted to Poland proper. Entire cities were repopulated (such as the formerly German metropolis of Breslau, which was suddenly renamed Wrocław and filled with refugee Poles from Lwów—now Lviv, in Ukraine). After millions died in the war, millions more were displaced from their ancestral homes. When the dust settled, Poland was in rubble...but almost exclusively populated by Poles.

Saddle on a Cow: Poland Under Communism

Like other Soviet satellites, Poland suffered under the communists. A postwar intimidation regime was designed to frighten people "on board" and coincided with government seizure of private property, rationing, and food shortages. The country enjoyed

POLAND

The Heritage of Communism

While Poland has been free, democratic, and capitalist since 1989, some adults carry lots of psychological baggage from living under communism. Although the young generally embrace the fast new affluence with enthusiasm, many older people tend to be nostalgic about that slower-paced time that came with more security. And even young professionals, with so much energy and hope now, don't condemn everything about that stretch of history. A friend who was 13 in 1989 recalled those days this way:

"My childhood is filled with happy memories. Under communism, life was family-oriented. Careers didn't matter. There was no way to get rich, no reason to rush, so we had time. People always had time.

"But there were also shortages—many things were 'in deficit.' Sometimes my uncle would bring us several toilet paper rolls, held together with a string—absolutely the best gift anyone could give. I remember my mother and father had to 'organize' for special events...somehow find a good sausage and some Coca-Cola.

"Boys in my neighborhood collected pop cans. Since drinks were very limited in Poland, cans from other countries represented a world of opportunities beyond our borders. Parents could buy their children these cans on the black market, and the few families who were allowed to travel returned home with a treasure trove of cans. One boy up the street from me went to Italy, and proudly brought home a Pepsi can. All of the boys in the neighborhood wanted to see it—it was a huge status symbol. But a month later, communism ended, you could buy whatever you wanted, and everyone's can collections were worthless.

"We had real chocolate only for Christmas. The rest of the year, for treats we got something called 'chocolate-like product,' which was sweet, dark, and smelled vaguely of chocolate. And we had oranges from Cuba for Christmas, too. Everybody was excited when the newspapers announced, 'The boat with the oranges from Cuba is just five days from Poland.' We waited with excitement all year for chocolate and those oranges. The smell of Christmas was so special. Now we have that smell every day. Still, my happiest Christmases were under communism."

a relatively open society under Premier Władysław Gomułka in the 1960s, but the impractical, centrally planned economy began to unravel in the 1970s. Stores were marked by long lines stretching around the block. Poles were issued ration coupons for food staples, and cashiers clipped off a corner when a purchase was made... assuming, of course, the item was in stock. It often wasn't.

The little absurdities of communist life—which today seem almost comical—made every day a struggle. For years, every elderly woman in Poland had hair the same strange magenta color. There was only one color of dye available, so if you had dyed hair, the choice was simple: Let your hair grow out (and look clownishly half red and half white), or line up and go red.

During these difficult times, the Poles often rose up—staging major protests in 1956, 1968, 1970, and 1976. Stalin famously noted that introducing communism to the Poles was like putting a saddle on a cow.

When an anti-communist Polish cardinal named Karol Wojtyła was elected Pope in 1978, then visited his homeland in 1979, it was a sign to his countrymen that change was in the air. In 1980, Lech Wałęsa, an electrician at the shipyards in Gdańsk, became the leader of the Solidarity movement, the first workers' union in communist Eastern Europe. After an initial 18-day strike at the Gdańsk shipyards, the communist regime gave in, legalizing Solidarity.

But the union grew too powerful, and the communists felt their control slipping away. On Sunday, December 13, 1981, Poland's head of state, General Wojciech Jaruzelski, declared martial law in order to "forestall Soviet intervention." (Whether the Soviets actually would have intervened remains a hotly debated issue.) Tanks ominously rolled through the streets of Poland on that snowy December morning, and the Poles were terrified.

Martial law lasted until 1983. Each Pole has his or her own chilling memories of this frightening time. During riots, the people would flock into churches—the only place they could be safe from the ZOMO (riot police). But Solidarity struggled on, going underground and becoming a united movement of all demographics, 10 million members strong (more than a quarter of the population).

In July of 1989, the ruling Communist Party agreed to hold open elections (reserving 65 percent of representatives for themselves). Their goal was to appease Solidarity, but the plan backfired: Communists didn't win a single contested seat. These elections helped spark the chain reaction across Eastern Europe that eventually tore down the Iron Curtain. Lech Wałęsa became Poland's first post-communist president.

Poland in the 21st Century

When 10 new countries joined the European Union in May 2004, Poland was the most ambivalent of the bunch. After centuries of being under other empires' authority, the Poles were hardly eager to relinquish some of their hard-fought autonomy to Brussels. Many Poles thought that EU membership would make things worse (higher prices, a loss of traditional lifestyles) before they got better. But most people agreed that their country had to join to survive in today's Europe. Today most Poles begrudgingly acknowledge that the benefits of EU membership have outweighed the drawbacks.

The most obvious initial impact of EU membership was the tremendous migration of young Poles seeking work in other EU countries (mostly Britain, Ireland, and Sweden, which waived visa requirements for Eastern European workers earlier than other EU nations). Many of them found employment at hotels and restaurants. Visitors to London and Dublin are still likely to notice a surprising language barrier at the front desks of hotels, and Polish-language expat newspapers have joined British gossip rags on newsstands. Those who remained in Poland were concerned about the "brain drain" of bright young people flocking out of their country. But with the recent global economic crisis, quite a few Polish expats have returned home.

Poland is by far the most populous of the recent EU members, with nearly 39 million people (about the same as Spain, or about half the size of Germany). This makes Poland the sixth-largest of the 27 EU member states—giving it serious political clout, which it has already asserted...sometimes to the dismay of the EU's more established powers.

On the American political spectrum, Poland may be the most "conservative" country in Europe. Like a nation of Newt Gingriches, Poles are phobic when it comes to "big government"—likely because they've been subjugated and manipulated by so many foreign oppressors over the centuries. For most of the 2000s, the country's right wing was represented by a pair of twin brothers, Lech and Jarosław Kaczyński. Their conservative Law and Justice Party is pro-tax cuts, fiercely Euroskeptic (anti-EU), and very Catholic. In the 2005 presidential election, Lech Kaczyński emerged as the victor; several months later, he took the controversial step of appointing his identical twin brother Jarosław as Poland's prime minister. The Kaczyński brothers were child actors who appeared in several popular movies together—their biggest hit was titled *Those Two Who Would Steal the Moon*. As teenagers, they would switch identities and take tests for each other.

The political pendulum swung back toward the center in October of 2007, when the Kaczyński brothers' main politi-

---

Polish Jokes

Through the dreary communist times, the Poles managed to keep their sense of humor. A popular target of jokes was the riot police, called the ZOMO. Here are just a few of the things Poles said about these unpopular cops:

- It's better to have a sister who's a whore than a brother in the ZOMO.
- ZOMO police are hired based on the 90-90 principle: They have to weigh at least 90 kilograms (200 pounds), and their I.Q. must be less than 90.
- ZOMO are dispatched in teams of three: one who can read, one who can write, and a third to protect those other two smart guys.
- A ZOMO policeman was sitting on the curb, crying. Someone came up to him and asked what was wrong. "I lost my dog!" he said. "No matter," the person replied. "He's a smart police dog. I'm sure he can find his way back to the station." "Yes," the ZOMO said. "But without him, I can't!"

The communists gave their people no options at elections: If you voted, you voted for the regime. Poles liked to joke that in some ways, this made communists like God—who created Eve, then said to Adam, "Now choose a wife." It was said that communists could run a pig as a candidate, and it would still win; a popular symbol of dissent became a pig painted with the words, "Vote Red."

There were even jokes about jokes. Under communism, Poles noted that there was a government-sponsored prize for the funniest political joke: 15 years in prison.

---

cal rival, the pro-EU Donald Tusk, led his Civic Platform Party to victory in the parliamentary elections. The name Kaczyński loosely means "duck"—so the Poles quipped that they were led by "Donald and the Ducks."

Tragically, the levity wasn't to last. On April 10, 2010, a plane carrying President Lech Kaczyński crashed in a thick fog near the city of Smolensk, Russia. All 96 people on board—including top government, military, and business officials, high-ranking clergy, and others—were killed, plunging the nation into a period of stunned mourning. Poles wondered why, yet again, an unprecedented tragedy had befallen their nation. (Ironically, the group's trip was intended to put a painful chapter of Poland's history to rest: a commemoration of the Polish officers and enlisted men killed in the Soviet massacre at Katyń.)

The ensuing presidential election pitted the deceased president's brother, Jarosław Kaczyński, against Donald Tusk's Civic

Bar Mleczny (Milk Bar)

When you see a "bar" in Poland, it doesn't mean alcohol—it means cheap grub. Eating at a *bar mleczny* (bar MLECH-neh) is an essential Polish sightsee-ing experience. These cafete-rias, which you'll see all over the country, are an incredibly cheap way to get a good meal...and, with the right attitude, a fun cul-tural experience.

In the communist era, the government subsidized the food at milk bars, allowing lowly workers to enjoy a meal out. The tradition continues, and today, Poland still foots the bill for most of your milk-bar meal. Prices are astoundingly low—my bill for a big meal usually comes to about $4-5—and, while communist-era fare was gross, today's milk-bar cuisine is usually quite tasty.

Milk bars usually offer many of the traditional tastes listed in the "Polish Food" section. Common items are soups (like *żurek* and *barszcz*), a variety of cabbage-based salads, *kotlet* (fried pork chops), pierogi (like ravioli, with various fillings), and *naleśniki* (pancakes). You'll see glasses of juice and (of course) milk, but most milk bars also stock bottles of water and Coke.

There are two types of milk bars: updated, modern cafeterias that cater to tourists (English menus), add some modern twists to their traditional fare, and charge about 50 percent more; and time-machine dives that haven't changed for decades. At truly traditional milk bars, the service is aimed at locals—which means no English menu and a confusing ordering system.

Every milk bar is a little different, but here's the general procedure: Head to the counter, wait to be acknowledged, and point to what you want. Handy vocabulary: *to* (sounds like "toe") means "this"; *i* (pronounced "ee") means "and."

If the milk-bar lady asks you any questions, you have three options: nod stupidly until she just gives you something; repeat one of the things she just said (assuming she's asked you to choose between two options, like meat or cheese in your pierogi); or hope that a kindly English-speaking Pole in line will leap to your rescue. If nothing else, ordering at a milk bar is an adventure in gestures. Smiling seems to slightly extend the patience of milk-bar staffers.

Once your tray is all loaded up, pay the cashier, do a dou-ble-take when you realize how cheap your bill is, then find a table. After the meal, it's generally polite, if not expected, to bus your own dishes to the little window (watch locals and imitate).

Platform compatriot, Bronisław Komorowski. Komorowski's victory—and Donald Tusk's re-election as prime minister in 2011 (the first re-election of a PM since the end of communism)—have given the centrist Civic Platform the reins of Poland for the foreseeable future.

Meanwhile, Poland's economy has just kept chugging along, even as the rest of Europe and much of the world were bogged down by an economic downturn. More than a quarter of Poland's trade is with neighboring Germany—another of Europe's healthiest economies—and Poland was the only European Union country that didn't have a recession in 2009. When I asked some Polish friends about this, they replied—cynically, but not without a hint of truth—"Well, when you have a backwards, agrarian economy, you're pretty resistant to international market fluctuations." Poland is a big, self-sustaining, insular economy. In recent years, Poland's relatively weak currency ("cheaper" than the euro, yet also shielded from euro volatility) and robust economy are luring foreign investment, paradoxically threatening the very autonomy that has buffered it so far. As Europe struggles to deal with its debt crisis and flagging economic might, it will be interesting to see the role that Poland plays.

Polish Food

Polish food is hearty and tasty. Since Poland is north of the Carpathian Mountains, its weather tends to be chilly, which lim-

its the kinds of fruits and vegetables that flourish here. Like other northern European countries (such as Russia or Scandinavia), dominant staples include potatoes, dill, berries, beets, and rye. Much of what you might think of as "Jewish cuisine" turns up on Polish menus (gefilte fish, potato pancakes, chicken soup, and so forth)—which makes sense, given that Poles and Jews lived in the same area for centuries under the same climatic and culinary influences.

Polish soups are a highlight. The most typical are *żurek* and *barszcz*. *Żurek* (often translated as "sour soup" on menus) is a light-colored soup made from a sourdough base, usually containing a hard-boiled egg and pieces of *kiełbasa* (sausage). *Barszcz*, better known to Americans as borscht, is a savory beet soup that you'll see in several varieties: *Barszcz czerwony* (red borscht) is a broth with a deep red color, sometimes containing dumplings or a hard-boiled egg. *Barszcz ukraiński* (Ukrainian borscht) is similar, but has vegetables mixed in (usually cabbage, beans, and carrots). In summer, try the "Polish gazpacho"—*chłodnik,* a cream soup with beets, onions, and radishes that's served cold. I never met a Polish soup I didn't like...until I was introduced to *flaki* (sometimes *flaczki*)—tripe soup.

Another familiar Polish dish is pierogi. These ravioli-like dumplings come with various fillings. The most traditional are minced meat, sauerkraut, mushroom, cheese, and blueberry; many restaurants also experiment with more exotic fillings. Pierogi are often served with specks of fatty bacon to add flavor. Pierogi are a budget traveler's dream: Restaurants serving them are everywhere, and they're generally cheap, tasty, and very filling.

Bigos is a rich and delicious sauerkraut stew cooked with meat, mushrooms, and whatever's in the pantry. *Gołąbki* is a dish of cabbage leaves stuffed with minced meat and rice in a tomato or mushroom sauce. *Kotlet schabowy* (fried pork chop)—once painfully scarce in communist Poland—remains a local favorite to this day. *Kaczka* (duck) is popular, as is fish: Look for *pstrąg* (trout), *karp* (carp, beware of bones), and *węgorz* (eel). Poles eat lots of potatoes, which are served with nearly every meal.

For a snack on the go, Poles love *zapiekanki* (singular *zapiekanek*): a toasted baguette with melted cheese, garlic, ketchup, rubbery mushrooms from a can, and sometimes onions or other toppings. It's like the poor cousin of a French-bread pizza, and a favorite late-night snack for bar-hopping young people. The bagel-like rings you'll see sold on the street, *obwarzanki* (singular *obwarzanek*), are also cheap, and usually fresh and tasty.

Poland has good pastries. A *piekarnia* is a bakery specializing in breads. But if you really want something special, look for a *cukiernia* (pastry shop). The classic Polish treat is *pączki,* glazed jelly doughnuts. They can have different fillings, but most typical is a wild-rose jam. *Szarlotka* is apple cake—sometimes made with chunks of apples (especially in season), sometimes with apple filling. *Sernik* is cheesecake, and *makowiec* is poppy-seed cake. *Winebreda* is an especially gooey Danish. *Babeczka* is like a cupcake filled with pudding. You may see *jabłko w cieście*—slices of apple cooked in dough, then glazed. *Napoleonka* is a French-style treat with layers of crispy wafers and custard.

Lody (ice cream) is popular. The tall, skinny cones of soft-serve ice cream are called *świderki,* sometimes translated as "American ice cream." The most beloved traditional candy is *ptasie mleczko* (birds' milk), which is like a semi-sour marshmallow covered with chocolate. E. Wedel is the country's top brand of chocolate, with outlets in all the big cities.

Thirsty? *Woda* is water, *woda mineralna* is bottled water (*gazowana* is with gas/carbonation, *niegazowana* is without), *kawa* is coffee, *herbata* is tea, *sok* is juice, and *mleko* is milk. Żywiec, Okocim, and Lech are the best-known brands of *piwo* (beer).

Wódka (vodka) is a Polish staple—the word means, roughly, "precious little water." Żubrówka, the most famous brand of vodka, comes with a blade of grass from the bison reserves in eastern Poland (look for the bottle with the bison). The bison "flavor" the grass...then the grass flavors the vodka. Poles often mix Żubrówka with apple juice, and call this cocktail *szarlotka* ("apple cake"); it also goes by the name *tatanka* (a Native American word for "bison"). For "Cheers!" say, "*Na zdrowie!*" (nah ZDROH-vyeh).

Unusual drinks to try if you have the chance are *kwas* (a cold, fizzy, Ukrainian-style non-alcoholic beverage made from day-old rye bread) and *kompot* (a hot drink made from stewed berries). Poles are unusually fond of carrot juice (often cut with fruit juice); Kubuś is the most popular brand.

"Bon appétit" *is* "*Smacznego*" (smatch-NEH-goh). To pay, ask for the *rachunek* (rah-KHOO-nehk).

Polish Language

Polish is closely related to its neighboring Slavic languages (Slovak and Czech), with the biggest difference being that Polish has lots of fricatives (hissing sounds—"sh" and "ch"—often in close proximity). Consider the opening line of Poland's most famous tongue-twisting nursery rhyme: *W Szczebrzeszynie chrząszcz brzmi w trzcinie* ("In Szczebrzeszyn, a beetle is heard in the reeds"—pronounced vuh shih-chehb-zheh-shee-nyeh khzhahshch bzh-mee vuh tzhuh-cheen-yeh...or something like that).

Polish intimidates Americans with long, difficult-to-pronounce words. But if you take your time and sound things out, you'll quickly develop an ear for it. One rule of thumb to help you out: The stress is always on the next-to-last syllable.

Polish has some letters that don't appear in English, and some letters and combinations are pronounced differently than in English:

ć, ci, and **cz** all sound like "ch" as in "church"
ś, si, and **sz** all sound like "sh" as in "short"
ż, ź, zi, and **rz** all sound like "zh" as in "leisure"
dż and **dź** both sound like the "dj" sound in "jeans"
ń and **ni** sound like "ny" as in "canyon"
ę and **ą** are pronounced nasally, as in French: "en" and "an"
c sounds like "ts" as in "cats"
ch sounds like "kh" as in the Scottish "loch"
j sounds like "y" as in "yellow"
w sounds like "v" as in "Victor"
ł sounds like "w" as in "with"

So to Poles, "Lech Wałęsa" isn't pronounced "lehk wah-LEH-sah," as Americans tend to say—but "lehkh vah-WEHN-sah."

The Polish people you meet will be impressed and flattered if you take the time to learn a little of their language.

As you're tracking down addresses, these words will help: *miasto* (mee-AH-stoh, town), *plac* (plahts, square), *rynek* (REE-nehk, big market square), *ulica* (OO-leet-sah, road), *aleja* (ah-LAY-yah, avenue), and *most* (mohst, bridge).

KRAKÓW

Kraków is easily Poland's best destination: a beautiful, old-fashioned city buzzing with history, enjoyable sights, tourists, and college students. Even though the country's capital moved from here to Warsaw 400 years ago, Kraków remains Poland's cultural and intellectual center. Of all of the Eastern European cities laying claim to the boast "the next Prague," Kraków is for real.

Kraków grew wealthy from trade in the late 10th and early 11th centuries. Traders who passed through were required to stop here for a few days and sell their wares at a reduced cost. Local merchants turned around and sold those goods with big price hikes...and Kraków thrived. In 1038, it became Poland's capital.

Tatars invaded in 1241, leaving the city in ruins. Krakovians took this opportunity to rebuild their streets in a near-perfect grid, a striking contrast to the narrow, mazelike lanes of most medieval towns. The destruction also paved the way for the spectacular Main Market Square—still Kraków's best attraction.

King Kazimierz the Great sparked Kraków's Golden Age in the 14th century. In 1364, he established the university that still defines the city (and counts Copernicus and Pope John Paul II among its alumni).

But Kraków's power waned as Poland's political center shifted to Warsaw. In 1596, the capital officially moved north. At the end of the 18th century, three neighboring powers—Russia, Prussia, and Austria—partitioned Poland, annexing all of its territory and dividing it among themselves. Warsaw ended up as a satellite of oppressive Moscow, and Kraków became a poor provincial backwater of Vienna. After Napoleon briefly reshuffled the map of

Kraków Essentials

English	Polish	Pronounced
Main Train Station	*Kraków Główny*	KROCK-oof GWOHV-nee
Old Town	*Stare Miasto*	STAH-reh mee-AH-stoh
Main Market Square	*Rynek Główny*	REE-nehk GWOHV-nee
Cloth Hall	*Sukiennice*	soo-kyeh-NEET-seh
Floriańska Street	*Ulica Floriańska*	OOH-leet-suh floh-ree-AHN-skah
Park around the Old Town	*Planty*	PLAHN-tee
Castle Hill	*Wawel*	VAH-vehl
Jewish Quarter	*Kazimierz*	kah-ZHEE-mehzh
Vistula River	*Wisła*	VEES-wah
Salt Mine	*Wieliczka*	vee-LEECH-kah
Planned Communist Suburb	*Nowa Huta*	NOH-vah HOO-tah

Europe in the early 19th century, Kraków was granted the status of a semi-independent city-state for about 30 years. The feisty Free City of Kraków, a tiny sliver wedged between three of Europe's mightiest empires, enjoyed an economic boom that saw the creation of the Planty park, the arrival of gas lighting and trams, and the construction of upscale suburbs outside the Old Town. Only after the unsuccessful Kraków Uprising of 1846 was Kraków forcefully brought back into the Austrian fold. But despite Kraków's reduced prominence, Austria's comparatively liberal climate allowed the city to become a haven for intellectuals and progressives (including a young revolutionary thinker from Russia named Vladimir Lenin).

The Nazis overran Poland in September of 1939. In the parts of the country that had no historical ties to Germany (including Kraków), the Nazis installed a ruling body called the *Generalgouvernement*, headed by former attorney Hans Frank. Germany wanted to quickly develop "Krakau" (as they called it) into the German capital of the nation. They renamed the Main Market Square "Adolf-Hitler-Platz," tore down statues of Polish figures (including the Adam Mickiewicz statue that dominates the Main Market Square today), and invested heavily in construction and industrialization (opening the door for Oskar Schindler to come and take over a factory from its Jewish owners). The German overlords imposed a "New Order" that included seizing businesses, rationing, and a strict curfew for Poles and Jews alike. A special set of "Jewish laws" targeted, then decimated, Poland's huge Jewish population.

Kraków's cityscape—if not its people—emerged from World War II virtually unscathed. But when the communists took over, they decided to give intellectual (and potentially dissident) Kraków an injection of good Soviet values—in the form of heavy industry. They built Nowa Huta, an enormous steelworks and planned town for workers, on Kraków's outskirts—dooming the city to decades of smog. Thankfully, Kraków is now much cleaner than it was 20 years ago.

Pope John Paul II was born (as Karol Wojtyła) in nearby Wadowice, and served as archbishop of Kraków before being called to Rome. Kraków might be the most Catholic town in Europe's most Catholic country; be sure to visit a few of its many churches. University life, small but thought-provoking museums, great restaurants, sprawling parks, and Jewish history round out the city's appeal.

Over the last few years, Kraków has gone through a boom and bust. The early 2000s were kind to the city, but tourist interest peaked around mid-2007; with uncertain economic times, many travelers seem to have retreated to more predictable destinations farther west—leaving local hoteliers scratching their heads and lowering their rates. Someday, this gem of a city will be as swamped with tourists as any big-league destination. Enjoy it now, while it's still relatively quiet.

Planning Your Time

Kraków and its important side-trips deserve at least two full days on the busiest itinerary. Most people can easily fill three days. More than any town in Europe, Kraków is made for aimless strolling.

Ideally, spend two full days in Kraków itself, plus a visit to Auschwitz (either as a side-trip on the third day, or en route to or from Kraków). In a pinch, spend one day sightseeing in Kraków, another at Auschwitz, and two evenings on the Main Market Square.

With only one full day in Kraków, follow this plan: Take my self-guided walk of Kraków's Royal Way to cover the city's core. Have lunch on or near the Main Market Square, and spend the rest of your time visiting any Old Town museums that interest you

Kraków's Old Town

KRAKÓW

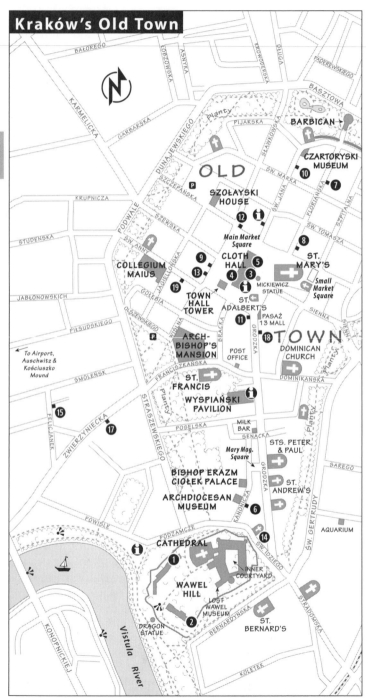

KRAKÓW

Sights
1. John Paul II Wawel Cathedral Museum
2. Sandomierska Tower
3. Gallery of 19th-Century Polish Art (Entrance)
4. Rynek Underground Museum (Tickets)
5. Rynek Underground Museum (Entrance)
6. John Paul II Center

Entertainment
7. Cukiarnia Jama Michalika
8. Jazz Club u Muniaka
9. Harris Piano Jazz Bar
10. Stalowa Magnolia
11. Polonia House/Dom Polonii
12. Bonerowski Palace
13. Pod Baranami Palace
14. St. Idziego/Giles Church

Services
15. Massolit Books
16. Frania Café/Laundry
17. Betty Clean Laundry
18. Kraków Bike Tours & Rental
19. Wypożyczalnia Rowerów Rent-a-Bike

Transportation
20. Trams #7, #13 & #24 to Kazimierz (2)
21. Kurniki Bus Stop (#304 to Wieliczka Salt Mine)

200 Meters
200 Yards

(such as the Gallery of 19th-Century Polish Art in the Cloth Hall, Jagiellonian University Museum, the museums at Wawel Castle, or Szołayski House), or head for the excellent Schindler's Factory Museum in Kazimierz. If you have any energy left by late afternoon, you could squeeze in a late visit to the Wieliczka Salt Mine (last English tour departs at 18:00, or at 17:00 Oct-May). Savor the Main Market Square over dinner or a drink, or enjoy traditional Jewish music and cuisine in Kazimierz.

With more time in Kraków, explore Kazimierz, the former Jewish quarter—a must for those interested in Jewish heritage, and illuminating for anyone. Or, if you're intrigued by the architecture of the communist era, head for the Nowa Huta suburb.

Auschwitz, an essential side-trip, requires the better part of a day for a round-trip visit (see next chapter). If you have more time, the Wieliczka Salt Mine nearby makes another good day trip. It's conceivably possible to fit Auschwitz and Wieliczka into the same day, but this requires an early start and a local driver—it's far more manageable to do them on separate days.

Orientation to Kraków

Kraków (Poles say KROCK-oof, but you can say KRACK-cow; it's sometimes spelled "Cracow" in English) is mercifully compact, flat, and easy to navigate. While the urban sprawl is big (with 757,000 people), the tourist's Kraków feels small. You can walk from the northern edge of the Old Town to the southern edge (Wawel Hill) in about 15 minutes.

Most sights—and almost all recommended hotels and restaurants—are in the Old Town (Stare Miasto), which is surrounded by a greenbelt called the Planty. In the center of the Old Town lies the Main Market Square (Rynek Główny, a.k.a. "the Square"). From the Main Market Square, the main train station is a 15-minute walk to the northeast; Kazimierz (the Jewish quarter) is a 20-minute walk to the southeast; and Wawel Hill (with a historic castle, museums, and Poland's national church) is a 10-minute walk south. Just beyond Wawel is the Vistula River.

Tourist Information

Kraków has many helpful TIs, called InfoKraków (www.info krakow.pl). Five branches are in or near the Old Town (all open daily May-Sept 9:00-19:00, Oct-April 9:00-17:00): in the **Planty** park, between the main train station and Main Market Square (in round kiosk at ulica Szpitalna 25, tel. 12-432-0110); just north of the Main Market Square on **ulica Św. Jana** (specializes in concert tickets, at #2, tel. 12-421-7787); in the **Cloth Hall** right on the Main Market Square (tel. 12-433-7310); in the **Wyspiański**

Pavilion just south of the Square on ulica Grodzka (plac Wszystkich Świętych 3, not at the window but inside the building, tel. 12-616-1886); and just west of **Wawel Hill** (also covers the entire region, Powiśle 11, mobile 513-099-688).

Other TI branches are in **Kazimierz** (daily 9:00-17:00, ulica Józefa 7, tel. 12-422-0471), **Nowa Huta** (Tue-Sat 10:00-14:00, closed Sun-Mon, os. Słoneczne 16, tel. 12-643-0303), and the **airport** (daily 9:00-19:00, tel. 12-285-5341).

At any TI, ask what's new in fast-changing Kraków, browse the brochures, and pick up the free map and the *Kraków Tourist Information Compendium* booklet. The TIs also offer a free room-finding service and sell tickets for bus tours and walking tours (though only for one walking-tour company, See Kraków; for other options, see "Tours in Kraków," later).

Sightseeing Pass: The TI's **Kraków Tourist Card** isn't a good value for most visitors. It covers public transportation, includes admission to several city museums (basically everything except the Wawel Hill sights and Wieliczka Salt Mine), and offers discounts to outlying sights and tours—but Kraków's museums are already cheap, and public transportation is mostly unnecessary (50 zł/2 days, 65 zł/3 days).

Warning: Many private travel agencies, room-booking services, and tour operators masquerade as TIs, with deceptive blue-and-white *i* signs. If I haven't listed them in this section, they're not a real TI.

Arrival in Kraków

By Train: Kraków's main train station (called "Kraków Główny") is just northeast of the Old Town. It shares a broad plaza (plac Dworcowy) with the giant, modern Galeria Krakowska shopping mall.

Taxis from the station are cheap and easy: From the tracks, take the elevator or stairs to the rooftop above you, where you'll find a giant parking lot where taxis wait. Be sure to use a taxi clearly marked with a company name and telephone number. The usual metered rate to downtown is a reasonable 10-15 zł.

Most hotels are within easy **walking** distance of the station. It's about a 15-minute stroll to the Main Market Square—just follow signs to the center (*wyjście do centrum* or *wyjście do miasta*). Arriving at the Kraków station can be confusing—when you get off the train, it's a bit of a hike to get to the station itself: From the tracks, you'll first walk down some stairs and pass through an underground corridor. When you emerge, turn left up the stairs and walk under the long green canopy to the yellow main terminal building. Exiting on the other side of the main terminal, you'll emerge into the wide-open plaza called plac Dworcowy, fronted by the Galeria Krakowska mall and an old-fashioned post office. Beyond the post office, a broad ramp leads down into a pedestrian underpass beneath the busy ring road; as you emerge from this underpass, bear right (following signs for *Rynek Główny/Main Market*) and head into the Planty park. You'll see the round TI kiosk on your left, and the Main Market Square is a few blocks straight ahead. If you're heading to hotels in Kazimierz, follow the same directions, but when you walk up the ramp into the Planty park, make a sharp right up the stairs to find a tram stop; from here, you can catch tram #7, #13, or #24 to Kazimierz (ride it three stops, to Miodowa).

By Bus: The bus station is right behind the main train station. To get into town, use the passage that takes you under the train tracks (following signs for *PKP*—the train station—and *centrum*). Once at the train station, follow the above directions.

To get *to* the bus station from the Old Town (such as to catch a bus to Auschwitz), first head to the main train station (go through the Planty park and use the underpass). From the train station's main terminal, walk under the long green canopy to the train platforms. Use the pedestrian underpass to go under the tracks (following signs for *dojście do dworca autobusowego*); when you emerge on the other side, the bus station is the blocky, modern building on your left (marked *RDA Dworzec Autobusowy*). Inside are the standard amenities (lockers and toilets), domestic and international ticket windows, and an electronic board showing the next several departures. Some bus departures, marked on the board with a *G,* leave from the upper *(gorna)* stalls, which you can see out the window. Other bus departures, marked with a *D,* leave from the lower *(dolna)* stalls; to find these, go down the easy-to-miss stairs (marked *zejście na dolna płytę*) on the left just beyond the ticket windows. Note that some minibuses, such as those to Auschwitz, also leave from, or near, this station (though the buses and minibuses that go to the Wieliczka Salt Mine leave from elsewhere).

By Car: *Centrum* signs lead you into the Old Town—you'll know you're there when you hit the ring road that surrounds the Planty park. Parking garages surround the Old Town. Your hotelier can advise you on directions and parking.

By Plane: The small, modern **John Paul II Kraków-Balice Airport** is about 10 miles west of the center, with separate international and domestic terminals (airport code: KRK, airport info: tel. 12-295-5800, www.krakowairport.pl). To get to downtown Kraków, you can take a speedy train, a slower public bus, or a taxi.

If you take the **train** downtown, first catch the free, blue shuttle bus from the airport to the nearby train station. The bus serves both the main international terminal (as you exit the terminal, turn right and look for the *PKP* sign for the bus stop) and the domestic terminal (bus stops in front). At the train station, you can buy the 10-zł ticket from the automated machine or from the conductor on the train (2/hour, 18 minutes, arrives at Kraków's main train station, uses platform 1, see train arrival instructions earlier).

To get to Kraków's main bus station downtown by **public bus,** catch bus #208, #292, or (at night) #902 in front of the airport (3.20 zł, 50-minute trip depending on traffic, see bus arrival instructions earlier).

For door-to-door service, hop in a **cab** at the taxi stand in front of the terminal (ask about the fare up front—should be around 70-80 zł, more expensive at night, about 30 minutes). You can also arrange a taxi transfer in advance (such as with recommended driver Andrew Durman, listed later, under "Tours in Kraków").

Note that many budget flights—including those on Wizz Air and Ryanair—use the **International Airport Katowice in Pyrzowice** (Międzynarodowy Port Lotniczy Katowice w Pyrzowicach, airport code: KTW, www.katowice-airport.com). This airport is about 18 miles from the city of Katowice, which is about 50 miles west of Kraków. Direct buses run sporadically between Katowice Airport and Kraków's main train station (50 zł, trip takes 1.75 hours, generally scheduled to meet incoming flights). You can also take the bus from Katowice Airport to Katowice's train station (hourly, 50 minutes), then take the train to Kraków (hourly, 1.5 hours). Wizz Air's website is useful for figuring out your connection: www.wizzair.com.

Helpful Hints

Sightseeing Schedules: Some sights are closed on Monday (including the Gallery of 19th-Century Polish Art, Szołayski House, and a few museums in Kazimierz), but many sights are open (including the churches and Jagiellonian University Museum, and in Kazimierz, all of the Jewish-themed sights). On Saturday, most of Kazimierz's Jewish-themed sights are closed.

Internet Access: Virtually every hotel in Kraków has an Internet terminal in its lobby and/or Wi-Fi in its rooms. Otherwise, take your pick of the city's many cheap Internet cafés—it seems there's one on every corner.

Post Office: The main post office (Poczta Główna) is at the intersection of Starowiślna and the Westerplatte ring road, a few blocks east of the Main Market Square (Mon-Fri 7:30-20:30, Sat 8:00-14:00, closed Sun).

Bookstore: For an impressive selection of new and used English books, try **Massolit Books,** just west of the Old Town. They also have a café with drinks and light snacks, and a good children's section (Sun-Thu 10:00-20:00, Fri-Sat 10:00-21:00, ulica Felicjanek 4, tel. 12-432-4150, http://massolit.com).

Laundry: Frania Café is a dream come true for a traveler with dirty laundry. Halfway between the Old Town and Kazimierz, this inviting café/pub has ample washers and driers, relaxing ambience, free Wi-Fi and a loaner laptop, a full bar serving up espresso drinks and laundry-themed hard drinks, very long hours, and a friendly staff. Those in search of a mellow hangout might want to come here even if they don't need to wash clothes (16 zł/load self-service, 26 zł for them to do it for you in 2 hours—consider dropping it off on your way to Kazimierz and picking it up on the way back, likely open daily 10:30-24:00, ulica Starowiślna 26, mobile 783-945-021, www.laundromat.pl).

Betty Clean is closer to the Old Town, but pricey (about 12 zł/shirt, 17 zł/pants, 1 zł/pair of socks or underwear, takes 24 hours, 50 percent more for express 3-hour service, Mon-Fri 7:30-19:30, Sat 8:00-15:30, closed Sun, just outside the Planty park at ulica Zwierzyniecka 6, tel. 12-423-0848).

Getting Around Kraków

Kraków's top sights and best hotels are easily accessible by foot. You'll only need wheels if you're going to the Kazimierz Jewish quarter or the Nowa Huta suburb.

By Public Transit: Trams and buses zip around Kraków's urban sprawl. While most trams are new and modern, a few rickety old trams with big windows (dubbed "aquariums" by locals) also rattle around the city. The same tickets are used for both trams and buses, and can be purchased at most kiosks or at the new automated machines you'll find at most stops. You can buy a ticket from the driver, but they sometimes run out and usually demand exact change, so it's safer to get one before you board. (Better yet, if you know in advance you'll be taking the tram, stock up on tickets ahead of time.) A *bilet jednoprzejazdowy* (basic single ticket, no transfers) costs 2.80 zł; a *bilet godzinny* (one-hour ticket) allows transfers and costs 3.60 zł. For a short ride, such as the one from the Old Town or train station to Kazimierz, buy a 15-minute ticket (2 zł). You can also get longer-term tickets for 24 hours (12 zł), 48 hours (20 zł), and 72 hours (28 zł). These prices are for a "one-zone" ticket, which covers virtually everything of interest in Kraków (including Nowa Huta and the Kościuszko Mound)— unless you're headed for the airport or Wieliczka Salt Mine, which are beyond the city limits and require a slightly more expensive *aglomeracyjny* ticket. Always validate your ticket when you board the bus or tram (24-, 48-, and 72-hour tickets must be validated only the first time you use them).

By Taxi: Just as in other Eastern European cities, only take cabs that are clearly marked with a company logo and telephone number. Kraków taxis start at 7 zł and charge about 3 zł per kilometer. Rides are usually very short and generally run less than 15-20 zł. You're more likely to get the fair metered rate by calling or hailing a cab, rather than taking one waiting at tourist spots. To call a cab, try **Radio Taxi** (tel. 19191).

By Bike: The riverfront bike path is enticing on a nice day; the Planty park, while inviting, can be a bit crowded for biking. **Kraków Bike Tours** rents a wide variety of new, good-quality bikes (10 zł/first hour, cheaper per hour for longer rentals, 50 zł/day, 60 zł/24 hours, daily 10:00-19:00, just off the Square at Grodzka 2; see listing later, under "Tours in Kraków"). Nearby at **Wypożyczalnia Rowerów Rent-a-Bike,** easygoing Michał Bisping rents cheaper bikes (5 zł/hour, 35 zł/day, April-Oct daily 9:00-dusk, less in bad weather, closed Nov-March, ulica Św. Anny 4, mobile 501-745-986).

Tours in Kraków

You have many options for touring Kraków (and beyond): with a local guide or driver, or by foot, bike, bus, buggy, or even golf cart.

Local Guides
Kraków has several affordable guides. I've enjoyed working with two in particular, both of whom can show you the sights in Kraków and also have cars for day-tripping into the countryside: **Marta Chmielowska** (by foot: 250 zł/half-day, 450 zł/day; by car: 300 zł, more for larger groups; mobile 603-668-008, martachm7 @gmail.com); or **Anna Gega** (by foot: 250 zł/4 hours, 350 zł/day; by car: 300 zł/4 hours, 500 zł/day—maybe more for long-distance trips; mobile 604-151-293, leadertour@wp.pl).

Either of these guides can also take you to **Auschwitz** for the day for around 600-700 zł. However, only official Auschwitz guides can legally give tours at the concentration camp museum. Therefore, your local guide will probably either do the tour herself (and pay to hire a Polish-speaking guide to tag along and act "official"), or send you with one of the regularly departing English tours. Because of the added expense of hiring the local guide, it's pricey to visit Auschwitz with Marta or Anna. You'll get a better value by going with one of the drivers listed next.

Drivers
Since Kraków is such a useful home base for day trips, it can be handy to splurge on a private driver for door-to-door service. **Andrew (Andrzej) Durman,** a Pole who lived in Chicago and speaks fluent English, is a gregarious driver, translator, miracle

Kraków at a Glance

▲▲▲Main Market Square Stunning heart of Kraków and a people magnet any time of day. **Hours:** Always open. See page 40.

▲▲Planty Once a moat, now a scenic park encircling the city. **Hours:** Always open. See page 36.

▲▲St. Mary's Church Landmark church with extraordinary wood-carved Gothic altarpiece. **Hours:** Mon-Sat 11:30-18:00, Sun 14:00-18:00. See page 37.

▲▲Cloth Hall Fourteenth-century market hall with 21st-century souvenirs. **Hours:** Summer Mon-Fri 9:00-18:00, Sat-Sun 9:00-15:00, sometimes later; winter Mon-Fri 9:00-16:00, Sat-Sun 9:00-15:00. See page 42.

▲▲St. Francis Basilica Lovely Gothic church with some of Poland's best Art Nouveau. **Hours:** Daily 6:00-19:45. See page 44.

▲▲Wawel Cathedral Poland's splendid national church, with tons of tombs, a crypt, and a climbable tower. **Hours:** April-Sept Mon-Sat 9:00-17:00, Sun 12:30-17:00; Oct-March Mon-Sat 9:00-16:00, Sun 12:30-16:00. See page 51.

▲▲Wawel Castle Grounds Historic hilltop with views, castle, cathedral, courtyard with chakras, and a passel of museums. **Hours:** Grounds open daily 6:00 until dusk, but many of the museums closed Mon, and Sun in winter. See page 55.

▲▲Gallery of 19th-Century Polish Art Worthwhile collection of paintings by should-be-famous artists, upstairs in the Cloth Hall. **Hours:** Tue-Sun 10:00-18:00, until 20:00 Fri-Sat, closed Mon. See page 61.

▲▲Old Cemetery Poignant Jewish burial site in Kazimierz, with graves from 1552 to 1800. **Hours:** Sun-Fri 9:00-16:00, sometimes until 18:00 May-Aug, closes earlier in winter and at sundown on Fri, closed Sat. See page 74.

▲▲Schindler's Factory Museum Historic building where Oskar Schindler saved more than 1,000 Jewish workers, now filled

KRAKÓW

with engaging exhibit about Kraków's WWII experience. **Hours:** April-Oct Mon 10:00-16:00 (closes at 14:00 first Mon of month), Tue-Sun 10:00-20:00; Nov-March Mon 10:00-14:00, Tue-Sun 10:00-18:00. See page 81.

▲**Czartoryski Museum** Varied collection, with European paintings and Polish armor, handicrafts, and decorative arts. **Hours:** Likely closed for restoration, otherwise Tue-Sat 10:00-18:00, Sun 10:00-16:00, closed Mon. See page 65.

▲**Rynek Underground Museum** Super-modern exhibit on medieval Kraków filling excavated cellars beneath the Main Market Square. **Hours:** Mon 10:00-20:00, Tue 10:00-16:00 (closed first Tue of month), Wed-Sun 10:00-22:00. See page 67.

▲**Jagiellonian University Museum: Collegium Maius** Proud collection of historic university, surrounding a tranquil courtyard where medieval professors lived. **Hours:** Entry by guided tour; 30-minute version—April-Oct departs every 20 minutes Mon-Fri 10:00-15:00, Tue and Thu until 18:00, Sat 10:00-14:00; no tours Sun; Nov-March 14:00-16:00; one-hour version—year-round Mon-Fri at 13:00, no tours Sat-Sun. See page 68.

▲**New Cemetery** Jewish graveyard with tombs from after 1800, partly restored after Nazi desecration. **Hours:** Sun-Fri 8:00-18:00, until 16:00 in winter, closed Sat. See page 74.

▲**Ethnographic Museum** Traditional rural Polish life on display. **Hours:** Tue-Sat 11:00-19:00, Thu until 21:00, Sun 11:00-15:00, closed Mon. See page 78.

▲**Pharmacy Under the Eagle** Small Podgórze exhibit about the Holocaust in Kraków, including three evocative historic films. **Hours:** April-Oct Mon 10:00-14:00, Tue-Sun 9:00-17:00; Nov-March Mon 10:00-14:00, Tue-Thu and Sat 9:00-16:00, Fri 10:00-17:00, closed Sun and the second Tue of each month. See page 79.

▲**Museum of Contemporary Art in Kraków** Today's thought-provoking art, displayed in renovated old warehouses behind Schindler's Factory Museum. **Hours:** Tue-Sun 11:00-19:00, closed Mon. See page 84.

worker, and all-around great guy. While not an officially licensed tour guide, Andrew is an eager conversationalist and loves to provide lively commentary while you roll. Although you can hire Andrew for a simple airport transfer or Auschwitz day trip, he also enjoys tackling more ambitious itineraries, from helping you track down your Polish roots to taking you on multiple-day journeys around Poland and beyond (prices are for up to four people if you book direct: 400 zł to Auschwitz—you can meet up with an English tour group there at your own expense or follow my self-guided tour, 200 zł to Wieliczka Salt Mine, 80 zł for transfer from Kraków-Balice Airport, 450 zł for transfer from Katowice Airport, 600 zł for an all-day trip into the countryside—such as into the High Tatras or to track down your Polish roots near Kraków, more to cover gas costs for trips longer than 100 km one-way; long-distance transfers for up to 4 people to Prague, Budapest, or Berlin for 1,600 zł or to Vienna for 1,800 zł; also available for multi-day trips—price negotiable, all prices higher for bigger van, tel. 12-411-5630, mobile 602-243-306, www.tour-service.pl, andrew@tour-service.pl).

Local guide Marta Chmielowska's husband, **Czesław** (a.k.a. Chester), can also drive you to nearby locations (300 zł for all-day trip to Auschwitz for up to 3 people, 350 zł for 4-8 people; to book, see Marta's contact information, above).

Walking Tours

Various companies run city walking tours in English daily in summer. Most do a 2.5-hour tour of the Old Town as well as a 2.5-hour tour of Kazimierz, the Jewish district (40-60 zł per tour, depending on company). Because the scene is continually evolving, it's best to pick up fliers locally (the TI works exclusively with one company, See Kraków, but hotel reception desks generally have more options), then choose the one that fits your interests and schedule. Four people can hire their own great local guide for about the same amount of money.

Crazy Guides

This irreverent company offers tours to the communist suburb of Nowa Huta and other outlying sights.

Bike Tours

Kraków Bike Tours is a well-established operation that runs 3- to 3.5-hour bike tours in English daily in summer. The tours make 25 stops in the Old Town, Kazimierz, and Podgórze (80 zł, includes loaner bike, April-Oct daily at 13:00, meet tour at their office down the passage at Grodzka 2—right at the bottom of the Square, tel. 12-430-2034, mobile 788-800-231, www.krakowbiketour.com, krakowbiketour@gmail.com).

Bus Tours

As Kraków is so easily seen on foot, taking a bus tour doesn't make much sense here. But they can be handy for reaching outlying sights. Various tour companies run bus-plus-walking itineraries (each of them around 100-130 zł), including Auschwitz (6 hours), Wieliczka Salt Mine (4 hours), and other regional side-trips. Look for fliers around town.

Buggy Tours

Romantic, horse-drawn buggies trot around Kraków from the Main Market Square. The going rate is a hefty 100 zł for a 30-minute tour.

Golf-Cart Tours

Several outfits around town (including on the Square) offer tours on a golf cart with recorded commentary (prices are for up to 4 people: 60 zł for one-way trip up to Wawel Hill, 120 zł for half-hour tour of Old Town or Kazimierz, 200 zł for hour-long tour of both the Old Town and Kazimierz).

Self-Guided Walk

Kraków's Royal Way

Most of Kraków's major sights are conveniently connected by this self-guided walking tour. This route is known as the "Royal Way" because the king used to follow this same path when he returned to Kraków after a journey. After the capital moved to Warsaw, most kings were still crowned and buried in Wawel Cathedral at the far end of town—and they followed this same route for both occasions. You could sprint through this walk in about an hour (less than a mile altogether), but it's much more fun if you take it slow.

• *Begin just outside the main gate at the north end of the Old Town.*

▲Barbican (Barbakan) and City Walls

Tatars invaded Kraków three times in the 13th century. After the first attack destroyed the city in 1241, Krakovians built this wall.

The original rampart had 47 watchtowers and eight gates. The big, round defensive fort standing outside the wall is a barbican. Structures like this provided extra fortification to weak sections. Imagine how it looked in 1500, when this barbican stood outside the town moat with a long bridge leading to the Florian Gate—the city's main entryway. Today you can pay to scramble along the passages and fortifications of the barbican, though there's little to see inside. The same ticket also lets you climb up onto the surviving stretch of Old Town walls flanking the Florian Gate (entry from inside walls).

Cost and Hours: 7 zł, May-Oct daily 10:30-18:00, last entry 30 minutes before closing, closed Nov-April.

• *Before entering the Old Town, look to the left and right of the barbican to see the...*

▲▲Planty

By the 19th century, Kraków's no-longer-necessary city wall had fallen into disrepair. Krakovians decided to tear down what remained, fill in the moat, and plant trees. (The name comes not from the English "plant," but from the Polish *plantovac,* or "flat"— since they flattened out this area to create it.) Today, the Planty is a beautiful park that stretches 2.5 miles around the entire perimeter of Kraków's Old Town.

• *Now enter the Old Town by walking through the...*

Florian Gate (Brama Floriańska)

Inside the gate, notice the little chapel with a replica of the famous **Black Madonna of Częstochowa,** probably the most important religious symbol among Polish Catholics. The original, located in Częstochowa (70 miles north of Kraków), is an Eastern Orthodox-style icon of mysterious origin with several mystical legends attached to it. After the icon's believed role in protecting a monastery from Swedish invaders in the mid-17th century, it was named "Queen and Protector of Poland."

• *Once through the gate, you're standing at the head of Kraków's historic (and now touristic) gamut...*

▲Floriańska Street (Ulica Floriańska)

On the inside of the city wall, you'll see a makeshift **art gallery,** where starving students hawk the works they've painted at the Academy of Fine Arts (across the busy street from the barbican). Portraits, still lifes, landscapes, local scenes, nudes...this might just be Kraków's best collection of art. If you were to detour along the gallery (to the right with your back to the gate), in a block you'd arrive at another fine collection—the eclectic Czartoryski Museum. (While it's currently closed for renovation, this museum is normally home to a rare Leonardo da Vinci oil painting.)

Standing at the top of Floriańska street, you can't miss two restaurant chains: **Coffee Heaven** (the local Starbucks) and **McDonald's.** When renovating the McDonald's building, they discovered a Gothic cellar—so they excavated it and added seating. Today, you can super-size your ambience by dining on a Big Mac and fries under a medieval McVault.

About halfway down the long block, on the left (at #45, round green sign), look for **Cukiarnia Jama Michalika** ("Michael's Cave"). This dark, atmospheric café, popular with locals for its coffee and pastries, began in 1895 as a simple bakery in a claustrophobic back room. A brothel upstairs scared off respectable patrons, so the owner attracted students by creating a cabaret act called "The Green Balloon." To this day, the cabaret—political satire set to music—still runs (in Polish only, Sun at 12:00; you may also see ads for a touristy folk show here). Around the turn of the 20th century, this was a hangout of the Młoda Polska (Young Poland) movement—the Polish answer to Art Nouveau. The walls are papered with sketches from poor artists who couldn't pay their tabs. Poke around inside, appreciating this unique art gallery. Consider having coffee and dessert here (Sun-Thu 9:00-22:00, Fri-Sat 9:00-23:00), but expect a grouchy greeting and a fee for the obligatory coat-check.

Continue strolling down Floriańska street. Two blocks ahead on the left (at #3, 50 yards before the big church), you'll see **Jazz Club u Muniaka.** In the 1950s, Janusz Muniak was one of the first Polish jazzmen. Now he owns this place, and jams regularly here in a cool cellar surrounded by jazzy art. If you hang around the bar before the show, you might find yourself sitting next to Janusz himself, smoking his pipe...and getting ready to smoke on the saxophone (for details, see "Entertainment in Kraków," later).

• *Continue into the Main Market Square, where you'll run into...*

▲▲St. Mary's Church (Kościół Mariacki)

A church has stood on this spot for 800 years. The original church was destroyed by the first Tatar invasion in 1241, but all subsequent versions—including the current one—have been built on the

KRAKÓW

same foundation. You can look down the sides to see how the Main Market Square has risen about seven feet over the centuries.

How many church towers does St. Mary's have? Technically, the answer is one. The shorter tower belongs to the church; the taller one is a municipal watchtower, from which you'll hear a bugler playing the hourly *hejnał* song. According to Kraków's favorite legend, during that first Tatar invasion, a town watchman saw the enemy approaching and sounded the alarm. Before he could finish the tune, an arrow pierced his throat—which is why, even today, the *hejnał* stops suddenly partway through. Today's buglers—12 in all—are firemen first, musicians second. Each one works a 24-hour shift up there, playing the *hejnał* on the hour, every hour (broadcast on national Polish radio at noon).

To see one of the most finely crafted Gothic altarpieces anywhere, it's worth paying admission to enter the church. The front door is open 14 hours a day and is free to those who come to pray, but tourists use the door around the right side (buy your ticket across the little square from this door).

Cost and Hours: 10 zł, audioguide-5 zł, Mon-Sat 11:30-18:00, Sun 14:00-18:00. The famous wooden altarpiece is open between noon and 18:00; try to be here by 11:50 for the ceremonial opening (Mon-Sat) or at 18:00 for the closing (except on Sat, when it's left open for the service on Sun).

Visiting the Church: The rusty neck-stock (behind the tourists' left door) was used until the 1700s to publicly humiliate wrongdoers.

Inside, you're drawn to one of the best medieval woodcarvings in existence—the exquisite, three-part **altarpiece** by German Veit Stoss (Wit Stwosz in Polish). Carved in 12 years and completed in 1489, it's packed with emotion rare in Gothic art. Get as close as you can, and study the remarkable details. Stoss used oak for the structural parts and linden trunks for the figures. When the altar doors are closed, you see scenes from the lives of Mary and Jesus. The open altar

depicts the Dormition (death) of the Virgin. The artist catches the apostles around Mary, reacting in the seconds after she collapses.

Kazimierz the Great
(1333-1370)

Out of the many centuries of Polish kings, only one earned the nickname "great," and he's the only one worth remembering: Kazimierz the Great.

K. the G., who ruled Poland from Kraków in the 14th century, was one of those larger-than-life medieval kings who left his mark on all fronts—from war to diplomacy, art patronage to womanizing. His scribes bragged that Kazimierz "found a Poland made of wood, and left one made of brick and stone." He put Kraków on the map as a major European capital. He founded many villages (some of which still bear his name) and replaced wooden structures with stone ones (such as Kraków's Cloth Hall). Kazimierz also established the Kraków Academy (today's Jagiellonian University), the second-oldest university in Central Europe. And to protect all these new building projects, he heavily fortified Poland by building a series of imposing forts and walls around its perimeter.

Most of all, Kazimierz is remembered as a progressive, tolerant king. In the 14th century, other nations were deporting—or even interning—their Jewish subjects, who were commonly scapegoated for anything that went wrong. But the enlightened and kindly Kazimierz actively encouraged Jews to come to Poland by granting them special privileges, often related to banking and trade—establishing the country as a safe haven for Jews in Europe.

Kazimierz the Great was the last of Poland's long-lived Piast dynasty. Although he left no male heir—at least, no legitimate one—Kazimierz's advances set the stage for Poland's Golden Age (14th-16th centuries). After his death, Poland united with Lithuania (against the common threat of the Teutonic Knights), the Jagiellonian dynasty was born, and Poland became one of Europe's mightiest medieval powers.

Mary is depicted in three stages: dying, being escorted to heaven by Jesus, and (at the very top) being crowned in heaven (flanked by two Polish saints—Adalbert and Stanisław). The six scenes on the sides are the Annunciation, birth of Jesus, visit by the Three Magi, Jesus' Resurrection, his Ascension, and Mary becoming the mother of the apostles at Pentecost.

There's more to St. Mary's than the altar. While you're admiring this church's art, notice the flowery Neo-Gothic painting covering the choir walls. Stare up into the starry, starry blue ceiling. As you wander around, consider that the church was renovated a century ago by three Polish geniuses from two very different artistic generations: the venerable positivist Jan Matejko and his Art Nouveau students, Stanisław Wyspiański and Józef Mehoffer

(we'll learn more about these two later on our walk). The huge silver bird under the organ loft in back is a crowned eagle, the symbol
of Poland.

Tower Climb: Several days a week in the summer, you can
actually climb up the 239 stairs to the top of the taller tower to
visit the *hejnał* fireman. While it's a huff—with some claustrophobic stone stairs, followed by some steep, acrophobic wooden
ones—the view up top is the best you'll find of the Square (5 zł,
buy ticket at little tent next to front door; open May-Sept Tue,
Thu, and Sat 9:00-11:30 & 13:00-17:30, closed Oct-April).

• *Leaving the church, enjoy the...*

▲▲▲Main Market Square (Rynek Główny), a.k.a. "The Square"

Kraków's marvelous Square, one of Europe's most gasp-worthy
public spaces, bustles with street musicians, colorful flower stalls,
cotton-candy vendors, loiter-
ing teenagers, businesspeople
commuting by foot, gawking
tourists, and the lusty coos of
pigeons. This Square is where
Kraków lives. It's often filled
with various special events,
markets, and festivals. The biggest are the seasonal markets
before Easter and Christmas,

but you're also likely to stumble on something special going on
here anytime between June and August.

The Square was established in the 13th century, when the city
had to be rebuilt after being flattened by the Tatars. At the time,
it was the biggest square in medieval Europe. It was illegal to sell
anything on the street, so everything had to be sold here on the
Main Market Square. It was divided into smaller markets, such
as the butcher stalls, the ironworkers' tents, and the still-standing
Cloth Hall (described later).

Notice the modern **fountain** with the glass pyramid at this
end of the Square. If you peer through the water and the glass bottom, you may see people moving around down there. A recent,
lengthy excavation of the surrounding area created a museum
of Kraków's medieval history that literally sprawls beneath the
Square (for more on the **Rynek Underground Museum,** see
"Sights in Kraków," later).

The statue in the middle of the Square is of Romantic
poet **Adam Mickiewicz** (1789-1855). His epic masterpiece, *Pan
Tadeusz,* is still regarded as one of the greatest works in Polish,
and Mickiewicz is considered the "Polish Shakespeare." A wistful,

The Młoda Polska (Young Poland) Art Movement

Polish art in the late 19th century was ruled by positivism, a school with a very literal, straightforward focus on Polish history (Jan Matejko led the charge; see page 158). But when the new generation of Kraków's artists came into their own in the early 1900s, they decided that the old school was exactly that. Though moved by the same spirit and goals as the previous generation—evoking Polish patriotism at a time when their country was being occupied—these new artists used very different methods. They were inspired by a renewed appreciation of folklore and peasant life. Rather than being earnest and literal (an 18th-century Polish war hero on horseback), the new art was playful and highly symbolic (the artist frolicking in a magical garden in the idyllic Polish countryside). This movement became known as Młoda Polska (Young Poland)—Art Nouveau with a Polish accent.

Stanisław Wyspiański (vees-PAYN-skee, 1869-1907) was the leader of Młoda Polska. He produced beautiful artwork, from simple drawings to the stirring stained-glass images in Kraków's St. Francis Basilica. Wyspiański was an expert at capturing human faces with realistic detail, emotion, and personality. The versatile Wyspiański was also an accomplished stage designer and writer. His patriotic play *The Wedding*—about the nuptials of a big-city artist and a peasant girl—is regarded as one of Poland's finest dramas. You'll find excellent examples of Wyspiański's art in Kraków's St. Francis Basilica and Szołayski House, and in Warsaw's National Museum.

Józef Mehoffer (may-HOH-fehr), Wyspiański's good friend and rival, was another great Młoda Polska artist. Mehoffer's style is more expressionistic and abstract than Wyspiański's, often creating an otherworldly effect. See Mehoffer's work in Kraków's St. Francis Basilica and at the artist's former residence (see the Józef Mehoffer House, later); and in Warsaw, at the National Museum.

Other names to look for include **Jacek Malczewski** (mahl-CHEHV-skee), who specialized in self-portraits, and **Olga Boznańska** (bohz-NAHN-skah), the movement's only prominent female artist. Both are featured in Warsaw's National Museum; Malczewski's works also appear in Kraków's Gallery of 19th-Century Polish Art.

nostalgic tale of Polish-Lithuanian nobility, *Pan Tadeusz* stirred patriotism in a Poland that had been dismantled by surrounding empires.

Near the end of the Square, you'll see the tiny, copper-domed **Church of St. Adalbert,** the oldest church in Kraków (10th century). This Romanesque structure predates the Square. Like St. Mary's (described earlier), it seems to be at an angle because it's aligned east-west, as was the custom when it was built. (In other words, the churches aren't crooked—the Square is.)

Drinks are reasonably priced at cafés on the Square (most around 10-15 zł). Find a spot where you like the view and the chairs, then sit and sip. Order a coffee, Polish *piwo* (beer, such as Żywiec, Okocim, or Lech), or a shot of *wódka* (Żubrówka is a good brand). For a higher vantage point, the Cloth Hall's **Café Szał** terrace, overlooking the Square and St. Mary's Church, has one of the nicest views in town (open daily until 24:00, terrace costs 2 zł to enter except free on Sun-Mon and after 20:00, 10-15-zł drinks, some light meals, enter through Gallery of 19th-Century Polish Art entrance).

As the Square buzzes around you, imagine this place before 1989. There were no outdoor cafés, no touristy souvenir stands, and no salesmen hawking cotton candy and quacking or chirping mouthpieces. The communist government shut down all but a handful of the businesses. They didn't want people to congregate here—they should be at home, resting, because "a rested worker is a productive worker." The buildings were covered with soot from the nearby Lenin Steelworks in Nowa Huta. The communists denied the pollution, and when the student "Green Brigades" staged a demonstration in this Square to raise awareness in the 1970s, they were immediately arrested. How things have changed.

• *The huge, yellow building right in the middle of the Square is the...*

▲▲Cloth Hall (Sukiennice)

In the Middle Ages, this was the place where cloth-sellers had their market stalls. Kazimierz the Great turned the Cloth Hall into a permanent structure in the 14th century. In 1555, it burned down, and was replaced by the current building. The letter *S* (at the top of the gable above the entryway) stands for King Sigismund the Old, who commissioned this version of the hall. As Sigismund fancied all things Italian (including women—he married an Italian princess), this structure is in the Italianate

Renaissance style. Sigismund kicked off a nationwide trend, and you'll still see Renaissance-style buildings like this one all over the country—making the style as typically Polish as it is typically Italian. We'll see more works by Sigismund's imported Italian architects at Wawel Castle.

Recently restored and gleaming, the Cloth Hall is still a functioning market—selling mostly souvenirs, including wood

carvings, chess sets, jewelry (especially amber), painted boxes, and trinkets (summer Mon-Fri 9:00-18:00, Sat-Sun 9:00-15:00, sometimes later; winter Mon-Fri 9:00-16:00, Sat-Sun 9:00-15:00). Cloth Hall prices are slightly inflated, but still cheap by American standards. You're paying a little extra for the convenience and the atmosphere, but you'll see locals buying gifts here, too.

WCs and telephones are at each end of the Cloth Hall. The upstairs of the Cloth Hall is home to the excellent **Gallery of 19th-Century Polish Art** (described later, under "Sights in Kraków").

• *Browse through the Cloth Hall passageway. As you emerge into the other half of the Square, the big tower on your left is the...*

Town Hall Tower

This is all that remains of a town hall building from the 14th century—when Kraków was the powerful capital of Poland. (The model to the right of the stairs shows the complete, original structure.) After the 18th-century partitions of Poland, Kraków's prominence took a nosedive. By the 19th century, Kraków was Nowheresville. As the town's importance crumbled, so did its town hall. It was cheaper to tear down the building than to repair it, and all that was left standing was this nearly 200-foot-tall tower. In summer, you can climb the tower, stopping along the way to poke around an exhibit on Kraków history—but the views from up top are disappointing.

Cost and Hours: 6 zł, April-Oct daily 10:30-18:00, last entry 30 minutes before closing, closed Nov-March.

Nearby: The **gigantic head** at the base of the Town Hall Tower (the opposite end from the Cloth Hall) is a sculpture by contemporary artist Igor Mitoraj, who studied here

in Kraków. Typical of Mitoraj's works, the head is an empty shell that appears to be wrapped in cloth. It was originally intended to be placed near the train station. But because of construction delays at the station, it found a home here on the Square. While some locals enjoy having a work by their fellow Krakovian in such a prominent place, others disapprove of its sharp contrast with the Square's genteel Old World ambience. Tourists enjoy playing peek-a-boo with the head's eyes.

• *When you're finished on the Square, we'll head toward Wawel Hill. But we'll take a one-block detour from the Royal Way to introduce you to one of Kraków's best churches. Leave on the street called ulica Bracka, in the middle of the bottom of the Square (next to the Deutsche Bank, straight ahead from the end of the Cloth Hall). Follow this one long block (and across the busy Franciszkańska street) directly to the side door of a big red-brick church. Go ye.*

▲▲St. Francis Basilica (Bazylika Św. Franciszka)

This beautiful Gothic church, which was Pope John Paul II's home church while he was archbishop of Kraków, features some

of Poland's best Art Nouveau in situ (in the setting for which it was intended). After an 1850 fire, it was redecorated by the two leading members of the Młoda Polska (Young Poland) movement: Stanisław Wyspiański and Józef Mehoffer. These two talented and fiercely competitive Krakovians were friends who apprenticed together under Poland's greatest painter, Jan Matejko. The glorious decorations of this church are the result of their great rivalry run amok. (For more Wyspiański or Mehoffer, visit the Szołayski House and the Mehoffer House— both described later, under "Sights in Kraków.")

Cost and Hours: Free, daily 6:00-19:45— but frequent services, so be discreet.

❍ **Self-Guided Tour:** To the right of the side door, notice the board displaying death announcements for community members. Entering through this door, turn left into the altar area to enjoy the paintings and stained-glass windows by **Stanisław Wyspiański.** The windows flanking the high altar represent the Blessed Salomea (left, the church's founder, buried in a side chapel) and St. Francis (right, the church's namesake). Salomea was a medieval Polish woman who became queen of Hungary, but later returned to Poland and entered a convent after her husband's death. Notice she's dropping a crown—repudiating the earthly world and giving herself over to the simple, stop-and-smell-God's-roses lifestyle of St. Francis.

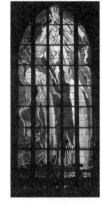

As you face the back of the church, look at the window in the rear of the nave: *God the Father Let It Be,* Wyspiański's finest masterpiece. The colors beneath the Creator change from yellows and oranges (fire) to soothing blues (water), depending on the light. Wyspiański was supposedly inspired by Michelangelo's vision of God in the Sistine Chapel, though he used a street beggar to model God's specific features. Wyspiański also painted the delightful floral designs decorating the walls of the nave—fitting for a church dedicated to a saint so famous for his spiritual connection to nature.

The chapel on the right side of the nave (as you face the back of the church) contains some evocative Stations of the Cross. This

is **Józef Mehoffer**'s response to Wyspiański's work. The centerpiece of the room is a replica of the Shroud of Turin—which, since it touched the original shroud, is also considered a holy relic.

Back out in the nave, the modern painting (with an orange-and-blue background, midway up the nave on the left as you face the back of the church) depicts **St. Maksymilian Kolbe,** the Catholic priest who sacrificed his own life to save a fellow inmate at Auschwitz. Kolbe is particularly beloved here, as he actually served at this church.

Just before going out the back door (below Wyspiański's stained-glass window), find the **silver plate** labeled "Jan Paweł II" on the second pew from the last (on right); this was Pope John Paul II's favorite place to pray when he lived in the Archbishop's Palace across the street.

• *Stepping outside (through the back door), look to the right. The light-yellow building across the street is the...*

Archbishop's Palace

This building (specifically, the window over the stone entryway) was Pope John Paul II's residence when he was the archbishop of Kraków. When he became Pope, it remained his home-away-from-Rome for

Karol Wojtyła (1920-2005):
The Life and Death of the Greatest Pole

The man who became John Paul II began his life as Karol Wojtyła, born to a humble family in the town of Wadowice near Kraków on May 18, 1920. Karol's mother died when he was a young boy. When he was older, he moved with his father to Kraków to study philosophy and drama at Jagiellonian University. Young Karol was gregarious and athletic—an avid skier, hiker, swimmer, and soccer goalie. During the Nazi occupation in World War II, he was forced to work in a quarry. In defiance of the Nazis, he secretly studied theology and appeared in illegal underground theatrical productions. When the war ended, he resumed his studies, now at the theology faculty.

After graduating in 1947, Wojtyła swiftly rose through the ranks of the Catholic Church hierarchy. By 1964, he was archbishop of Kraków, and just three years later, he became the youngest cardinal ever in the Roman Catholic Church. Throughout the 1960s, he fought an ongoing battle with the regime when they refused to allow the construction of a church in the Kraków suburb of Nowa Huta. After years of saying Mass for huge crowds in open fields, Wojtyła finally convinced the communists to allow the construction of the Lord's Ark Church in 1977. A year later, just as Poland was facing its darkest hour, Karol Wojtyła was called to the papacy—the first non-Italian pope in more than four centuries. In 1979, he paid a visit to his native Poland. In a series of cautiously provocative speeches, he demonstrated to his countrymen the potential for mass opposition to communism.

Imagine you're Polish in the 1970s. Your country was devastated by World War II, and has struggled under an oppressive regime ever since. Food shortages are epidemic. Lines stretch around the block even to buy a measly scrap of bread. Life is bleak, oppressive, and hopeless. Then someone who speaks your language—someone you've admired your entire life, and one of the only people you've seen successfully stand up to the regime—becomes one of the world's most influential people. A Pole like you is the leader of a billion Catholics. He makes you believe that the impossible can happen. He says to you again and again: *"Nie lękajcie się"*—"Have no fear." And you begin to believe it.

In addition to encouraging his countrymen, the Pope had a knack for challenging the communists. He'd push at them strongly enough to get his point across, but never went so far as to jeopardize the stature of the Church in Poland. Gentle but pointed wordplay was his specialty. The inspirational role he played in the lives of Lech Wałęsa and the other leaders of Solidarity gave them the courage to stand up to the communists (for more on Solidarity, see page 206). Many people (including Mikhail Gorbachev) credit Pope John Paul II for the collapse of Eastern European communism.

Even as John Paul II's easy charisma attracted new worshippers to the Church (especially young people), his conservatism on issues such as birth control, homosexuality, and female priests pushed away many Catholics. Under his watch, the Church struggled with embarrassing pedophilia scandals in the US, Ireland, and elsewhere. Many still fault him for turning a blind eye and not putting a stop to these abuses much earlier. By the end of his papacy, John Paul II's failing health and old-fashioned politics had caused him to lose stature in worldwide public opinion. And yet, approval of the Pope never waned in Poland. His countrymen—even the relatively few atheists and agnostics—saw John Paul II both as the greatest hero of their people...and as a member of the family, like a kindly grandfather.

When Pope John Paul II died on April 2, 2005, the mourning in Poland was particularly deep and sustained. Though the Pope's passing was hardly unexpected, it created an overwhelming wave of grief that flooded the country for weeks. Musical performances of all kinds were canceled for a week after his death, and the irreverent MTV-style music channel simply went off the air out of respect.

Since John Paul II's death, Kraków has improvised some modest collections that celebrate his legacy. While there's still no definitive museum about the man, you'll find items relating to his life at the Archdiocesan Museum and John Paul II Center (both on Kanonicza street below the castle), and at the John Paul II Wawel Cathedral Museum (facing the cathedral); all of these are described in this chapter.

A speedy six years after his death, Karol Wojtyła was beatified in May of 2011; sainthood is all but certain to follow. Out of 265 popes, only two have been given the title "great." There's already talk in Rome of increasing that number to three. Someday soon we may speak of this man as "John Paul the Great." His countrymen already do.

KRAKÓW

KRAKÓW

visits to his hometown. After a long day of saying formal Mass during his visits to Kraków, he'd wind up here. Weary as he was, before going to bed he'd stand in the window for hours, chatting casually with the people assembled below—about religion, but also about sports, current events, and whatever was on their minds. In 2005, when the Pope's health deteriorated, this street filled with his supporters, even though the Pope was in Rome. For days, somber locals focused their vigil on this same window, their eyes fixed on a black crucifix that had been placed here. At 21:37 on the night of April 2, 2005, the Pope passed away in Rome. Ten thousand Krakovians were in this street, under this window, listening to a Mass broadcast on loudspeakers from the church. When the priest announced the Pope's death, every single person simultaneously fell to their knees in silence. For the next several days, thousands of the faithful continued to stand in this street, staring intently at the window where they last saw the man they considered to be the greatest Pole.

• Now turn right, walk along the side of the church, pass a few monuments and a tram stop, and turn right again down busy...

Grodzka Street

Now you're back on the Royal Way proper. At the corner of Grodzka street stands the modern, copper-colored **Wyspiański Pavilion.** In addition to housing a handy TI (inside—not the ticket window out front) and a conference center, this building features three new stained-glass windows based on designs Wyspiański once submitted for a contest to redecorate Wawel Cathedral. While these designs were rejected back then, they were finally realized on the hundredth anniversary of his death (in 2007). Visible from inside the building during the day (step inside to see them), and gloriously illuminated to be seen outside the building at night, they represent three Polish historical figures: the gaunt St. Stanisław (Poland's first saint), the skeletal Kazimierz the Great (in the middle), and the swooning King Henry the Pious.

Now continue down Grodzka street. This lively thoroughfare, connecting the Square with Wawel, is teeming with shops—and some of Kraków's best restaurants (see "Eating in Kraków," later). Survey your options now, and choose (and maybe reserve) your favorite for dinner tonight. This street is also characterized by its fine arcades over the sidewalks. While this might seem like a charming Renaissance feature, the arcades were actually added by the Nazis after they invaded in 1939; they wanted to convert Kraków into a city befitting its status as the capital of their Polish puppet state.

This is also a good street to find some of Kraków's **milk bars**. The most traditional one is about two blocks down, on the right (at #45), with a simple *Bar Mleczny* sign. These government-sub-sidized cafeterias are the locals' choice for a quick, cheap, filling, lowbrow lunch. Prices are deliriously cheap (soup costs less than a dollar), and the food isn't bad. Or, for an even quicker bite, buy an *obwarzanek* (ring-shaped roll, typically fresh) from a street vendor.

• *One more block ahead, the small square on your right is...*

Mary Magdalene Square (Plac Św. Marii Magdaleny)

Back when Kraków was just a village, this was its main square. Today it offers a great visual example of Kraków's deeply religious character. In the Middle Ages, Kraków was known as "Small Rome" for its many churches. Today, there are 142 churches and monasteries within the city limits (32 in the Old Town alone)—more per square mile than anywhere outside Rome. You can see several of them from this spot: The nearest, with the picturesque white facade and red dome, is the **Church of Saints Peter and Paul** (Kraków's first Baroque church, and a popular tourist concert venue). The statues lining this church's facade are the 11 apostles (minus Judas), plus Mary Magdalene, the square's namesake. The next church to the right, with the twin towers, is the Romanesque **St. Andrew's** (now with a Baroque interior). According to legend, a spring inside this church provided water to citizens who holed up here during Tatar invasions in the 13th century. If you look farther down the street, you can see three more churches. And the square next to you used to be a church, too—it burned in 1855, and only its footprint survives.

• *Go through the square (admiring the sculpture on the column that won Kraków's distinguished "ugliest statue" award in 2002), and turn left down...*

Kanonicza Street (Ulica Kanonicza)

With so many churches around here, the clergy had to live some-where. Many lived on this well-preserved street—supposedly the oldest street in Kraków. As you walk, look for the cardinal hats over three different doorways. The Hotel Copernicus, on the left, is named for a famous guest who stayed here five centuries ago. On the right at #17, the **Bishop Erazm Ciołek Palace** hosts a good exhibit of medieval art and Orthodox icons. Next door, the yellow house on the right (#19) is where Karol Wojtyła lived for

10 years after World War II—long before he became Pope John Paul II. Today this building houses the **Archdiocesan Museum,** which features a few sparse exhibits about Kraków's favorite son. Across the street is the **John Paul II Center,** which has another modest exhibit about the late pontiff, and also provides information about a major complex being built in his honor. These two exhibits are worth visiting if you want to know more about the man. All three of these sights are described later, under "Sights in Kraków."

• *At the end of Kanonicza street, our self-guided walk is finished. But there's still much more to see. Across the busy street, a ramp leads up to the most important piece of ground in all of Poland: Wawel.*

Sights in Kraków

Wawel Hill

Wawel (VAH-vehl), a symbol of Polish royalty and independence, is sacred territory to every Polish person. A castle has stood here since the beginning of Poland's recorded history. Today, Wawel—awash in tourists—is the most vis-ited sight in the country. Crowds and an overly complex admissions system for the hill's many historic sights can be exasperating. Thankfully, a stroll through the cathedral and around the castle grounds requires no tickets, and—with the help of the following commentary—is enough. I've described these sights in the order of a handy self-guided walk. The many museums on Wawel (all described in this section) are mildly interesting, but can be skipped (grounds open daily from 6:00 until dusk, inner courtyard closes 30 minutes earlier).

• *From Kanonicza street—where my self-guided walk ends—head up the long ramp to the castle entry.*

Entry Ramp

Huffing up this ramp, it's easy to imagine how this location—rising above the otherwise flat plains around Kraków—was both strategic and easy to defend. When Kraków was part of the Habsburg Empire in the 19th century, the Austrians turned this castle complex into a fortress, destroying much of its delicate beauty. When Poland regained its independence after World War I, the castle was returned to its former glory. The bricks you see on your left as you climb the ramp bear the names of Poles from around the world who donated to the cause.

The jaunty equestrian statue ahead is **Tadeusz Kościuszko** (1746-1817)—a familiar name to many Americans. Kościuszko was a hero of the American Revolution and helped design West Point. When he returned to Poland, he fought bravely but unsuccessfully against the Russians (during the Partitions that would divide Poland's territory among three neighboring powers). Kościuszko also gave his name to several American towns, a county in Indiana, a type of mustard from Illinois, and the tallest mountain in Australia.

• *Hiking through the Heraldic Gate next to Kościuszko, you pass the ticket office (if you'll be going into the museums, use the other ticket office, with shorter lines, on top of the hill—see "Tickets and Reservations," later). As you crest the hill, on your left is...*

▲▲Wawel Cathedral

Poland's national church is its Westminster Abbey. While the history buried here is pretty murky to most Americans, to Poles, this

church is *the* national mausoleum. It holds the tombs of nearly all of Poland's most important rulers and greatest historical figures.

Cost and Hours: It's usually free to walk around the main part of the church. You must buy a 12-zł ticket to climb up the tallest tower, visit the crypt and the royal tombs, and tour the John Paul II

Wawel Cathedral Museum. Buy this ticket at the house across from the cathedral entry, where you can also rent an audioguide (7 zł). The cathedral is open April-Sept Mon-Sat 9:00-17:00, Sun 12:30-17:00, closes one hour earlier Oct-March, last entry 15 minutes before closing (tel. 12-429-9516, www.katedra-wawelska.pl). Note that the cathedral's museum (described later) is closed on Sunday.

Cathedral Exterior

Go around to the far side of the cathedral to take in its profile. This uniquely eclectic church is the product of centuries of haphazard additions...yet somehow, it works. It began as a simple, stripped-down Romanesque church in the 12th century. (The white base of the nearest tower is original. In fact, anything at Wawel that's made of white limestone like this was probably part of the earliest Romanesque structures.) Kazimierz the Great and his predecessors gradually surrounded the cathedral with some 20 chapels, which were further modified over the centuries—making this beautiful church a happy hodgepodge of styles. To give you a sense of the historical sweep, scan the chapels from left to right: 14th-century Gothic, 12th-century Romanesque (the base of the tower), 17th-century Baroque (the inside is Baroque, though the exterior is a copy of its Renaissance neighbor), 16th-century Renaissance, and 18th- and 19th-century Neoclassical. (This variety in styles is even more evident in the chapels' interiors, which we'll see soon.)

Pay attention to the two particularly interesting domed chapels to the right of the tall tower. The gold one is the Sigismund Chapel, housing memorials to the Jagiellonian kings—including Sigismund the Old, who was responsible for Kraków's Renaissance renovation in the 16th century. Poles consider this chapel, made with 80 pounds of gold, to be the finest Renaissance chapel north of the Alps. The copper-domed chapel next to it, home to the Swedish Waza dynasty, resembles its neighbor (but it's a copy built 150 years later, and without all that gold). The tallest tower, called the Sigismund Tower, has a clock with only an hour hand.

Go back around and face the front entry for more architectonic silliness. You see Gothic chapels (with pointy windows)

flanking the door, a Renaissance ceiling, lavish Baroque decoration over the door, and some big bones (thought to have come from extinct animals). Years ago, these were taken for the bones of giants and put here as an oddity to be viewed by the public. (Back then, there were no museums, so notable items like these were used to lure people to the church.) It's said that as long as the bones hang here, the cathedral will stand. The door is the original from the 14th century, with fine wrought-iron work. The *K* with the crown stands for Kazimierz the Great. The black marble frame is made of Kraków stone from nearby quarries.

Cathedral Interior

The cathedral interior is slathered in Baroque memorials and tombs, decorated with tapestries, and soaked in Polish history.

◐ Self-Guided Tour: After you step inside, you'll follow the one-way, clockwise route that leads you through the choir, then around the back of the apse, then back to the entry.

At the entry, look straight ahead to see the silver tomb under a **canopy,** inspired by the one in St. Peter's Basilica at the Vatican. It contains the remains of the first Polish saint, Stanisław (from the 11th century).

Go behind this canopy into the ornately carved **choir** area. For 200 years, the colorful chair to the right of the high altar has been the seat of Kraków's archbishops, including Karol Wojtyła, who served here for 14 years before becoming pope.

Now you'll continue into the left aisle. From here, if you have a ticket, you can enter two of the optional attractions: Seventy claustrophobic wooden stairs lead up to the 11-ton **Sigismund Bell** and pleasant views of the steeples and spires of Kraków. Then, closer to the front of the church, descend into the little **crypt** (with a rare purely Romanesque interior), which houses the remains of Adam Mickiewicz—the Romantic poet whose statue dominates the Main Market Square.

Now continue around the apse (behind the main altar). After curving around to the right, look for the red-marble tomb (on the right) of The Great One—**Kazimierz,** of course. (Look for *Kazimierz Wielki*—at his feet is what appears to be a beaver.) You may notice that there's one VIP (Very Important Pole) who's missing...Karol Wojtyła, a.k.a. John Paul II. Even so, a few more steps toward the entrance, on the left, is the **Chapel of the Blessed John Paul II.** The late pontiff left no specific requests for his body, and the Vatican controversially (to Poles, at least) chose to entomb him in Vatican City, instead of sending him back home to Wawel. While Karol Wojtyła's remains are in St. Peter's Basilica, this chapel was recently converted to honor him—with a plaque in the floor and an altar with his picture. Someday, Poles hope, he may be moved here (but, the Vatican says, don't hold your breath).

On the right is the white sarcophagus of **St. Jadwiga** (with a dog at her feet). This 14th-century "King" of Poland advanced the fortunes of her realm by partnering with the king of Lithuania. The resulting Jagiellonian dynasty fought off the Teutonic Knights and helped Christianize Lithuania. All the flowers here demonstrate how popular she remains among Poles today; she was sainted by Pope John Paul II in 1997. Across from Jadwiga, peek into the gorgeous 16th-century **Sigismund Chapel,** with its silver altar (this is the gold-roofed chapel you just saw from outside). Then, look into the **Waza Chapel:** Remember that its exterior matches the restrained, Renaissance style of the Sigismund Chapel, but the interior is clearly Baroque, slathered with gold and silver.

Just beyond is a door leading back outside. If you don't have a ticket, your tour is finished—head out here. But those with a ticket can keep circling around.

To the left of the main door, take a look at the Gothic **Holy Cross Chapel,** with its seemingly Orthodox-style 14th-century frescoes.

In the back corner of the church is the entrance to the **royal tombs** (you'll exit outside the church, so be sure you're done in here first). The first big room houses Poland's greatest war heroes: Kościuszko (of American Revolution fame), Jan III Sobieski (who successfully defended Vienna from the Ottomans; he's in the simple black coffin with the gold inscription *J III S*), Sikorski, Poniatowski, and so on. Then you'll wander through several rooms of second-tier Polish kings, queens, and their kids. Marshal Józef Piłsudski, the WWI hero who seized power and ruled Poland from 1926 to 1935, has the last grave (in the room on the right, just before you exit). His tomb was moved here so the rowdy soldiers who came to pay their respects wouldn't disturb the others.

• *Nearby (and covered by the same ticket as the tower and crypt) is the cathedral's museum.*

John Paul II Wawel Cathedral Museum

This small museum, up the little staircase across from the cathedral entry, was recently spiffed up and re-dedicated to Kraków's favorite archbishop. It fills four rooms with artifacts relating to both the cathedral and John Paul II.

Downstairs is the Royal Room, with vestments, swords, regalia, holy robes, and items that were once buried with the kings, as well as early treasury items (from the 11th through 16th centuries). Upstairs are a later treasury collection (17th through 20th centuries) and a "Papal Room" with items from John Paul II's life: his armchair, vestments, and miter (pointy pope hat—notice how the golden decorations on this one incorpo-

rate the Black Madonna of Częstochowa), plus souvenirs from his travels.

Admission to this museum is included with your ticket to the cathedral's special options (Sigismund Bell tower, plus crypt and royal tombs), and its collection is worth a quick look, especially if you're interested in John Paul II (April-Sept Mon-Sat 9:00-17:00, Oct-March Mon-Sat 9:00-16:00, closed Sun year-round; pick up free brochure at entrance, tel. 12-429-3321).

• *When you're finished with the cathedral sights, stroll around the...*

▲▲Wawel Castle Grounds

In the rest of the castle, you'll uncover more fragments of Kraków's history, and have the opportunity to visit several museums. While I consider the museums skippable, if you want to visit them, buy tickets before you enter the inner courtyard.

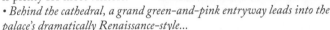

KRAKÓW

❍ Self-Guided Walk: This tour, which doesn't enter any of the attractions, is plenty for most visitors.

• *Behind the cathedral, a grand green-and-pink entryway leads into the palace's dramatically Renaissance-style...*

Inner Courtyard: If this space seems to have echoes of Florence, that's because it was designed and built by young Florentines after Kazimierz's original castle burned down. Notice

the three distinct levels: The ground floor housed the private apartments of the higher nobility (governors and castle administrators); the middle level held the private apartments of the king; and the top floor—much taller, to allow more light to fill its large spaces—were the public state rooms of the king. The ivy-covered wing to the right of where you entered served as the headquarters of the notorious Nazi governor of German-occupied Poland, Hans Frank. (He was tried and executed in Nürnberg after the war.) At the far end of the courtyard is a false wall, designed to create a pleasant Renaissance symmetry, and also to give the illusion that the castle is bigger than it is. Looking through the windows, notice that there's nothing but air on the other side. When foreign dignitaries visited, these windows could be covered to complete the illusion. The entrances to most Wawel museums are around this courtyard, and some believe that you'll find something even more special: chakra.

Adherents to the Hindu concept of **chakra** believe that a powerful energy field connects all living things. Some believe that, mirroring the seven chakra points on the body (from head to groin), there are seven points on the surface of the earth where this energy is most concentrated: Delhi, Delphi, Jerusalem, Mecca, Rome, Velehrad...and Wawel Hill—specifically over there in the corner (immediately to your left as you enter the courtyard). Look for peaceful people (here or elsewhere on the castle grounds) with their eyes closed. One thing's for sure: They're not thinking of Kazimierz the Great. The smudge marks on the wall are from people pressing up against this corner, trying to absorb some good vibes from this chakra spot.

The Wawel administration seems creeped out by all this. They've done what they can to discourage this ritual (such as putting up information boards right where the power is supposedly most focused), but believers still gravitate from far and wide to hug the wall. Give it a try...and let the Force be with you. (Just for fun, ask a Wawel tour guide about the chakra, and watch her squirm—they're forbidden to talk about it.)

• *If you want to visit some of the* **castle museums** *(you can enter four of the five from this courtyard), you'll first need to buy tickets elsewhere. Stick with me for a little longer to finish up our tour of the grounds, and we'll wind up near a ticket office.*

Head back out to the side of the cathedral to survey the...

Field of History: This hilltop has seen lots of changes over the years. Kazimierz the Great turned a small fortress into a mighty Gothic castle in the 14th century. Today, you'll see the cathedral and a castle complex, but little remains of Kazimierz's grand fortress, which burned to the ground in 1499. In the grassy field across from the cathedral, you'll see the **foundations** of two Gothic churches that were destroyed when the Austrians took over Wawel in the 19th century and needed a parade ground for their troops. (They built the red-brick hospital building beyond the field, now used by the Wawel administration.)

• *Head across to the gap in the buildings beyond the field, to the...*

Viewpoint over the Vistula: Belly up to the wall and enjoy the panorama over the Vistula River and Kraków's outskirts. From here, you can see some unusual landmarks, including the odd wavy-roofed building just across the river (which houses the Manggha Japanese art gallery). The symmetrical little bulge that tops the highest hill on the horizon is the **Kościuszko Mound**.

Now look directly below you, along the riverbank, to find a fire-belching monument to the **dragon** that was instrumental in the founding of Kraków. Once upon a time, a prince named Krak founded a town on Wawel Hill. It was the perfect location—except for the fire-breathing dragon who lived in the caves under the hill and terrorized the town. Prince Krak had to feed the dragon all of the town's livestock to keep the monster from going after the townspeople. But Krak, with the help of a clever shoemaker, came up with a plan. They stuffed a sheep's skin with sulfur and left it outside the dragon's cave. The dragon swallowed it, and before long, developed a terrible case of heartburn. To put the fire out, the dragon started drinking water from the Vistula. He kept drinking and drinking until he finally exploded. The town was saved, and Kraków thrived.

If you want to head down to see the Vistula and the dragon close up, take a shortcut through the nearby **Dragon's Den** (Smocza Jama, enter at the little copper-roofed brick building). It's just a 135-step spiral staircase and a few underground caverns—worthwhile only as a quick way to get from the top of Wawel down to the banks of the Vistula (3 zł, pay at machine—coins only, April-Oct daily 10:00-17:00, July-Aug until 18:00, closed Nov-March).

If you'd like a higher viewpoint on the riverfront, you can pay 4 zł to climb 137 stairs to the top of the **Sandomierska Tower** (at the far end of the hill, past the visitors center, no elevator). But I'd skip it—disappointingly, the view from up top is only through small windows (May-Sept daily 10:00-18:00, June-Aug until 19:00, Oct Sat-Sun only 10:00-17:00, closed Nov-April).

• *Our Wawel tour is finished. If you'd like to explore some of the museums, you can buy your tickets in the nearby visitors center (head back into the main Wawel complex—with the empty field—and turn right); here you'll also find WCs, a café, a gift shop, and other amenities. Or go down to the riverfront park: Walk downhill (through the Dragon's Den, or use the main ramp and simply circle around the base of the hill) to reach the park—one of the most delightful places in Kraków to simply relax, with beautiful views back on the castle complex.*

Wawel Castle Museums

There are five museums and exhibits in Wawel Castle (not including the cathedral and Cathedral Museum, the Dragon's Den, or the Sandomierska Tower—all described above). A sixth exhibit—featuring Leonardo da Vinci's masterful painting *Lady with an Ermine*—will likely be on display at least through 2014. Each venue has its own admission and slightly different hours (tel. 12-422-5155, ext. 219, www.wawel.krakow.pl). The castle sights don't have an audioguide, but English descriptions are posted. If you're visiting all of the sights, start with the Royal State Rooms and/or Royal Private Apartments (which share an entrance), then see the Oriental Art exhibit (on your way back down from the Royal State Rooms), the Crown Treasury and Armory, and finally the Leonardo exhibit (back near where you entered). Then head back out into the outer courtyard for the Lost Wawel exhibit.

Tickets and Reservations: Each sight has individual ticket prices (listed below). A 62-zł combo-ticket includes the Royal State Rooms, Royal Private Apartments, and Crown Treasury and Armory; for another 17 zł, you can add any other sight.

Wawel has two ticket windows. Most people line up at the top of the entry ramp, but it's faster to buy tickets at the visitors center at the far corner of the castle grounds (across the field from the cathedral, near the café). You can buy tickets directly at the door for two of the exhibits: Oriental Art and Lost Wawel.

A limited number of tickets are sold for the Royal State Rooms, Royal Private Apartments (entry by guided, included tour only), and Crown Treasury and Armory. Boards show how many tickets for each of these are still available on the day you're there. Tickets come with an assigned entry time (though you can usually sneak in before your scheduled appointment). In the summer, ticket lines can be long, and sights can sell out by midday. You can make a free reservation for the tour of the Royal Private Apartments, but if you book the Royal State Rooms and the Crown Armory and Treasury in advance, you'll pay a 16-zł reservation fee for up to nine people (tel. 12-422-1697). Frankly, the sights aren't worth all the fuss—if they're sold out, you're not missing much.

Hours: Unless otherwise noted, the museums are open April-Oct Tue-Fri 9:30-17:00, Sat-Sun 11:00-17:00, closed Mon; Nov-March Tue-Sat 9:30-16:00, closed Sun-Mon; last entry one hour before closing.

Exceptions: In summer (April-Oct), Lost Wawel and the Crown Treasury and Armory are free and open on Mondays (9:30-13:00). Off-season (Nov-March), everything closes on Monday, but Lost Wawel, the Royal State Rooms, and the Leonardo exhibit (Jan-March only) remain open on Sunday.

▲Royal State Rooms (Komnaty Królewskie)

While precious to Poles, these rooms are mediocre by European standards. Still, this is the best of the Wawel museums. First, climb up to the top floor and wander through some ho-hum halls with paintings and antique furniture. Along the way, you'll walk along the outdoor gallery (enjoying views down into the courtyard). Finally, you'll reach the Throne Room, with 30 carved heads in the ceiling. According to legend, one of these heads got mouthy when

the king was trying to pass judgment—so its mouth has been covered to keep it quiet. Continue into some of the palace's finest rooms, with 16th-century Brussels tapestries (140 of the original series of 300 survive), remarkably decorated wooden ceilings, and gorgeous leather-tooled walls. Wandering these halls (with their period furnishings), you get a feeling for the 16th- and 17th-century glory days of Poland, when it was a leading power in Eastern Europe. The Senate Room, with its throne and elaborate tapestries, is the climax.

Cost and Hours: 18 zł, see hours above, plus Nov-March also open—and free—Sun 10:00-16:00, enter through courtyard.

Royal Private Apartments (Prywatne Apartamenty Królewskie)

The rooms, which look similar to the State Rooms, can only be visited with a guided (and included) tour.

Cost and Hours: 25 zł, request English tour when buying your ticket—they depart 3/hour, see hours listed above, enter through courtyard.

Oriental Art (Sztuka Wschodu)

While small, this exhibit displays swords, carpets, banners, vases, and remarkable Turkish tents used by the Ottomans during the 1683 Battle of Vienna. These are trophies of Jan III Sobieski, the Polish king who led a pan-European army to victory in that battle.

Cost and Hours: 8 zł, tickets sold at the door, see hours listed earlier, enter through courtyard; don't miss entry on your way back downstairs from Royal State Rooms.

Crown Treasury and Armory (Skarbiec i Zbrojownia)

This is a decent collection of swords, saddles, and shields; ornately decorated muskets, crossbows, and axes; and cannons in the basement. Off in a smaller side room are some of the most precious items. Look for the regalia given to Jan III Sobieski as thanks for his defeat of the Ottoman invaders in the Battle of Vienna: giant swords consecrated by the pope and the mantle (robe) of the Order of the Holy Ghost from France's King Louis XIV. Nearby is the 13th-century coronation sword of the Polish kings, and some gorgeously inlaid rifles.

Cost and Hours: 18 zł, see hours listed earlier, plus April-Oct also open—and free—Mon 9:30-13:00, enter through courtyard.

▲▲Leonardo da Vinci's *Lady with an Ermine*

The single best and most famous painting in Kraków is normally displayed at the Czartoryski Museum. But while that space is closed for renovation (at least through 2014, and likely longer), you'll most likely find the canvas at Wawel Castle. It's well worth the price of entry to view this rare, small (21 x 16 inches), but magnificently executed portrait of a teenage girl—a rare surviving work by one of history's greatest minds. (If you have your heart set on seeing this painting, make sure it's here before making the trip—it may be on loan or in storage.)

Cost and Hours: 10 zł, see hours listed earlier, plus Jan-March also open Sun 10:00-16:00, enter through courtyard.

Visiting the Museum: Spend some time lingering over the canvas (dating from 1489 or 1490). The girl is likely Cecilia Gallerani, the young mistress of Ludovico Sforza, the duke of Milan and Leonardo's employer. The ermine (white during winter) suggests chastity (thus bolstering Cecilia's questioned virtue), but is also a naughty reference to the duke's nickname, Ermellino— notice that his mistress is sensually, um, "stroking the ermine."

Painted before the *Mona Lisa*, the portrait was immediately recognized as revolutionary. Cecilia turns to look at someone, her gaze directed to the side. Leonardo catches this unguarded, informal moment, an unheard-of gesture in the days of the posed, front-facing formal portrait. Her simple body language and far-away gaze speak volumes about her inner thoughts and personality. Leonardo tweaks the generic Renaissance "pyramid" composition, turning it to a three-quarters angle, and softens it with curved lines that trace from Cecilia's eyes and down her cheek and sloping shoulders before doubling back across her folded arms. The background—once gray and blue—was painted black in the 19th century.

Lady with an Ermine is one of only three surviving oil paintings by Leonardo. It's better preserved than her famous cousin in Paris *(Mona Lisa)*, and—many think—simply more beautiful. Can we be sure it's really by the enigmatic Leonardo? Yep—the master's fingerprints were literally found pressed into the paint (he was known to work areas of paint directly with his fingertips).

▲Lost Wawel (Wawel Zaginiony)

This exhibit traces the history of the hill and its various churches and castles. Begin by viewing the model of the entire castle complex in the 18th century (pre-Austrian razing). From here, the one-way route leads through scarcely explained excavations of a 10th-century church. The collection includes models of the cathedral at various historical stages (originally Romanesque—much simpler, before all the colorful, bulbous domes, chapels, and towers were added—then Gothic, and so on). Circling back to the entrance, find the display of fascinating decorative tiles from 16th-century stoves that once heated the place.

Cost and Hours: 8 zł, tickets sold at the door, see hours listed earlier, plus April-Oct also open—and free—Mon 9:30-13:00; Nov-March also open—and free—Sun 9:30-13:00; enter near snack bar across from side of cathedral.

National Museum Branches

Kraków's National Museum (Muzeum Narodowe) is made up of a series of small but interesting collections scattered throughout the city (www.muzeum.krakow.pl). I've listed the best of the National Museum's branches below. All of these are free to enter on Sunday.

▲▲Gallery of 19th-Century Polish Art (Galeria Sztuki Polskiej XIX Wieku)

This surprisingly enjoyable collection of works by obscure Polish artists fills the upper level of the Cloth Hall. While you probably won't recognize any of the Polish names in here—and this collection isn't quite as fine as Warsaw's National Gallery—some of these paintings are just plain good. It's worth a visit to see some Polish canvases in their native land, and to enjoy views over the Square from the hall's upper terraces.

Cost and Hours: 12 zł, free on Sun, dry audioguide-5 zł, comprehensive guidebook-40 zł, Tue-Sun 10:00-18:00, until 20:00 Fri-Sat, closed Mon, last entry 30 minutes before closing, entrance on side of Cloth Hall facing Adam Mickiewicz statue, tel. 12-424-4600.

Background: Keep in mind that during the 19th century—when every piece of art in this museum was created—there was no "Poland." The country had been split up among its powerful neighbors in a series of three Partitions, and would not appear again on the map of Europe until after World War I. Meanwhile, the 19th century was a period of national revival throughout Europe, when various until-then-marginalized ethnic groups began to take pride in what made them different from their neighbors. So the artists you see represented here were grappling with trying to forge a national identity at a time when they didn't even have a nation. You'll sense a pessimism that comes from a country that feels abused by foreign powers, mingled with a resolute spirit of national pride.

Ⓞ Self-Guided Tour: The small collection fills just four rooms. On a quick visit, skip the museum's audioguide and guide-

book and just enjoy the canvases, focusing on the highlights I mention here.

Entering the Cloth Hall, buy your ticket and head up the stairs—pausing to peek out onto the inviting café terrace for a fine view of the Square and St. Mary's. Then continue up to the main exhibit.

The first two small rooms don't feature much of interest.

You enter **Room I** (Bacciarelli Room), with works from the Enlightenment; straight ahead is **Room II** (Michałowski Room), featuring Romantic works from 1822 to 1863.

The two larger rooms merit a linger. From Room I, turn right into **Room III** (Siemiradzki Room). This hall features art of the Academy, which was "conformist" art embraced by the art critics of the day. Entering the room, turn right and survey the canvases counterclockwise. The space is dominated by the works of Jan Matejko, a remarkably productive painter who specialized in epic historical scenes that he presented in such a way as to comment on his own era. The first big canvas is his depiction of Wenyhora, a (possibly fictional) late-18th-century Ukrainian soothsayer who, according to legend, foretold Poland's hardships—the three Partitions, Poland's pact with Napoleon, and its difficulties regaining nationhood. Like many Poles of the era, Matejko was preoccupied with Poland's tragic fate, imbuing this scene with an air of inevitable tragedy. A similar gloominess is reflected in the *Death of Ellenai*, by Jacek Malczewski. The main characters in a Polish Romantic poem, Ellenai and Anhelli, have been exiled to a remote cabin in Siberia (in Russia—one of the great powers occupying Poland). Just when they think things can't get worse, Ellenai dies. Anhelli sits immobilized by grief.

Farther down is a gigantic canvas by Matejko: Tadeusz Kościuszko—a hero of the American Revolution, now back in his native Poland fighting the Russians—doffs his hat after his unlikely victory at the battle at Racławice. In this battle (which ultimately had little bearing on Russia's drive to overtake Poland), a ragtag army of Polish peasants defeated the Russian

forces. Kościuszko is clad in an American uniform, symbolizing Matjeko's respect for the American ideals of democracy and self-determination.

To the left, a smaller Matejko painting shows the last Grand Master of the fearsome Teutonic Knights swearing allegiance to the Polish king in 1525. This historic ceremony took place in the Main Market Square in Kraków, the capital at the time. Notice the Cloth Hall and the spires of St. Mary's Church in the background. Matejko has painted his own face on one of his favorite historical figures, the jester Stańczyk (at the foot of the throne).

Dominating the far wall is *Nero's Torches*, by Henryk Siemiradzki. On the left, Roman citizens eagerly gather to watch

Christians being burned at the stake (on the right). The symbolism is clear: The meek and downtrodden (whether Christians in the time of Rome, or Poles in the heyday of Russia and Austria) may be persecuted now, but we have faith that their noble ideals will ultimately prevail.

On the next wall, Pantaleon Szyndler's *Bathing Girl* evokes the orientalism popular in 19th-century Europe, when romanticized European notions of the Orient (such as harem slave girls) were popular artistic themes. Already voyeuristic, the painting was originally downright lewd until Szyndler painted over a man leering at the woman from the left side of the canvas.

The predominantly pessimistic theme continues with Matejko's *Rejtan: The Fall of Europe,* in which a prince, who has just been poisoned, clutches his chest and breathes his last. On a lighter note, Tadeusz Ajdukiewicz's portrait of Helena Modrzejewska depicts a popular actress of the time attending a party in this very building.

Finally, backtrack through Room I and continue into **Room IV** (Chełmoński Room). Featuring works of the late 19th century, this section includes Realism and the first inklings of Symbolism and Impressionism. Just as elsewhere in Europe (including Paris, where many of these artists trained), artists were beginning to throw off the conventions of the Academy and embrace their own muse.

As you proceed counterclockwise through the room, the next stretch of canvases features landscapes and genre paintings. Tune into a couple of appealing nature scenes: Józef Chełmoński's small and misty *Cranes,* and Wladyslaw Malecki's *A Gathering of Storks,* in which the majestic birds stand under big willows in front of the setting sun. Even seemingly innocent wildlife paintings have a political message: Storks are particularly numerous in Poland, making them a subtle patriotic symbol.

Linger over Józef Brandt's excellent battle scenes (often involving a foe from the East). The Jewish artist Samuel Hirszenberg's *School of Talmudists* features young Jewish students poring over the Talmud (including one, deeply lost in thought, who may be pondering more than ancient Jewish law).

Dominating the end of the room is Józef Chełmoński's energy-charged *Four-in-Hand,* depicting a Ukrainian horseman giving a lift to a pipe-smoking nobleman.

Heading back toward the entrance, on the right wall, watch for Witold Pruszkowski's *Water Nymphs*. Based on Slavic legends (and wearing traditional Ukrainian costumes), these mischievous ladies have just taken one victim (see his hand in the

foreground) and are about to descend on another (seen faintly in the upper-right corner). Beyond this painting are some travel pictures from Italy and France (including some that are very Impressionistic, suggesting a Parisian influence).

Flanking the door are two of this room's best works. First, on the right, is Władysław Podkowiński's gripping *Frenzy* (whose

title, tellingly, has variously been translated as *Ecstasy* or *Insanity*). A pale, sensuous woman—possibly based on a socialite for whom the artist fostered a desperate but unrequited love—clutches an all-fired-up black stallion. This sexually charged painting caused a frenzy indeed at its 1894 unveiling—leading the unbalanced artist to attack his own creation with a knife (you can still see the slash marks in the canvas).

On the other side of the door is Jacek Malczewski's poignant *Introduction*, showing a young painter's apprentice on a bench contemplating his future. Surrounded by nature and with his painter's tools beside him, it's easy to imagine this as a self-portrait of the artist as a young man...wondering if he's choosing the correct path.

Szołayski House (Kamienica Szołayskich)

This restored mansion, just a few steps from the Main Market Square, has been in transition in recent years. You'll most likely find high-quality temporary exhibits showcasing Art Nouveau works by the Młoda Polska movement. The collection typically features masterpieces by the movement's founder, Stanisław Wyspiański, but many of these are currently in restoration and/or storage—so for now, your best dose of his work can be found inside St. Francis Basilica.

Cost and Hours: 9 zł, free on Sun, open Wed-Sat 10:00-18:00, Sun 10:00-16:00, closed Mon, Tue only temporary exhibits open, last entry 30 minutes before closing, 1 block northwest of the Square at ulica Szczepańska 11, tel. 12-292-8183.

Bishop Erazm Ciołek Palace
(Pałac Biskupa Erazma Ciołka)

This branch of the National Museum features two separate art collections. Upstairs, the extensive "Art of Old Poland" section shows off works from the 12th through the 18th centuries, with room after room of altarpieces, sculptures, paintings, and more. The "Orthodox Art of the Old Polish Republic" section on the ground floor offers a taste of the remote Eastern reaches of Poland, with icons and other ecclesiastical art from the Orthodox faith. You'll see a sizeable section of the iconostasis (wall of icons) from the town of Lipovec. Both collections are covered by the same ticket and are very well-presented in a modern facility; while items are labeled in English, there's not much description.

Cost and Hours: 12 zł, free on Sun, audioguide-5 zł, Tue-Sat 10:00-18:00, Sun 10:00-16:00, closed Mon, Kanonicza 17, tel. 12-424-9371.

▲Czartoryski Museum (Muzeum Czartoryskich)

This eclectic collection, displaying armor, handicrafts, decorative arts, and paintings, is one of Kraków's best-known (and most

overrated) museums. It's closed for several years (at least through 2014, and likely longer) for a major restoration, during which most of its collection is scheduled to be temporarily exhibited at a castle outside of town (not worth the trip). At least one of its three top paintings—a Leonardo, a Rembrandt, and a Raphael—may be on view elsewhere in Kraków (the Leonardo will probably be at Wawel Castle; confirm this and the location of the other paintings at any TI).

Background: The museum's collection came about, in part, thanks to Poland's 1791 constitution (Europe's first), which inspired Princess Izabela Czartoryska to begin gathering bits of Polish history and culture. She fled with the collection to Paris after the 1830 insurrection, and 45 years later, her grandson returned it to its present Kraków location. When he ran out of space, he bought part of the monastery across the street, joining the buildings with a fancy passageway. The Nazis took the collection to Germany, and although most of it has been returned, some pieces are still missing.

The museum owns three undisputed masterpieces, which are in varying states of accessibility. Art lovers will want to ask around for the scoop on their latest locations. While the museum is closed, its top painting—**Leonardo da Vinci's *Lady with an Ermine***—can likely be found at Kraków's Wawel Castle (described earlier), though there's a possibility it will be on loan to another city or simply in storage. **Rembrandt van Rijn's** *Landscape with the Good Samaritan* (1638) may be on display in another city (or possibly in Kraków). And then there's **Raphael's** *Portrait of a Young Man*, arguably the most famous and most valuable stolen artwork of all time. Quite likely a self-portrait (but possibly a portrait of Raphael by another artist), it depicts a Renaissance dandy, clad in a fur coat, with a self-satisfied smirk. Painted (perhaps) by the Renaissance master in 1513 or 1514, and purchased by a Czartoryski prince around the turn of the 19th century, the work was seized by the occupying Nazis during World War II. Along with the paintings by Leonardo and Rembrandt, this Raphael decorated the Wawel Castle residence of Nazi governor Hans Frank. But when Frank and the Nazis fled the invading Red Army at the end of the war, many of their pilfered artworks were lost—including the Raphael. For decades, this canvas was synonymous with art theft—the (literal) poster boy for Nazi crimes against culture. Then, dramatically, the Polish government announced in 2012 that the priceless painting had been found, safe and sound (in a bank vault in an undisclosed location). The hope is that the "Czartoryski Raphael," as it's called, will eventually be returned to this museum.

Cost and Hours: If museum is open—around 12 zł, free on Sun, audioguide-15 zł, Tue-Sat 10:00-18:00, Sun 10:00-16:00, closed Mon, last entry 30 minutes before closing, 2 blocks north of the Main Market Square at ulica Św. Jana 19, tel. 12-422-5566, www.czartoryski.org.

Visiting the Museum: If the museum is open, you'll wander through rooms of ornate armor (including a ceremonial Turkish tent from the 1683 siege of Vienna, plus feathered Hussar armor), tapestries, treasury items, majolica pottery, and Meissen porcelain figures. Rounding out the exhibits are painting galleries (including Italian, French, and Dutch High Renaissance and Baroque, as well as Czartoryski family portraits) and ancient art (mostly sculptures and vases).

More National Museum Branches

While less interesting than the branches listed above, the National Museum's **Main Branch** (Gmach Główny) is worth a visit for museum completists. It features 20th-century Polish art and temporary exhibits (10 zł, west of the Main Market Square at aleja 3 Maja 1). The brand-new **Europeum** collection, housed in a restored granary, features works by European masters, including Breughel and Veneziano, along with a range of lesser-known artists (just west of the Old Town at Plac Sikorskiego 6). You can also check out the museum of Wyspiański's friend and rival, the **Józef Mehoffer House** (Dom Józefa Mehoffera, 6 zł, ulica Krupnicza

26, tel. 12-421-1143), and the former residence of their mentor, the **Jan Matejko House** (Dom Jana Matejki, 8 zł, ulica Floriańska 41, tel. 12-422-5926).

Other Attractions

The following sights are worth considering if you're looking to fill out your Kraków sightseeing experience.

▲Rynek Underground Museum (Podziemia Rynku)

KRAKÓW

Recent work to renovate the Square's pavement unearthed a wealth of remains from previous structures. Now you can do some urban spelunking with a visit to this high-tech medieval-history museum, which is literally underground—beneath all the photo-snapping tourists on the Square above.

Cost and Hours: 19 zł, free on Tue, open Mon 10:00-20:00, Tue 10:00-16:00 (but closed first Tue of each month), Wed-Sun 10:00-22:00, last entry 1.25 hours before closing, enter at north end of Cloth Hall near the fountain, Rynek Główny 1, tel. 12-426-5060, www.podziemiarynku.com.

Reservations: Advance reservations are recommended, as the museum allows 30 people to enter every 15 minutes. You can reserve online or by phone (see contact information above), or drop by the information office a few hours (or ideally up to a day) before your visit. (This office faces the Town Hall Tower, on the opposite side of the Cloth Hall.) If you already have a reservation, report to the museum entrance.

Visiting the Museum: You'll enter through a door near the north end of the Cloth Hall (close to the fountain, facing St. Mary's). Climb down a flight of stairs, buy your ticket, then follow the numbered panels through the exhibit (all in English except a few unimportant video clips). Cutting-edge museum technology illuminates life and times in medieval Kraków: Touchscreens let you delve into topics that intrigue you, 3-D virtual holograms resurrect old buildings, lots of surround-sound effects convincingly immerse you in a medieval burg, and video clips illustrate everyday life on unexpected surfaces (such as a curtain of fog).

All of this is wrapped around large chunks of early structures that still survive beneath the Square; several "witness columns" of rock and dirt are accompanied by diagrams helping you trace the layers of history. Interactive maps emphasize Kraków's Europe-wide importance as an intersection of major trade routes, and several models, maps, and digital reconstructions give you a good look at Kraków during the Middle Ages—when the Old Town looked barely different from today. You'll see a replica of a blacksmith's shop, and learn how "vampire prevention burials" were used to ensure that the suspected undead wouldn't return from the grave. In the middle of the complex, look up through the glass of the Square's fountain to see the towers of St. Mary's above.

Deeper in the exhibit, explore the long corridors of ruined buildings that once ran alongside the length of the Cloth Hall. In this area, you'll find a series of five rooms, each showing a brief, excellent film outlining a different period of Kraków's history. These "Kraków Chronicles" provide a big-picture context to what otherwise seems like a loose collection of cool museum gizmos, and also help you better appreciate what you'll see outside the museum's doors.

▲Jagiellonian University Museum: Collegium Maius

Kraków had the second university in Central Europe (founded in 1364, after Prague's), boasting such illustrious grads over the

centuries as Copernicus and Pope John Paul II. With around 150,000 students (including 500 Norwegian med students), this city is still very much a university town, and Jagiellonian University proudly offers tours of its historic oldest building, the 15th-century Collegium Maius (one block west of the Main Market Square at ulica Jagiellońska 15). In the Middle Ages, professors were completely devoted to their scholarly pursuits. They were unmarried and lived, ate, and slept here in an almost monastic environment. They taught downstairs and lived upstairs. In many ways, this building feels more like a monastery than a university.

Tours: Student guides lead visitors through the musty and mildly interesting interior of the complex. You'll choose between two different guided tours: 30 minutes (very popular) or one hour. It's smart to call ahead to find out when the shorter tour is scheduled in English, and to reserve for either tour (tel. 12-663-1307 or 12-663-1521, www.maius.uj.edu.pl).

The **30-minute tour** books up long in advance—especially on Tuesday afternoons, when it's free. Its "main exhibition" route includes the library, refectory (with a gorgeously carved Baroque staircase), treasury (including Polish filmmaker Andrzej Wajda's honorary Oscar), assembly hall, and some old scientific instruments (12 zł, a few tours per day in English, 20 people maximum, leaves every 20 minutes Mon-Fri 10:00-15:00, Tue and Thu until 18:00 in April-Oct, Sat 10:00-14:00, last tour departs 40 minutes before closing, no tours Sun). On Tuesday afternoons, entrance is free (April-Oct 15:00-18:00, last tour departs 17:20; Nov-March 14:00-16:00, last tour departs at 15:20).

The **one-hour tour** adds some more interiors, room after room of more old scientific instruments, medieval art (mostly church sculptures), a Rubens, a small landscape from the shop of Rembrandt, and Chopin's piano (16 zł, usually in English year-round Mon-Fri at 13:00, no tours Sat-Sun).

Aside from the courtyard, the only part of the Collegium Maius you can see without a tour is an interactive exhibit that allows you to tinker with replicas of old scientific tools (7 zł, open Mon-Sat 9:00-13:30, closed Sun).

Before you leave, enjoy a cup of hot chocolate at the chocolate shop (down the stairs near the entrance)—widely regarded as the best in town.

Archdiocesan Museum (Muzeum Archidiecezjalne)

This museum, in a building where John Paul II lived both as a priest and as a bishop, does its best to capture some of his story. The museum consists of several parts: the underwhelming ground-floor collection of sacral art (with altars, paintings, and vestments); various temporary exhibits; and the top-floor museum devoted to John Paul II. Wandering past the scores of paintings and photographs, the late pontiff's cult of personality is almost palpable. Unfortunately, since the collection mostly consists of elaborate gifts received by the Holy Father from around the world, it offers little intimacy or insight into the man himself. Still, admirers of John Paul II will appreciate it.

Cost and Hours: 5 zł, Tue-Fri 10:00-16:00, Sat-Sun 10:00-15:00, closed Mon, Kanonicza 19-21, tel. 12-421-8963, www.muzeumkra.diecezja.pl.

John Paul II Center (Centrum Jan Pawła II)

This modest exhibition space, across the street from the Archdiocesan Museum, is also the headquarters for the construction of a sprawling John Paul II Center on the outskirts of Kraków. The new complex will include the Sanctuary of Blessed John Paul II (already open and displaying papal relics), a museum, meeting spaces, a retreat center with accommodations, and other facilities for John Paul II pilgrims (scheduled to be fully open in 2015). In the meantime, in this small center, you can see exhibits (with photographs, artifacts, and English descriptions), watch films (subtitled in English) about the late pontiff, and get construction updates.

Cost and Hours: Free, daily 10:00-16:00, Kanonicza 18, tel. 12-429-6471, www.janpawel2.pl.

Kraków Aquarium

Landlocked Kraków and marine life don't quite seem to go together. But this facility—the brainchild of an armchair ichthyologist and expat American—is surprisingly modern and engaging, and one of the only truly kid-friendly attractions in town. With 130 different species of fish, reptiles, snakes, and even tamarinds (cute little monkeys) thoughtfully displayed on two floors, it offers a refreshing break from historic old Kraków. High-tech touchscreen displays give you more detail on each of the animals, and everything's kid-oriented and well-described in English. Rounding out the collection are items from the former Natural History Museum that once filled this building, including the skeleton of a 30,000-year-old woolly rhinoceros and two mammoth skulls.

Cost and Hours: Adults-20 zł, kids under 16-14 zł, family ticket for 2 adults and 2 kids-59 zł, Mon-Fri 9:00-19:00, Sat 9:00-20:00, Sun 10:00-12:00, near Wawel Hill just outside the Planty park at ulica Św. Sebastiana 9, tel. 12-429-1049, www.aquarium krakow.com.

Kazimierz (Jewish Quarter)

The neighborhood of Kazimierz (kah-ZHEE-mezh), 20 minutes by foot southeast of Kraków's Old Town, is the historic heart of Kraków's once-thriving Jewish community. After years of neglect, the district has been rediscovered by Krakovians and tourists alike. Visitors expecting a polished, touristy scene like Prague's Jewish Quarter will be surprised...and maybe disappointed. This is basically a local-feeling, slightly run-down neighborhood with a handful of Jewish cemeteries, synagogues, and restaurants, and often a few pensive Israeli tour groups wandering the streets. But for many, this is where you'll find the true soul of the European Jewish experience.

Try to visit any day except Saturday, when most Jewish-themed sights are closed (except the Old Synagogue, High Synagogue, and Galicia Jewish Museum). Monday comes with a few closures: the Ethnographic Museum, Museum of Contemporary Art in Kraków, and Museum of Municipal Engineering (along with Schindler's Factory Museum, but only on the first Monday of the month).

Note that it's respectful for men to cover their heads while visiting a Jewish cemetery or synagogue. While some of these sights offer loaner yarmulkes, it's easiest to just bring your own hat.

Getting to Kazimierz: From the Old Town, it's about a 20-minute **walk,** which gets you out of the fairy-tale tourist zone and into the real, soot-stained, workaday Kraków (that's a good thing). From the Main Market Square, walk down ulica Sienna (near St. Mary's Church). At the fork, bear right through the Planty park. At the intersection with the busy Westerplatte ring road, you'll continue straight ahead (bear right at fork, then continue straight across the busy ring road) down Starowiślna for 15 more minutes. To hop the **tram,** go to the stop on the left-hand side of ulica Sienna (at the intersection with Westerplatte, across the street from the Poczta Główna, or main post office). Catch tram #7, #13, or #24 and go two stops to Miodowa. Walking or by tram, at the intersection of Starowiślna and Miodowa, you'll see a small park across the street and to the right. To reach the heart of Kazimierz—ulica Szeroka—cut through this park. You can also take this tram from near the train station (see "Arrival in Kraków," earlier). To return to the Old Town, catch tram #7, #13, or #24 from the intersection of Starowiślna and Miodowa (kitty-corner from where you got off the tram), and go two stops back to the Poczta Główna stop.

Orientation: Start your visit to Kazimierz on **ulica Szeroka** (which is more of a long, parking-lot square than a street), surrounded by Jewish-themed restaurants, hotels, and synagogues.

Check in at the **Jarden Bookshop** at the top of the square (Mon-Fri 9:00-18:00, Sat-Sun 10:00-18:00, ulica Szeroka 2, tel. 12-429-1374, www.jarden.pl, jarden@jarden.pl). While there are many new bookstores in Kazimierz (mostly inside the various museums and synagogues), this is the original. It serves as a sort of TI for the neighborhood, and sells a wide variety of fairly priced books on Kazimierz and Jewish culture in the region (including a good 4-zł Kraków map of Jewish monuments and the well-illustrated 18-zł *Jewish Kraków* guidebook). They also run several tours (prices based on the number of people; I've listed the price per person for 2 people): Jewish Kazimierz overview (70 zł, 2 hours, walking tour), Kazimierz and the WWII ghetto (90 zł, 3 hours, walking, the best overview), *Schindler's List* sights (120 zł, 2 hours, by car), and Auschwitz-Birkenau (180 zł, 6-7 hours, by car). Call to reserve ahead, as tours are by appointment only. Pairs or singles may be able to join an already scheduled tour (which lowers the price for everybody).

There's also an official **TI** just a few blocks off the bottom of ulica Szeroka, at ulica Józefa 7 (daily 9:00-17:00, tel. 12-422-0471).

Several Kazimierz restaurants offer live traditional Jewish **klezmer music** nightly in summer, and the district is home to many of the city's best bars, cafés, nightspots, and hangouts.

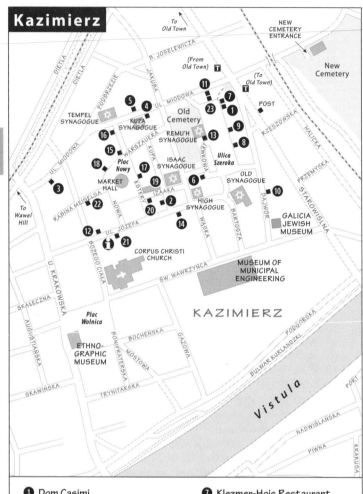

Kazimierz

KRAKÓW

1. Dom Casimi
2. Karmel Hotel & Warsztat
3. Tournet Guest House
4. Maayan Guest Rooms
5. Hostel Momotown
6. Arka Noego Restaurant
7. Klezmer-Hois Restaurant
8. Ariel Restaurant
9. Awiw Restaurant
10. Bagelmama
11. Rest. Samoobsługowa Polakowski

KRAKÓW

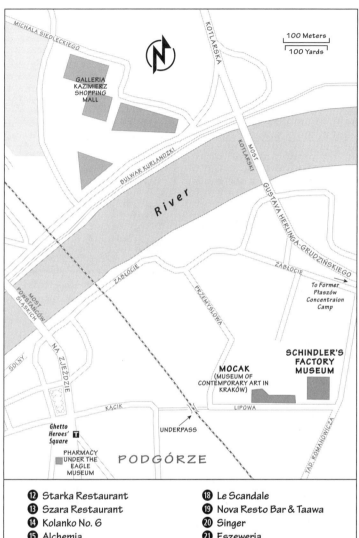

12 Starka Restaurant

13 Szara Restaurant

14 Kolanko No. 6

15 Alchemia

16 Miejsce

17 Kolory

18 Le Scandale

19 Nova Resto Bar & Taawa

20 Singer

21 Eszeweria

22 Mleczarnia & Stajnia

23 Jarden Bookshop

Central Kazimierz

Ulica Szeroka is the core of Kazimierz; within a few blocks of here, you'll find two cemeteries (quite different and both worth a visit), six synagogues, and three museums, as well as the lively market square called plac Nowy.

▲▲Old Cemetery (Stary Cmentarz)

This small cemetery was used to bury members of the Jewish community from 1552 to 1800. It has been renovated—so in a way, it actually feels "newer" than the New Cemetery. After the New Cemetery (described next) was opened in 1800, this one gradually fell into disrepair. What remained was further desecrated by the Nazis during World War II. In the 1950s, it was discovered, excavated, and put back together as you see here. Shattered grave-

stones form a mosaic wall around the perimeter. As in all Jewish cemeteries, you'll see many small stones stacked on the graves (originally placed over desert graves to cover the body and prevent animals from disturbing it). Behind the little synagogue to the left, the tallest tombstone next to the tree belonged to Moses Isserles (a.k.a. Remu'h), an important 16th-century rabbi. He is believed to have been a miracle worker, and his grave was one of the only ones that remained standing after World War II. Notice the written prayers crammed into the cracks and crevices of the tombstone.

Cost and Hours: 5 zł, also includes entry to attached Remu'h Synagogue—described later; very sporadic hours according to demand—especially outside peak season—but generally open Sun-Fri 9:00-16:00, can be open until 18:00 May-Aug, closes earlier off-season and by sundown on Fri, always closed Sat, enter through Remu'h Synagogue at ulica Szeroka 40.

▲New Cemetery (Nowy Cmentarz)

This much larger site has graves of those who died after 1800.

Nazis also vandalized this cemetery, selling many of its gravestones to stonecutters, and using others as pavement in their concentration camps. Many of the gravestones have since been returned to their original positions. Other headstones could not be replaced, and were used to create the moving mosaic wall and Holocaust monument (on the right as you enter). Most gravestones are in one of four languages: Hebrew (generally the oldest, especially if there's no other language, though some are newer "retro" tombstones); Yiddish (sounds like a mix of German and Hebrew, and uses the Hebrew alphabet); Polish (Jews who assimilated into the Polish community); and German (Jews who assimilated into the German community). The earliest graves are simple stones, while later ones imitate graves in Polish Catholic cemeteries—larger, more elaborate, and with a long stone jutting out to cover the body. Notice that some new-looking graves have old dates. These were most likely put here well after the Holocaust (or even after the communist era) by relatives of the dead.

Cost and Hours: Free, Sun-Fri 8:00-18:00, until 16:00 in winter, closed Sat. It's tricky to find: Go under the railway bridge at the east end of ulica Miodowa, and jog left as you emerge. The cemetery is to your right (enter through gate with small *cmentarz żydowski* sign).

Synagogues

Six different synagogues in Kazimierz welcome visitors. Each of the interiors is a variation on the same theme: a large central prayer hall, often with an altar-like ark (facing east, toward Jerusalem) where the Torah is kept. The elevated platform in the center, sometimes surrounded by a cage-like structure, is the equivalent of a pulpit in a Christian church. You may see segregated areas (often a balcony or an arcade) where women would worship separately from men. Some synagogues have been converted into museums, while others are still used for services. The first two synagogues listed below are on Kazimierz's main square, ulica Szeroka; the next four are all within three blocks to the west.

Remu'h Synagogue, which is tight, cozy, and dates from 1553, has been carefully renovated and is fully active (included in 5-zł entry fee for Old Cemetery, same unpredictable hours as Old Cemetery, ulica Szeroka 40).

The **Old Synagogue** (Stara Synagoga), the oldest surviving Jewish building in Poland, is now a good three-room museum on

local Jewish culture, with informative English descriptions. Most of the exhibits are displayed in the impressive main prayer hall (8 zł, free on Mon, good 50-stop audioguide-10 zł; April-Oct Mon 10:00-14:00, Tue-Sun 10:00-17:00; Nov-March Mon 10:00-14:00, Wed-Thu and Sat-Sun 9:00-16:00, Fri 10:00-17:00,

Jewish Kraków

After King Kazimierz the Great encouraged Jews to come to Poland in the 14th century, a large Jewish community settled in and around Kraków. According to legend, Kazimierz (the king) established Kazimierz (the village) for his favorite girlfriend—a Jewish woman named Ester—just southeast of the city walls. (If you have a 50-zł note, take a look at it: That's Kazimierz the Great on the front, and on the back are his capital, Cracovia, and the most important town he founded, Casmirus.)

It's a cute legend, but the village of Kazimierz didn't really become a Jewish enclave until much later. By the end of the 15th

century, there were large Jewish populations in both Kazimierz and in Kraków. Kraków's Jewish community and the university students clashed, and when a destructive fire broke out in 1495, the Jews were blamed. The king at the time forced all of Kraków's Jews to move to Kazimierz.

Kazimierz was an autonomous community, with its own Town Hall, market square, and city walls (though many Jews still commuted into Kraków's Main Market Square to do business). Within Kazimierz, the Christian (west) and Jewish (east) neighborhoods were also separated by a wall. But by 1800, the walls came down, Kazimierz became part of Kraków, and the Jewish community flourished.

By the start of World War II, 65,000 Jews lived in Kraków

closed Tue; ulica Szeroka 24, tel. 12-422-0962).

The recently renovated **High Synagogue**—so called because its prayer room is upstairs—displays changing exhibits, most of which focus on the people who lived here before and after the Holocaust (9 zł, daily 10:00-19:00, shorter hours in winter, just around the corner from the Old Synagogue at ulica Józefa 38, tel. 12-430-6889).

Isaac Synagogue (Synagoga Izaaka), one of Kraków's biggest, was built in the 17th century. On the walls in the prayer hall are giant wall paintings of prayers for worshippers who couldn't afford to buy books (with translations posted below). It also serves as the local center for the Hasidic Jewish group Chabad, with a kosher restaurant and a library (5 zł; Sun-Thu 9:00-18:00, open later in summer depending on sunset—until 20:00 in July-Aug, Fri 9:00-15:00, closed Sat, a block west of ulica Szeroka at ulica Kupa 18, tel. 12-430-2222). In addition to its Sabbath services, this is Kraków's only synagogue that has daily prayers (at 8:30).

(mostly in Kazimierz)—making up more than a quarter of the city's population. When the Nazis arrived, they immediately sent most of Kraków's Jews to the ghetto in the eastern Polish city of Lublin. Soon after, they forced Kraków's remaining 15,000 Jews into a walled ghetto at Podgórze, across the river. The Jews' cemeteries were defiled, and their buildings ransacked and destroyed. In 1942, the Nazis began transporting Kraków's Jews to death camps (including Płaszów—just on Kraków's outskirts—and Auschwitz). Many others were worked to death in the Podgórze ghetto. Only a few thousand Kraków Jews survived

the war. During World War II, Poland was the only Nazi-controlled country where residents could be executed for helping Jews—making even more remarkable the number of Poles who risked their lives to help escapees.

Today's Kraków has only about 200 Jewish residents. During the communist era, this waning population was ignored or mistreated. But in recent years, Kazimierz has enjoyed a renaissance of Jewish culture—thanks largely to the popularity of *Schindler's List* (which was partly filmed here). Look for handwritten letters from Steven Spielberg and the cast in local restaurants (such as Ariel) and hotels. While few Jews live here now, the spirit of the Jewish tradition lives on in the many synagogues, as well as in the soulful cemeteries.

Tempel Synagogue (Synagoga Templu) has the grandest interior—big and dark, with elaborately decorated, gilded ceilings and balconies—and the most lived-in feel of the bunch (5 zł, Sun-Fri 10:00-16:00, sometimes until 18:00, closed Sat, corner of ulica Miodowa and ulica Podbrzezie).

The smaller **Kupa Synagogue** (Synagoga Kupa), clean and brightly decorated, sometimes hosts temporary exhibits (Miodowa 27).

▲Galicia Jewish Museum (Galicja Muzeum)

This museum focuses on the present rather than the past. With a series of photographs displayed around a restored Jewish furniture factory, the permanent "Traces of Memory" exhibit shows today's remnants of yesterday's Judaism in the area around Kraków (a region known as "Galicia"). From forgotten synagogues to old Jewish gravestones flipped over and used as doorsteps, these giant postcards of Jewish artifacts (with good English descriptions) ensure that an important part of this region's heritage won't be forgotten. Complementing this permanent collection are good temporary exhibits.

Cost and Hours: 15 zł, daily 10:00-18:00, 1 block east of ulica Szeroka at ulica Dajwór 18, tel. 12-421-6842, www.galiciajewish museum.org. The museum also serves as a sort of cultural center, with a good bookstore, café, and programming that caters to both locals and visitors (pick up the monthly program).

Kazimierz Market Square (Plac Nowy)

The natives shop at plac Nowy's market stalls. This is a gritty, factory-workers-on-lunch-break contrast to Kraków's touristy Main Market Square (stalls open Tue-Sun 6:00-14:00, a few also open later, closed Mon). Consider dropping by here for some shopping, people-watching, or a quick, cheap, and local lunch. For dessert, buy some fruit from a vendor. There's a fun antique shop at #3. This square also has the highest concentration of nightlife in town, and several fun and funky spots are open during the day as stay-awhile cafés (see "Entertainment in Kraków," later).

▲Ethnographic Museum (Muzeum Etnograficzne)

This clever and refreshingly good museum hides a few blocks west of the Jewish area of Kazimierz, in the former town hall. It sits on plac Wolnica, which was Kazimierz's primary market square and was once almost as big as Kraków's. On the ground floor, you'll find models of traditional rural Polish homes, as well as musty replicas of the interiors (like an open-air folk museum moved inside). The exhibit continues upstairs, where each in a long lineup of traditional Polish folk costumes is identified by specific region. You'll see exhibits on village lifestyles, rustic tools, and musical instruments (including a Polish bagpipe). A highlight is the explanation of traditional holiday celebrations—from elaborate crèche scenes at Christmas, to a wall of remarkably painted Easter eggs. Some items are labeled in English, but it's mostly in Polish. The top floor features temporary exhibits.

Cost and Hours: 9 zł, free on Sun, open Tue-Sat 11:00-19:00, Thu until 21:00, Sun 11:00-15:00, closed Mon, ulica Krakowska 46, tel. 12-430-6023, www.etnomuzeum.eu.

Museum of Municipal Engineering (Muzeum Inżynierii Miejskiej)

This pleasant museum fills the immaculately restored red-brick buildings of an old tram depot in a quiet part of Kazimierz. Exhibits include a history of the town's public-transit system (including several antique trams); old Polish-made cars and motorcycles (among them the tiny commie-era Polski Fiat); typography and historical printing presses; and a hands-on area for kids called "Around the Circle."

Cost and Hours: 8 zł, family ticket-24 zł, Tue-Sun 10:00-

16:00, until 18:00 on Tue and Thu June-Sept, closed Mon, Św. Wawrzyńca 15, tel. 12-421-1242.

Near Kazimierz: Podgórze

The neighborhood called Podgórze (POD-goo-zheh), directly across the Vistula from Kazimierz, has one of Kraków's most famous sights: Schindler's Factory Museum.

Background: This is the neighborhood where the Nazis forced Kraków's Jews into a ghetto in early 1941. (*Schindler's List* and the films in the Pharmacy Under the Eagle museum depict the sad scene of the Jews loading their belongings onto carts and trudging over the bridge into Podgórze.) Non-Jews who had lived here were displaced to make way for the new arrivals. The ghetto was surrounded by a wall with a fringe along the top that resembled Jewish gravestones—a chilling premonition of what was to come. A short section of this wall still stands along Lwowska street. The tram continued to run through the middle of Podgórze, without stopping—giving Krakovians a chilling glimpse at the horrifying conditions inside the ghetto.

Getting There: To get to Ghetto Heroes' Square, continue through Kazimierz on tram #7, #13, or #24 (described earlier, under "Getting to Kazimierz") to the stop called plac Bohaterow Getta. You can also simply continue walking along Starowiślna, about 10 minutes past the other Kazimierz sights—it's just across the bridge.

Ghetto Heroes' Square (plac Bohaterow Getta)

This unassuming square is the focal point of the visitor's Podgórze. Today the square is filled with a recent monument consisting of several empty metal chairs. This is intended to remind view-

ers that the Jews of Kazimierz were forced to carry all of their belongings—including furniture—to the ghetto on this side of the river. It was also here that many Jews waited to be sent to extermination camps. The small, gray building at the river end of Ghetto Heroes' Square feels like a train car inside, evocative of the wagons that carried people from here to certain death.

▲Pharmacy Under the Eagle (Apteka pod Orłem)

This small but newly modernized museum, on Ghetto Heroes' Square, tells the story of Tadeusz Pankiewicz, a Polish Catholic pharmacist who chose to remain in Podgórze when it became a Jewish ghetto. During this time, the pharmacy was an important meeting point for the ghetto residents, and Pankiewicz and

Oskar Schindler (1908-1974) and His List

Steven Spielberg's instant-classic, Oscar-winning 1993 film, *Schindler's List*, brought the world's attention to the inspiring story of Oskar Schindler, the compassionate German businessman who did his creative best to save the lives of the Jewish workers at his factory in Kraków. Spielberg chose to film the story right here in Kazimierz, where the historical events actually unfolded. Today the Schindler's Factory Museum gives visitors the chance to learn not just about the man and his workers, but about the historical context of their story: the Nazi occupation of Poland.

Oskar Schindler was born in 1908 in the Sudetenland (currently Moravia in the Czech Republic, then predominantly German). Early on, he displayed an idiosyncratic interpretation of ethics that earned him both wealth and enemies. As Nazi aggressions escalated, Schindler (who was very much a Nazi) carried out espionage against Poland; when Germany invaded the country in 1939, Schindler smelled a business opportunity. Early in the Nazi occupation of Poland, Schindler came to Kraków and lived in an apartment at ulica Straszewskiego 7 (a block from Wawel Castle, but unmarked and not available for tours). He took over the formerly Jewish-owned Emalia factory at ulica Lipowa 4, which produced metal pots and pans that were dipped into protective enamel (later the factory also began producing armaments for the Nazi war effort). The factory was staffed by about 1,000 Jews from the nearby Płaszów Concentration Camp, which was managed by the ruthless SS officer Amon Göth (depicted in *Schindler's List*—based on real events—shooting at camp inmates for sport from his balcony).

At a certain point, Schindler began to sympathize with his Jewish workers, and gradually did what he could to protect them and offer them better lives. Schindler fed them far better than most concentration-camp inmates, and allowed them to sell some of the pots and pans they made on the black market to

his staff heroically aided and hid Jewish victims of the Nazis. (Pankiewicz survived the war and was later acknowledged by Israel as one of the "Righteous Among the Nations"—non-Jews who risked their lives to help the Nazis' victims during World War II.) Today the pharmacy hosts an exhibit about the Jewish ghetto. You'll learn about people who worked in the pharmacy, hear Pankiewicz telling stories about that tense time, and watch film footage from that era: Kazimierz before the Nazis arrived; the forced transition to the Podgórze ghetto; and secret surveillance footage of Płaszów Concentration Camp, on Kraków's outskirts.

Cost and Hours: 10 zł, free on Mon, some English descrip-

make money. After he saw many of his employees and friends murdered during an SS raid in 1943, he ramped up these efforts even further. He would come up with bogus paperwork to classify those threatened with deportation as "essential" to the workings of the factory—even if they were unskilled. He sought and was granted permission to build a "concentration camp" barracks for his workers on the factory grounds, where they lived in far better conditions than those at Płaszów. These lucky few became known as *Schindlerjuden*—"Schindler's Jews."

As the Soviet army encroached on Kraków in October of 1944, word came that the factory would need to be relocated west, farther from the front line. While Schindler could easily have simply turned his workers over to the concentration-camp system and certain death—as most other industrialists did—he decided to bring them with him to his new factory at Brünnlitz (Brněnec, in today's Czech Republic). He assembled a list of 700 men and 300 women who worked with him, along with 200 other Jewish inmates, and at great personal expense, moved them to Brünnlitz. At the new factory, Schindler and the 1,200 people he had saved produced grenades and rocket parts—virtually all of them, the workers later claimed, mysteriously defective.

After the war, Schindler—who had spent much of his fortune protecting his Jewish workers—hopped around Germany and Argentina, repeatedly attempting but failing to break back into business (often with funding from Jewish donors). He died in poverty in 1974. In accordance with his final wishes, he was buried in Jerusalem, and today, his grave is piled high with small stones left there by appreciative Jewish visitors. He has since been named one of the "Righteous Among the Nations" for his efforts to save Jews from the Holocaust. Thomas Keneally's 1982 book *Schindler's Ark* brought the industrialist's tale to a wide audience that included Steven Spielberg, who vaulted Schindler to the ranks of a pop-culture icon.

tions, good 45-minute audioguide-10 zł; April-Oct Mon 10:00-14:00, Tue-Sun 9:00-17:00; Nov-March Mon 10:00-14:00, Tue-Thu and Sat 9:00-16:00, Fri 10:00-17:00; closed Sun and the second Tue of each month; plac Bohaterow Getta 18, tel. 12-656-5625.

▲▲Schindler's Factory Museum (Fabryka Emalia Oskara Schindlera)

One of Europe's best museums about the Nazi occupation fills the actual factory building (named "Emalia") where Oskar Schindler and his Jewish employees worked. It's worth ▲▲▲ to those interested in World War II history generally, or in Schindler specifically, but it's fascinating to anyone. While the museum tells the story of Schindler and his workers, it broadens its perspective to

KRAKÓW

take in the full experience of all of Kraków during the painful era of Nazi rule—making it the single best WWII museum in this country that was so profoundly affected by that war. It's loaded with in-depth information (all in English), and touchscreens throughout invite you to

learn more and watch eyewitness interviews. Scattered randomly between the exhibits are replicas of everyday places from the age—a photographer's shop, a tram car, a hairdresser's salon—designed to give you a taste of 1940s Kraków. Throughout the museum are calendar pages outlining wartime events, which you can stamp with seals and symbols from each era, then take along with you.

Cost and Hours: 19 zł, limited free entry on Mon (first-come, first-served, so consider reserving ahead on their website); open April-Oct Mon 10:00-16:00 (except closes at 14:00 first Mon of month), Tue-Sun 10:00-20:00; Nov-March Mon 10:00-14:00, Tue-Sun 10:00-18:00; last entry 1.5 hours before closing, tel. 12-257-1017, www.mhk.pl.

Getting There: It's in a depressed industrial area a five-minute walk from Ghetto Heroes' Square (plac Bohaterow Getta): Head up Kącik street (use the pedestrian underpass, then head to the left of the big, glass skyscraper), go under the railroad underpass marked *Kraków-Zabłocie,* and continue two blocks, past MOCAK (the Museum of Contemporary Art in Kraków, described later) to the second big building on the left (ulica Lipowa 4). Look for signs to *Emalia.*

⊙ Self-Guided Tour: You'll begin on the ground floor, where you'll buy your ticket and have the chance to tour the special exhibits. There's also a "film café" with refreshments. Then head upstairs to the first floor.

First Floor: The 35-minute **film**, called *Lipowa 4* (this building's address), sets the stage with interviews of both Jews and non-

Jews describing their wartime experience (subtitled in English, runs continuously 10:15-15:50). From here, the one-way route winds through the permanent exhibit, called "**Kraków Under Nazi Occupation 1939-1945.**" "Stereoscopic" (primitive 3-D) photos of prewar Kraków capture an idyllic age when culture flourished and the city's Jews (more than one-quarter of the population) blended more or less smoothly with their Catholic-Pole neighbors. A video explains the Nazi invasion of Poland in early September of 1939: It took them only a few weeks to overrun the country (which desperately awaited the promised-for help of their British and French allies, who never arrived). Watch the film clip of SS soldiers marching through the Main Market Square—renamed "Adolf-Hitler-Platz"—and read stories about how the Nazis' *Generalgouvernement* attempted to reshape the life of its new capital, "Krakau." You'll see the story of a newly German-owned shop selling Nazi propaganda, and learn how professors at Kraków's Jagiellonian University were arrested to prevent them from fomenting rebellion among their students. During this time, Polish secondary schools were closed—effectively prohibiting learning among Poles, whom the Nazis considered inferior. But Polish students continued to meet clandestinely with their teachers. The exhibit also details how early Nazi policies targeted Jews, with roundups, torture, and execution. (Down the staircase is an eerie simulation of a cellar prison.) As the Nazis ratcheted up their genocidal activities, troops swept through Kraków on March 3, 1941, forcing all the remaining Jews in town to squeeze into the newly created Podgórze ghetto.

Second Floor: Climb upstairs using the long **staircase,** which was immortalized in a powerful scene in *Schindler's List.* At the top of the stairs on the right is a small room that served as "Schindler's office" for the film; more recently, they've determined that his actual office was elsewhere (we'll see it soon).

You'll walk through a corridor lined by a replica of the wall that enclosed the **Podgórze ghetto,** and see exhibits about the horrific conditions there (including a replica of the cramped living quarters). The Nazis claimed that Jews had to be segregated here, away from the general population, because they "carried diseases."

Continue into the office of Schindler's secretary, with exhibits about Schindler's life and video touchscreens that play testimo-

nial footage of Schindler's grateful employees. Then proceed into the actual **Schindler's office.** The big map (with German names for cities) was uncovered only in recent years when the factory was being restored. Because Schindler's short tenure here was the only time in the factory's history that these Polish place names would appear in German, it's believed that this map was hung over his desk. Nearby is a giant monument of enamel pots and pans, like those that were made in this factory, and walls lined with names from The List.

Continuing through the exhibit, you'll learn more about everyday life, including the Polish resistance (see the Home Army's underground print shop). More eyewitness accounts relate the terrifying days of March 13 and 14, 1943, when the Podgórze ghetto was liquidated, sending survivors to the nearby Płaszów Concentration Camp. The replica of the Płaszów quarry, where inmates were forced to work in unimaginably difficult conditions,

provides a poignant memorial for those who weren't fortunate enough to be on Schindler's list.

Now head all the way back down to the ground floor.

Ground Floor: Exhibits here capture the uncertain days near the end of the war in the summer of 1944, when Nazis arrested between 6,000 and 8,000 suspected saboteurs after the Warsaw Uprising, and sent them to Płaszów (see the replica of a basement hideout for 10 Jews who had escaped the ghetto); and later, when many Nazis had fled Kraków, leaving residents to await the Soviet Union's Red Army (see the replica air-raid shelters). The Red Army arrived here on January 18, 1945—at long last, the five years, four months, and twelve days of Nazi rule were over. The Soviets caused their own share of damage to the city before beginning a whole new occupation that would last for generations...but that's a different museum.

Finally, walk along the squishy floor into the Hall of Choices, where six rotating pillars tell the stories of people who chose to act—or not to act—when they witnessed atrocities. Think about the ramifications of the choices they made...and what you would have done in their shoes. The final room holds two books: a white book listing those who tried to help, and a black book listing Nazi collaborators.

Before heading back to downtown Kraków, consider paying a visit to the excellent—and very different—museum that fills the buildings on the factory grounds, behind this main building.

▲Museum of Contemporary Art in Kraków (Muzeum Sztuki Współczesnej w Krakowie)

Called "MOCAK" for short, this museum exhibits a changing array of innovative and thought-provoking works by contemporary artists, often with heavy themes tied to the surrounding sites. With the slogan *Kunst macht frei* ("Art will set you free"—a pointed spin on the Nazis' *Arbeit macht frei* concentration-camp motto), the museum occupies warehouse buildings once filled by Schindler's

workers. Now converted to wide-open, bright-white halls, the buildings house many temporary exhibits as well as two permanent ones (the MOCAK Collection in the basement, and the library in the smaller side building). Pick up the floor plan as you enter. It's all well-described in English, and engaging even for non-art-lovers.

Cost and Hours: 10 zł, free on Tue, open Tue-Sun 11:00-19:00, closed Mon, Lipowa 4, tel. 12/263-4001, www.mocak.pl.

Outside of Central Kraków

Each of these three sights—an impressive salt mine, a purpose-built communist town, and an unusual earthwork—requires a bus or tram ride to reach.

▲▲Wieliczka Salt Mine (Kopalnia Soli Wieliczka)

Wieliczka (veel-EECH-kah), a salt mine 10 miles southeast of Kraków, is beloved by Poles. Deep beneath the ground, the mine is filled with sculptures that miners have lovingly carved out of the salt. You'll explore this unique gallery—learning both about the art and about medieval mining techniques—on a required tour. Though the sight is a bit overrated, it's unique and practically obligatory if you're in Kraków for at least two days.

Cost and Hours: Visits cost 75 zł and are by guided tour only. English tours are offered daily year-round (June-Sept every half-hour 8:30-18:00, Oct-May every hour 9:00-17:00), with the exception of a few holidays when the mine is closed. If you miss the English-language tour (or decide to just show up and take whatever's going next), you can rent an audioguide for an extra 10 zł. The mine is in the town of Wieliczka at ulica Daniłowicza 10 (tel. 12-278-7302, www.kopalnia.pl).

You'll pay an extra 10 zł for permission to use your camera—but be warned that flash photos often don't turn out, thanks to the irregular reflection of the salt crystals. Dress warmly—the mine is a constant 57 degrees Fahrenheit.

Your ticket includes a dull **mine museum** at the end of the tour. It adds an hour to the mine tour and is discouraged by locals

("1.5 miles more walking, colder, more of the same"). Make it clear when you buy your ticket that you're not interested in the museum.

Getting There: The salt mine, 10 miles from Kraków, is best reached by **bus #304** (3.20-zł *aglomeracyjny* ticket, 3/hour, 40-minute trip, catch bus at Kurniki stop across from church near Galeria Krakowska mall, get off at stop called Wieliczka Kopalnia Soli). You can also get there by **minibus** (2.50 zł, 4/hour or with demand, *Wieliczka Soli* sign in window, 30-40 minutes), but the departure point for the minibuses is constantly changing—ask the TI where you can find them now (likely near the main post office). These options are better than taking the train, which deposits you in the town of Wieliczka, far from the mine.

Background: Wieliczka Salt Mine has been producing salt since at least the 13th century. Under Kazimierz the Great, one-third of Poland's income came from these precious deposits. Wieliczka miners spent much of their lives underground, leaving for work before daybreak and returning after sundown, rarely emerging into daylight. To pass the time, and to immortalize their national pride and religiosity in art, 19th-century miners began to carve figures, chandeliers, and eventually even an elaborate chapel out of the salt. Until a few years ago, the mine still produced salt. Today's miners—about 400 of them—primarily work on maintaining the 200 miles of chambers. This entire network is supported by wooden beams (because metal would rust).

Visiting the Mine: From the lobby, your guide leads you 380 steps down a winding staircase. From this spot you begin a 1.5-mile stroll, generally downhill (more than 800 steps down altogether), past 20 of the mine's 2,000 chambers (with signs explaining when they were dug), finishing 443 feet below the surface. When you're done, an elevator beams you back up.

The tour shows how the miners lived and worked, using horses who spent their whole adult lives without ever seeing the light of day. It takes you through vast underground caverns, past subterranean lakes, and introduces you to some of the mine's many sculptures (including one of Copernicus—who actually visited here in the 15th century—as well as an army of salt elves, and this region's favorite son, Pope John Paul II). Your jaw will drop as you enter the enormous  **Chapel of St. Kinga,** carved over three decades in the early 20th century. Look for the salt-relief carving of the Last Supper (its 3-D details are astonishing, considering it's just six inches deep).

While advertised as two hours, your tour finishes in a deep-down shopping zone 1.5 hours after you started (they hope you'll hang out and shop). Note when the next elevator departs (just 3/hour), and you can be outta there on the next lift. Zip through the shopping zone in two minutes, or step over the rope and be immediately in line for the great escape (you'll be escorted 300 yards to the skinny industrial elevator, into which you'll be packed like mine workers).

▲Nowa Huta

Nowa Huta (NOH-vah HOO-tah, "New Steel Works"), an enormous planned workers' town, offers a glimpse into the stark, grand-scale aesthetics of the communists. Since it's five miles east of central Kraków and a little tricky to see on your own, skip it unless you're determined. But architects and communist sympathizers may want to make a pilgrimage here.

Getting There: Trams #4 and #15 go from near Kraków's Old Town (catch the tram on the ring road near Kraków's main train station, at the Basztowa stop) along Pope John Paul II Avenue (aleja Jana Pawła II) to Nowa Huta's main square, plac Centralny (about 30 minutes total). From there, tram #4 (but not #15) continues a few minutes farther to the main gate of the Tadeusz Sendzimir Steelworks, and then it returns to Kraków.

Tours: True to its name, Mike Ostrowski's **Crazy Guides** is a loosely run operation that takes tourists to Nowa Huta in genuine communist-era vehicles (mostly Trabants and Polski Fiats). While the content is good, Mike and his comrades are laid-back, very informal, and sometimes crude. If you're offended by a foul-mouthed guide who reminds you of a scruffy college student, or if you don't like the idea of careening down the streets of Kraków in a car that feels like a cardboard box with a lawnmower engine, skip this tour. For the rest of us, it's a fun and convenient way to experience Nowa Huta (129 zł/person for 2.5-hour Nowa Huta tour; 169 zł/person for 4-hour Communism Deluxe tour that also includes their makeshift "museum"—a communist-era apartment that's decorated to give you a taste of the way things were; 159 zł/person for 4-hour Real Kraków tour that covers the basic Nowa Huta trip plus outlying sights; other crazy experiences also available, cash only, reserve ahead and they'll pick you up at your hotel, mobile 500-091-200, www.crazyguides.com, info@crazyguides.com).

Background: Nowa Huta was the communists' idea of paradise. It's one of only three towns outside the Soviet Union that were custom-built to showcase socialist ideals. (The others are Dunaújváros—once called Sztálinváros—south of Budapest, Hungary; and Eisenhüttenstadt—once called Stalinstadt—near Brandenburg, Germany.) Completed in just 10 years (1949-1959),

Nowa Huta was built primarily because the Soviets felt that smart and sassy Kraków needed a taste of heavy industry. Farmers and villagers were imported to live and work in Nowa Huta. Many of the new residents, who weren't accustomed to city living, brought along their livestock (which grazed in the fields around unfinished buildings). For commies, it was downright idyllic: Dad would cheerily ride the tram into the steel factory, mom would dutifully keep house, and the kids could splash around at the man-made beach

and learn how to cut perfect red stars out of construction paper. But Krakovians had the last laugh: Nowa Huta, along with Lech Wałęsa's shipyard in Gdańsk, was one of the home bases of the Solidarity strikes that eventually brought down the regime. Now, with the communists long gone, Nowa Huta remains a sooty suburb of Poland's cultural capital, with a whopping 200,000 residents.

Touring Nowa Huta: Nowa Huta's focal point used to be known simply as **Central Square** (plac Centralny), but in a fit of poetic justice, it was recently renamed for the anti-communist Ronald Reagan. This square is the heart of the planned town. A map of Nowa Huta looks like a clamshell: a semi-circular design radiating from Central/Reagan Square. Numbered streets fan out like spokes on a wheel, and trolleys zip workers directly to the immense factory.

Believe it or not, the inspiration for Nowa Huta was the Renaissance (which, thanks to the textbook Renaissance design of the Cloth Hall and other landmarks, Soviet architects considered typically Polish). Notice the elegantly predictable arches and galleries that would make Michelangelo proud. The settlement was loosely planned on the gardens of Versailles (comparing aerial views of those two very different sites—both with axes radiating from a central hub—this becomes clear). When first built (before it was layered with grime), Nowa Huta was delightfully orderly, primly painted, impeccably maintained, and downright beautiful... if a little boring. It was practical, too: Each of the huge apartment blocks is a self-contained unit, with its own grassy inner courtyard, school, and shops. Driveways (which appear to dead-end at underground garage doors) lead to vast fallout shelters.

Today's Nowa Huta is a far cry from its glory days. Wander around. Poke into the courtyards. Reflect on what it would be like to live here. It may not be as bad as you imagine. Ugly as they seem from the outside, these buildings are packed with happy little apartments filled with color, light, and warmth.

The wide boulevard running northeast of Central/Reagan Square, now called Solidarity Avenue (aleja Solidarności, lined with tracks for tram #4), leads to the **Tadeusz Sendzimir Steelworks.** Originally named for Lenin, this factory was supposedly built using plans stolen from a Pittsburgh plant. It was designed to be a cog in the communist machine—reliant on iron ore from Ukraine, and therefore worthless unless Poland remained in the Soviet Bloc. Down from as many as 40,000 workers at its peak, the steelworks now employs only about 10,000. Today there's little to see other than the big sign, stern administration buildings, and smokestacks in the distance. Examine the twin offices flanking the sign—topped with turrets and a decorative frieze inspired by Italian palazzos, these continue the Renaissance theme of the housing districts.

Another worthwhile sight in Nowa Huta is the **Lord's Ark Church** (Arka Pana, several blocks northwest of Central/Reagan

Square on ulica Obrońców Krzyża). Back when he was archbishop of Kraków, Karol Wojtyła fought for years to build a church in this most communist of communist towns. When the regime refused, he insisted on conducting open-air Masses before crowds in fields—until the communists finally capitulated. Consecrated on May 15, 1977, the Lord's Ark Church has a Le Corbusier–esque design that looks like a fat, exhausted Noah's Ark resting on Mount Ararat—encouraging Poles to persevere through the floods of communism. While architecturally interesting, the church is mostly significant as a symbol of an early victory of Catholicism over communism.

▲Kościuszko Mound (Kopiec Kościuszki)

On a sunny day, the parklands west of the Old Town are a fine place to get out of the city and commune with Krakovians at play. On the outskirts of town is the Kościuszko Mound, a nearly perfectly conical hill erected in 1823 to honor the Polish and American military hero, Tadeusz Kościuszko. The mound incorporates soil that was brought here from battlefields where the famous general fought, both in Poland and in the American Revolution. Later, under Habsburg rule, a citadel with a chapel was built around the mound, which provided a fine lookout over this otherwise flat terrain. And more recently, the hill was reinforced with steel and cement to prevent it from eroding away. You'll pay to enter the walls and walk to the top—up a curlicue path that makes the mound resemble a giant soft-serve cone—and inside you'll find a modest Kościuszko museum. While not too exciting, this is a pleasant place for an excursion on a nice day.

Cost and Hours: 10 zł, includes museum, mound open daily 9:00-dusk, museum open daily 9:30-16:30, café, tel. 12-425-1116, www.kopieckosciuszki.pl.

Getting There: Ride tram #1 (from in front of the Wyspiański Pavilion or the main post office) to the end of the line, called Salvator, then follow the well-marked path uphill for 20 minutes.

Shopping in Kraków

Two of the most popular Polish souvenirs—amber and pottery—come from areas far from Kraków. Amber *(bursztyn)* is found on northern Baltic shores. "Polish pottery," with distinctive blue-and-white designs, is made in the region of Silesia, west of Kraków (mostly in the town of Bolesławiec). Because neither of these items actually comes from Kraków, you won't find any great bargains. Somewhat more local are the many wood carvings you'll see.

The **Cloth Hall,** smack-dab in the center of the Main Market Square, is the most convenient place to pick up any Polish souvenirs. It has a great selection, respectable prices, and the city's highest concentration of pickpockets (summer Mon-Fri 9:00-18:00, Sat-Sun 9:00-15:00, sometimes later; winter Mon-Fri 9:00-16:00, Sat-Sun 9:00-15:00).

A small but swanky mall called **Pasaż 13** is a few steps off the southeast corner of the Main Market Square, where Grodzka street enters the Square. Enter the mall under the balcony marked *Pasaż 13* (Mon-Sat 9:00-21:00, Sun 11:00-17:00).

Two new, enormous shopping malls lie just beyond the tourist zone. The gigantic **Galeria Krakowska,** with 270 shops, shares a square with the train station (Mon-Sat 9:00-22:00, Sun 10:00-21:00, can't miss it right next to the main train station). Note that nearby landmarks are signposted inside this massive, labyrinthine mall (*PKP/PKS* leads to the train and bus stations; *Stare Miasto* goes to the Old Town). Only slightly smaller is the **Galeria Kazimierz** (Mon-Sat 10:00-22:00, Sun 10:00-20:00, just a few blocks east of the Kazimierz sights, along the river at Podgórska 24).

Entertainment in Kraków

As a town full of both students and tourists, Kraków has plenty of fun options, especially at night.

In the Old Town
Main Market Square
Intoxicating as the Square is by day, it's even better at night...
pure enchantment. Have a meal or nurse a drink at an outdoor
café, or just grab a bench and enjoy the scene. There's often live,
al fresco music coming from somewhere (either at restaurants, at
a temporary stage set up near the Town Hall Tower, or from talented buskers). You could spend hours doing slow laps around the
Square after dark, and never run out of diversions.

Concerts
You'll find a wide range of musical events, from tourist-oriented
"Chopin's greatest hits" in quaint old ballrooms, to folk-dancing
shows, to serious philharmonic performances. Popular venues
include churches (such as the churches of Sts. Peter and Paul on
ulica Grodzka, St. Adalbert on the Square, or St. Idziego/Giles at
the foot of Wawel Hill), various gardens around town (July-Aug
only), and fancy mansions on the Main Market Square (including the Polonia House/Dom Polonii at #14, near ulica Grodzka;
the Bonerowski Palace near the top of the Square at ulica Św.
Jana 1; and the Pod Baranami Palace, at #27). Because Kraków's
live-music scene is continually evolving, it's best to inquire locally
about what's on during your visit. Hotel lobbies are stocked with
fliers for upcoming concerts. But to get all of your options, visit
any TI. The TI on ulica Św. Jana, which specializes in cultural
events, can book tickets for most concerts (no extra fee) and tell
you how to get tickets for the others. The free, monthly *Karnet*
cultural-events book lists everything (half in Polish and half in
English, also online at www.karnet.krakow.pl).

Jazz
For something a little more edgy, delve into Kraków's thriving
jazz scene. Several popular clubs hide on the streets surrounding
the Main Market Square (open nightly, most shows start around
21:30). The most famous and best for all-around jazz in a sophisticated cellar environment is **Jazz Club u Muniaka** (10-20-zł cover,
open nightly 19:00-1:00 in the morning, live music nightly from
21:30, best music when the owner Janusz plays on Thu-Sat, ulica
Floriańska 3, tel. 12-423-1205; described earlier on my self-guided
walk). **Harris Piano Jazz Bar,** right on the Square (at #28), is more
casual and offers a mix of traditional and updated "fusion" jazz,
plus blues (free most nights, 10-zł cover for more serious shows
on Sat, music nightly from 21:30, tel. 12-421-5741, www.harris
.krakow.pl). **Stalowa Magnolia** is a bit more youthful, clubby-
feeling, and snooty, with jazz about two nights a week and rock or
pop the other nights (no cover on weeknights, on weekends 15-zł
cover for men and free for women, music nightly from 22:00, ulica
Św. Jana 15, tel. 12-422-8472, www.stalowemagnolie.com).

KRAKÓW

Nightlife in the Old Town

The entire Old Town is crammed with nightclubs and discos pumping loud music on weekends. On a Saturday, the pedestrian streets can be more crowded at midnight than at noon. However, with the exception of the jazz clubs mentioned earlier, most of the nightspots in the Old Town are garden-variety dance clubs, completely lacking the personality and creativity of the Kazimierz nightspots described next. Worse, to save money, local young people stand out in front of nightclubs to drink their own booze (BYOB), rather than pay high prices for the drinks inside—making the streets that much more crowded and noisy. For low-key hanging out, people choose a café on the Square; otherwise, they head for Kazimierz.

In Kazimierz

Aside from the Old Town's gorgeous Square, Kraków's best area to hang out after dark is Kazimierz, the former Jewish quarter.

Klezmer Music

Several restaurants offer traditional Jewish klezmer music most evenings for a steep 25-zł cover charge (plus the cost of food). On most summer evenings, a klezmer concert or two can be found at theater venues (generally 50 zł; look for posters and fliers around town). The music is lively and evocative, but this is a fairly sedate scene—most of the people around you will be going to bed right after the show. If you'd like to stay up a bit later, there's no better way to spend your time than exploring the bars of Kazimierz (described next).

Bars and Clubs

Squeezed between centuries-old synagogues and cemeteries are wonderful hangouts running the full gamut from sober and tasteful to wild and clubby. The classic recipe for a Kazimierz bar: Find a dilapidated old storefront, fill the interior with ramshackle furniture, turn the lights down low, and pipe in old-timey jazz music from the 1920s. Sprinkle with alcohol. Serves one to two dozen hipsters. After a few clubs of this type caught on, a more diverse cross-section of nightspots began to move in, including some loud dance clubs. The whole area is bursting with life—it's the kind of place where people just spontaneously start dancing—and locals still outnumber tourists. I've listed websites for places that feature periodic live music and other events.

On and near Plac Nowy: The highest concentration of bars ring the plac Nowy market square. While most of these are nondescript, a few stand out. **Alchemia**, one of the first—and still one of the best—bars in Kazimierz, is candlelit, cluttered, and claustrophobic, with cave-like rooms crowded with rickety old furniture,

plus a cellar used for live performances (Estery 5, www.alchemia
.com.pl). Hiding just a half-block down the street is **Miejsce** ("The
Place"), which is brighter and more minimalist than the norm,
with stripped-down walls and carefully chosen Scan-design old
furniture—it's run by the owners of a design firm specializing in
decor from the 50s, 60s, and 70s (Estery 1). Fronting the square,
Kolory has a pleasant Parisian brasserie ambience (Estery 10),
while **Le Scandale** is all black leather and serves Italian food (plac
Nowy 9). Late at night, the little windows in the plac Nowy **market hall** do a big business selling *zapiekanki* (baguette with toppings) to hungry bar-hoppers.

On Rabina Meiselsa street, just a half-block off plac Nowy,
two places share a long courtyard: **Mleczarnia**, a top-notch beer
garden with rickety tables squeezed under the trees and its cozy
old-fashioned pub across the street (at #20); and **Stajnia**, at the
far end of the courtyard, where scenes from *Schindler's List* were
filmed. Its interior feels like a Polish village drenched in red light
and turned into a dance hall.

Near Isaac Synagogue: A block east of plac Nowy, a few
more places cluster on the wide street in front of Isaac Synagogue.
The huge **Nova Resto Bar** dominates the scene with a long covered terrace, a vast interior, and seating in their courtyard—all
with a cool-color-scheme Las Vegas polka-dot style. This feels
upscale and a bit pretentious compared to many of the others,
but it's *the* place to be seen (25-40-zł meals, Estery 18). Upstairs
is the similarly trendy music club **Taawa** (www.taawa.pl). Facing
this double-decker wall of style are some smaller, more accessible
options: **Singer** is classy and mellow, with most of its tables made
of old namesake sewing machines (Estery 20), while **Warsztat** has
an exploding-instruments-factory ambience (Izaaka 3; also recommended later, under "Eating in Kraków").

On Józefa Street: More good bars are just a short block
south. Along Józefa, you'll find a pair of classic Kazimierz joints:
Eszeweria, which wins the "best atmosphere" award, feels like a
Polish speakeasy that's been in mothballs for the last 90 years—
a low-key, unpretentious, and inviting hangout (Józefa 9). Their
less enticing but still enjoyable sister bar, Esze, is across the street.
A block up, look for **Kolanko No. 6,** with a cozy bar up front,
a pleasant beer garden in the inner courtyard, and a fun events
hall in back (Józefa 17, www.kolanko.net; also recommended later,
under "Eating in Kraków").

In Podgórze: If you run out of diversions in the heart of
Kazimierz, head south. With the construction of a new pedestrian
bridge over the river just south of this area, Kazimierz's nightlife
scene is spreading to **Podgórze,** just across the river. Here in this
fast-evolving zone, prices are a bit lower.

Sleeping in Kraków

Healthy competition—with new, cleverly run places cropping up all the time—keeps Kraków's accommodation prices reasonable and makes choosing a hotel fun rather than frustrating. Rates are soft; hoteliers don't need much of an excuse to offer you 10 to 20 percent off, especially on weekends or off-season. I've focused my accommodations in two areas: in and near the Old Town; and in Kazimierz, a local-style, more affordable neighborhood that is home to both the old Jewish quarter and a thriving dining and nightlife zone.

While the Old Town used to be sleepy, it's now jam-packed with discos that thump loud music on weekend nights to attract roving gangs of rowdy students, backpackers, and obnoxious "stag parties" of drunken louts from the UK in town for a weekend of carousing. The "quiet after 22:00" law is flagrantly ignored. Kazimierz is also home to various hip dance clubs. Because of all these clubs, virtually all of my accommodations come with some risk of noise; to help your odds, ask for a quiet room when you reserve, and bring earplugs.

In the Old Town

While you could stay away from the center, accommodations values here are so good that there's little sense in sleeping beyond the Planty park. Most of my listings are inside (or within a block or two of) the former city walls.

The Old Town has four basic types of accommodations: small, well-run guest houses (my favorite); big hotels (comfortable but overpriced); apartments (cheap, but you're on your own); and funky youth hostels. I've listed the best of each type.

Guest Houses

These good-value pensions almost invariably come with lots of stairs (no elevators), and are run by smart, can-do, entrepreneurial owners. They're all located in the heart of the Old Town along busy pedestrian streets, and most don't have air-conditioning—so they can be noisy with the windows open in the summer, especially on weekends. (Light sleepers should request quiet rooms.) These places book up fast, especially in summer—reserve as far ahead as possible. Don't expect a 24-hour reception desk; it's always smart to tell them your arrival time, especially if it's late in the day.

$$ Tango House, run by tango dance instructor Marcin Miszczak, is in a well-located building with an ancient-feeling stairwell decorated with faded Art Nouveau paintings. Its eight long, skinny, stylish rooms have parquet floors (tiny Sb-220 zł, standard Sb-300 zł, Db-340 zł, big Db-380 zł, prices can be soft

Sleep Code

(3 zł = about $1, country code: 48)
S = Single, **D** = Double/Twin, **T** = Triple, **Q** = Quad, **b** = bathroom, **s** = shower only. Unless otherwise noted, credit cards are accepted, and breakfast is included. Everyone listed here speaks English.

To help you easily sort through these listings, I've divided the accommodations into three categories based on the price for a double room with bath during high season:

$$$ **Higher Priced**—Most rooms 400 zł or more.
$$ **Moderately Priced**—Most rooms between 300-400 zł.
$ **Lower Priced**—Most rooms 300 zł or less.

Prices can change without notice; verify the hotel's current rates online or by email. For the best prices, always book direct.

in slow times, about 100 zł cheaper Nov-March, Wi-Fi, ask for quieter courtyard room to avoid rowdy street noise on weekends, ulica Szpitalna 4, tel. 12-429-3114, www.tangohouse.pl, info @tangohouse.pl).

$ Golden Lion Guest House has 12 smallish rooms with modern flair on a bustling pedestrian street a block off the Main Market Square (Sb-180 zł, Db-300 zł, 10 percent cheaper Nov-Feb, ask for quieter room in back, air-con in some rooms, guest computer, Wi-Fi, guest kitchen, no parking, ulica Szewska 19, tel. 12-422-9323, www.goldenlion.pl, reservation@goldenlion.pl, Łodziński family and Tyson, a smelly boxer dog).

$ Globtroter Guest House offers 18 rustic-feeling rooms with high ceilings and big beams around a serene garden courtyard. Jacek (Jack), who really understands and respects travelers, conscientiously focuses on value—keeping prices as low as possible by not offering needless extras (June-Aug: Sb-190 zł, Db-310 zł; April-May and Sept-Oct: Sb-170 zł, Db-290 zł; Nov-March: Sb-120 zł, Db-180 zł; ask for 10 percent discount with this book, 2 people can cram into a single to save money—a little more than the Sb price, larger suites for up to five also available, no breakfast at hotel but you can buy 14-zł breakfast from nearby restaurant, guest computer, Wi-Fi, fun 700-year-old brick cellar lounge down below, go down passageway at #7 at the square called plac Szczepański, tel. 12-422-4123, www.globtroter-krakow.com, globtroter@globtroter-krakow.com).

$ La Fontaine B&B, run by a French-Polish family, offers 14 rooms and 9 apartments in two different buildings just off the

KRAKOW

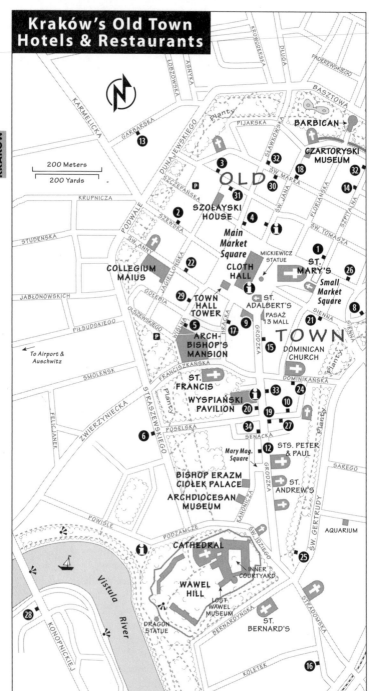

Kraków's Old Town Hotels & Restaurants

KRAKÓW

1. Tango House
2. Golden Lion Guest House
3. Globtroter Guest House
4. La Fontaine B&B #1
5. La Fontaine B&B #2
6. Hotel Maltański
7. Hotel Pugetów
8. Hotel Gródek
9. Wentzl Hotel, Wierzynek Rest. & Słodki Wentzl
10. Hotel Wawel
11. Hotel Classic
12. Hotel Senacki & Bar Grodzki
13. Hotel Amber
14. Kraków City Apts.
15. Grodzka Apt. House
16. Nathan's Villa Hostel
17. Mama's Hostel
18. Restauracja Farina
19. Miód Malina Restaurant
20. Restauracja pod Aniołami
21. Aperitif Restaurant
22. Chimera Cafeteria
23. Restauracja Jarema
24. Ancora Restaurant
25. Pod Wawelem Beer Hall
26. Cyklop Pizza
27. Pizzeria Trzy Papryczki
28. Pizza Garden
29. Aqua e Vino
30. Indus Tandoor
31. Polskie Smaki
32. U Babci Maliny (2)
33. Kwandras Lunch Bar
34. Bar Mleczny

Main Market Square (one of them has lots of stairs and no elevator; the other does have an elevator). Tastefully decorated with
French flair, it's cute as a poodle. Each room has a little lounge
with a microwave and fridge—most on the hall, some inside the
room (Sb-224 zł, Db-239 zł, extra bed-60 zł, apartment for up
to four-297 zł, apartment for up to six-465 zł, gigantic apart-
ment-639 zł, 30 percent cheaper Nov-Easter, air-con, low slanted
ceilings in some rooms, Wi-Fi, guest kitchen, free self-service
laundry machine—or pay them 25 zł to wash clothes for you, ulica
Sławkowska 1, tel. 12-422-6564, www.bblafontaine.com, biuro
@bblafontaine.com). They also have six newer rooms and two
apartments in another, equally convenient Old Town location, just
south of the Square; you'll check in at the main hotel, then walk
five minutes to your room (similar prices to main hotel).

Hotels

For this section, I've listed the official, published "rack rates"—
which are very soft. Most hotels discount their rates substantially,
especially in slow times. Consider asking several hotels for their
lowest price during your visit, and take the best deal.

$$$ Donimirski Boutique Hotels, with three different loca-
tions in or near Kraków's Old Town, set the bar for splurge hotels
in Kraków (website for all: www.donimirski.com). All Donimirski
hotels offer my readers a 15 percent discount. You can expect any of
these hotels to have some of the friendliest staff in Kraków and all
of the classy little extras that add up to a memorable hotel experi-
ence. **Hotel Maltański**—my home away from home in Kraków—
has 16 rooms in the beautifully renovated former royal stables, just
outside the Planty park and only two blocks from Wawel Castle
(Sb-430 zł, Db-510 zł, 80 zł more for "deluxe" room with air-
con, cheaper Nov-March, no elevator but only 2 floors, Wi-Fi,
parking-50 zł/day, ulica Straszewskiego 14, tel. 12-431-0010,
maltanski@donimirski.com). **Hotel Pugetów,** with seven small
but plush and cozy rooms and a fun breakfast cellar, is on the
other side of town, in a slightly dingy but convenient neighbor-
hood between the Main Market Square and Kazimierz (Sb-280
zł, Db-490 zł, Db suite-640 zł, cheaper Nov-March, air-con,
cable Internet, parking-50 zł/day, ulica Starowiślna 13-15, tel.
12-432-4950, pugetow@donimirski.com). **Hotel Gródek**—by
far the fanciest and most central of the bunch—offers 23 rooms
a three-minute walk behind St. Mary's Church on a quiet dead-
end street overlooking the Planty park. This place is easily the
best splurge in town, with a handy location, gorgeously decorated
rooms, and a top-notch breakfast served in a room surrounded by a
mini-museum of artifacts discovered during the recent renovation
(Sb-470 zł, bigger "deluxe" Sb-630 zł, Db-610 zł, bigger "deluxe"

Db-690 zł, suite-920 zł, cheaper Nov-March, guest computer, Wi-Fi, good cellar restaurant serves Polish cuisine, parking-50 zł/day, Na Gródku 4, tel. 12-431-9030, grodek@donimirski.com). If you have a car, ask about rooms at their countryside castle, Zamek Korzkiew. Their fifth property, Hotel Kościuszko, has five stars and reasonable prices, but is located far from the center.

$$$ Wentzl Hotel is your splurge-right-on-the-Square option, with 18 rooms. The decor is over-the-top-classy Old World with modern touches, like state-of-the-art TVs and bathrooms. When reserving, request a room with a view on the Square—which can be noisy, especially on weekends—or one of the three quieter back rooms (Sb-665 zł, Db-700 zł, bigger "deluxe" rooms cost 50 zł more, air-con, elevator, Wi-Fi, Rynek Główny 19, tel. 12-430-2664, www.wentzl.pl, hotel@wentzl.pl).

$$$ Hotel Wawel has 39 rooms on a well-located street that's quieter than the Old Town norm. It feels plush for the price, though its colorful decor verges on gaudy; above the swanky marble lobby are hallways creatively painted with the history of the building and images from around Kraków (Sb-340 zł, Db-480 zł, extra bed-100 zł/adult or 50 zł/child, rates are soft so ask for best price, 20 percent less Nov-March, non-smoking, air-con, elevator—but doesn't go to top floor, guest computer, Wi-Fi, ulica Poselska 22, tel. 12-424-1300, www.hotelwawel.pl, hotel@hotelwawel.pl).

$$$ Hotel Classic, a modern home in old Kraków (on a nondescript street just inside the Planty park), has 30 Scan-designed rooms, a sleek marble lobby, professional staff, decent prices, and little character (April-Oct: Sb-495 zł, Db-540 zł, suite-740 zł, cheaper Nov-March, Rick Steves readers get a 20 percent discount on weekdays and 25 percent discount Fri-Sun with a 2-night minimum stay, non-smoking floor, air-con, elevator, Wi-Fi and cable Internet, request one of the few quiet back rooms to avoid weekend disco noise from across the street, ulica Św. Tomasza 32, tel. 12-424-0303, www.hotel-classic.pl, hotel@hotel-classic.pl).

$$$ Hotel Senacki is a business-class place renting 20 aging rooms with parquet floors between Wawel Castle and the Main Market Square. Nine of the rooms have air-conditioning for no extra charge—if you'll be here in summer, request this when you reserve. Top-floor "attic" rooms have low beams, skylight windows, and a flight of stairs after the elevator (prices change constantly with demand, but generally Sb-400 zł, Db-500 zł, deluxe Db-550 zł, extra bed-90 zł, cheaper Nov-March, non-smoking rooms, elevator—but doesn't go to "attic" rooms, Wi-Fi, parking-50 zł/day, ulica Grodzka 51, tel. 12-422-7686, www.osti-hotele.pl, senacki @osti-hotele.pl).

$$ Hotel Amber sits on a grimy but safe and quiet street just outside the Planty park, less than a 10-minute walk from the

Square. With 18 rooms, attentive service, and modern style, it's a good-value alternative to the places inside the Old Town (Sb-350 zł, standard Db-438 zł, bigger "superior" Db-479 zł, "deluxe" Db with fancier touches-499 zł, cheaper Nov-March, air-con, elevator, Wi-Fi, Garbarska 10, tel. 12-421-0606, www.hotel-amber.pl, office@hotel-amber.pl).

Apartments

You can save money by staying in your own apartment rather than a hotel. Apartments come with great locations, simple kitchens, and relatively low prices, but no reception desk or big-hotel services (such as having your room cleaned daily)...you're on your own. Apartments aren't just for long stays—these places welcome even one-nighters. While the apartments themselves are neat and modern, most are in old buildings with dreary entryways and stairways. Be sure to clearly communicate your arrival time.

$ **Kraków City Apartments,** conscientiously run by Andzej and Katarzyna, is 10 clean, modern apartments tucked away in a quiet courtyard at the corner of the Old Town (small Db-200 zł, standard Db-260 zł, bigger apartment-350 zł, 20 percent cheaper Oct-April, non-smoking, elevator in one building, Wi-Fi, ulica Szpitalna 34, tel. 12-431-0041, mobile 504-235-925, www.krakow apartments.info, info@krakowapartments.info).

$ **Grodzka Apartment House** offers 11 new-feeling, stylishly decorated apartments around a courtyard along one of Kraków's most happening streets, just a few steps off the Main Market Square. The studio apartments are as nice as a hotel room and a good value (studio-250 zł, 1-bedroom-330 zł, 2-bedroom-450 zł, prices soft, cheaper Nov-March, no breakfast but can buy 25-zł breakfast at nearby café, reception open daily 11:00-21:00, some apartments have street noise—light sleepers ask for quiet room, lots of stairs with no elevator, Wi-Fi, go down the passage at Grodzka 4, tel. 12-421-4835, mobile 660-541-085, www.grodzka .net.pl, info@grodzka.net.pl, Mikołaj). They also have more apartments (though not quite as nice) in two other Old Town buildings.

Hostels

New hostels are born—and go extinct—every other day in Kraków. But these three are well-established.

$ **Nathan's Villa Hostel,** in an up-and-coming neighborhood between Wawel Hill and Kazimierz, is well-run by an energetic young Bostonian and his wife. It's loose, easygoing, and fun, with 120 beds in 21 cleverly painted rooms, a bar, a beer garden, an art gallery, a cheap BBQ every night in summer, and plenty of back-packer bonding. Their advertising promises advice on how to "get hammered," and the bar has regular drinking contests...if that's not your scene, sleep elsewhere (bunk in 4-bed room-65 zł, in 6-bed room-60 zł, in 8-bed room-55 zł, in 10-bed room-45 zł, D-160 zł, Db-180 zł, apartment with kitchenette for up to four-280 zł, rates are 5 zł/person less Nov-Feb; includes breakfast, sheets, laundry facilities, and lockers; guest computer, Wi-Fi, non-smoking, no curfew or lockout time, ulica Św. Agnieszki 1, tel. 12-422-3545, www.nathansvilla.com, krakow@nathansvilla.com).

$ Mama's Hostel is ideally located (just steps off the Main Market Square) and more dignified than most hostels—like an old apartment taken over by vagabonds with good manners, but who still know how to have a good time. With 54 beds in 7 rooms and mellow public spaces, it's a winner (60 zł/person in a 6-bed room, 55 zł in a 10-bed room, 50 zł in a 12-bed room, D-180 zł; includes sheets, breakfast, and lockers; non-smoking, no curfew, lots of stairs with no elevator, guest computer, Wi-Fi, kitchen, pay laundry, ulica Bracka 4, tel. 12-429-5940, www.mamashostel.com .pl, hostel@mamashostel.com.pl).

$ Hostel Momotown, in Kazimierz (described next), is a smidge more institutional and less party-oriented than the above options, but still loose and friendly. Run by Paweł Momot, it has 52 dorm beds and a fun garden for hanging out (bunk in 4-bed dorm-60 zł, in 6-bed dorm-55 zł, in 8-bed dorm-55 zł, in 10-bed dorm-45 zł, includes breakfast and sheets, towels-2.50 zł, guest computer, Wi-Fi, kitchen, laundry, lockers, ulica Miodowa 28, tel. 12-429-6929, www.momotownhostel.com, info@momotown hostel.com). Two blocks away, they also rent 14 basic but cheap private rooms that share a kitchenette, overlooking Kazimierz's main square, ulica Szeroka (Sb-140 zł, Db-180 zł).

In Kazimierz

Sleep in Kazimierz to be close to Kraków's Jewish heart—or simply to experience a cheaper, less touristy, more local-feeling neighborhood outside the Old Town. With the highest concentration of pubs and nightclubs in town, Kazimierz rivals the Old Town for nightlife—which means that all of these places can be subject to some noise, especially on weekends. Keep in mind that these accommodations put you a 20-minute walk or a 5-minute tram ride from the medieval ambience of Kraków's old center. Some of the klezmer music restaurants listed under "Eating in Kraków" also rent rooms, but they're generally an afterthought to the food and music, and not a good value. Note that Hostel Momotown—listed above—is also in Kazimierz.

$$ Dom Casimi is nicely located, with 12 rooms at the top of ulica Szeroka in the heart of Jewish Kazimierz (Sb-155-260 zł, Db-220-370 zł, Tb-240-430 zł, price depends on size, season, and style of room—pricier rooms have antique furniture, rates are soft so ask for best price, stairs with no elevator, Wi-Fi and cable Internet, free loaner bikes for guests, ulica Szeroka 7/8, tel. 12-426-1193, www.casimi.pl, casimi@casimi.pl).

$$ Karmel Hotel, with 11 rooms on a pleasant side street near the heart of Kazimierz, offers elegance at a reasonable price (Sb-260 zł, tight twin Db-298 zł, more spacious "komfort plus" Db with one big bed and air-con-398 zł, pricier suites also available, extra bed-70 zł, about 15-20 percent less Nov-March, upstairs with no elevator, guest computer, Wi-Fi, some night noise on weekends, ulica Kupa 15, tel. 12-430-6697, www.karmel.com.pl, hotel@karmel.com.pl).

$ Tournet Guest House, well-run by friendly Piotr and Sylwia Działowy, is a great budget option offering 19 clean, colorful rooms near the edge of Kazimierz toward Wawel Hill. The "basic" rooms don't include breakfast (7.50 zł extra) or TV sets (basic Sb-110 zł, standard Sb-150 zł, basic Db-140 zł, standard Db-200 zł, Tb-250 zł, extra bed-50 zł, 10 zł/person less Nov-March, lots of stairs with no elevator, Wi-Fi, reception open 7:00-22:00, ulica Miodowa 7, tel. 12-292-0088, www.nocleg.krakow.pl, tournet@accommodation.krakow.pl).

$ Maayan Guest Rooms offers 11 simple, cozy, cheap rooms surrounding the 17th-century Kupa Synagogue. You can walk through the balconies overlooking the synagogue's prayer hall (S-70 zł, Sb-120 zł, D-100 zł, Db-180 zł, T-160 zł, Tb-210 zł, cash only, no breakfast, non-smoking, guest computer, Wi-Fi, café, bike rental, some nightclub noise on weekends—ask for quiet room, ulica Miodowa 27, tel. 12-431-0170, maayanhotel@gmail .com).

Eating in Kraków

Kraków has a wide array of great restaurants—for every one I've listed, there are two or three nearly as good. (The downside is a lack of variation; little distinguishes one place from another.) Polish food is rivaled by Italian in popularity. As the restaurant scene changes constantly, I've chosen places that are well-established and have a proven track record for reliably good food.

In the Old Town

Kraków's Old Town is loaded with dining options. Prices are reasonable even on the Main Market Square. And a half-block away, they get even better. All of these eateries (except the milk bars) are likely to be booked up on weekends—always reserve ahead.

Restauracja Farina, with a fish-and-bottles theme, features a welcoming atmosphere and Polish and Mediterranean cuisine with an emphasis on fresh fish (30-35-zł pastas, 30-60-zł main dishes). They serve some special seafood dishes (60-100 zł) only on the days that they get their fresh delivery (about twice weekly; open daily 12:00-23:00, 2 blocks north of the Square at ulica Św. Marka 16, at intersection with ulica Św. Jana, tel. 12-422-1680).

Miód Malina ("Honey Raspberry") is a delightful Polish-Italian fusion restaurant filled with the comforting aroma of its wood-fired oven. The menu is half Polish and half Italian—yet, remarkably, they do both cuisines equally well. For example, you can start with borscht and follow it with lasagna Bolognese. Sit in the cozy, warmly painted interior, or out in the courtyard (19-zł pierogi, 25-zł pastas, 40-70-zł main dishes, reservations smart, daily 12:00-23:00, ulica Grodzka 40, tel. 12-430-0411).

Restauracja pod Aniołami ("Under Angels") offers a dressy, candlelit atmosphere on a wonderful covered patio, or in a deep, steep, romantic cellar with rough wood and medieval vaults. Peruse the elaborately described menu of medieval noblemen's dishes. The cuisine is traditional Polish, with an emphasis on grilled meats and trout (on a wood-fired grill). Every meal begins with *smalec* (spread made with lard, fried onion, bacon, and apple). Don't go here if you're in a hurry—only if you want to really slow down and enjoy your dinner. Reservations are smart (15-30-zł starters, 40-70-zł main dishes, daily 13:00-24:00, ulica Grodzka 35, tel. 12-421-3999).

Aperitif is a stylish bistro serving tasty international cuisine with Mediterranean flair on the appealing Small Market Square (Mały Rynek) behind St. Mary's Church. It's classy but casual, with a cozy interior and a pleasant garden in back. Their 19- or 25-zł lunch specials, served on weekdays, are a great deal (22-26-zł pastas, 35-50-zł main dishes, daily 10:00-23:00, ulica Sienna 9, tel. 12-432-3333).

Chimera, just off the Main Market Square, is a cafeteria that serves fast traditional meals to a steady stream of students. You'll order at the counter, then eat outside on their quiet courtyard (good salad buffet: small plate-12 zł, big plate-16 zł; 12-19-zł main dishes, good for vegetarians, daily 9:00-22:00, near university at ulica Św. Anny 3). I'd skip their expensive full-service restaurant (in the basement), which shares an entryway.

Restauracja Jarema (yah-RAY-mah) offers a tasty reminder that Kraków used to rule a large swath of Ukraine and Lithuania. They serve eastern Polish/Ukrainian cuisine (with well-described specialties) amid 19th-century aristocratic elegance—you'll feel like you're dining in an old mansion. It's very sedate and feels a bit tired, but the food satisfies (30-55-zł main dishes, several good vegetarian options, daily 12:00-22:00, usually live music from 19:00, reservations wise, across the street from barbican at plac

Matejki 5, tel. 12-429-3669).

Fine Dining: **Ancora** attempts to bring a touch of modern class and creativity to Kraków's otherwise staid and predictable culinary landscape. Chef Adam Chrząstowski, who worked under world-famous chef Thomas Keller, offers modern international food with a Polish accent. It's not cheap—you're basically paying Square-view prices for a sleek minimalist dining room tucked alongside the Dominican Church—but the food is a notch above (30-40-zł starters, 55-70-zł main dishes; fixed-price meals: 155 zł/5 courses, 190 kn/7 courses; daily 11:00-22:30, Dominikańska 3, tel. 12-357-3355).

Beer Hall: **Pod Wawelem** ("Under Wawel") is a rollicking Austrian-style beer hall right on the Planty park near Wawel Castle. It's packed with locals seeking big, sloppy, greasy portions of meaty fare, with giant mugs of various beers on tap (including Polish and Bavarian). Choose between the bustling interior, or the outdoor terrace right on the Planty (20-30-zł main dishes, different specials every day—such as giant schnitzel, pork ribs, or roasted chicken; daily 12:00-24:00, ulica Św. Gertrudy 26-29, tel. 12-421-2336).

Pizza: Two well-established places in the Old Town are reliable choices. **Cyklop,** with 10 tables wrapped around the cook and his busy oven, has good wood-fired pizzas (14-23-zł one-person pizzas, 15-26-zł two-person pizzas, daily 11:00-23:00, near St. Mary's Church at Mikołajska 16, tel. 12-421-6603). **Pizzeria Trzy Papryczki** ("Three Peppers"), whose wood-fired pizzas aren't quite as good as Cyklop's, has better ambience, either inside or out in the welcoming garden (17-25-zł one-person pizzas, 20-29-zł two-person pizzas, daily 11:00-23:00, ulica Poselska 17, tel. 12-292-5532). But the best pizza in town is at **Pizza Garden,** run by Stanisław, who worked at a respected New York City pizzeria for a decade and has brought the art of brick-oven pizza back home. The catch is that his place is well outside the Old Town, about a 10-minute walk across the river from Wawel Hill (the walk is mostly along the pretty riverside parkland and across Dębnicki Bridge, with great views back on the castle). This makes it a good post-Wawel lunch or dinner spot (16-30-zł one-person pizzas, 20-25-zł two-person pizzas, Mon-Wed 13:00-22:00, Thu-Sun 13:00-23:00; cross Dębnicki Bridge, then look right to find M. Konopnickiej 11/1; tel. 12-266-7309).

Serious Italian: The Italian-owned **Aqua e Vino** offers good food in a mellow, mod, black-and-white cellar decorated with giant stills from old movies. Probably the most authentic Italian eatery in town, it has a loyal following among the Italian expat community (20-40-zł pastas, 45-65-zł main dishes, daily 12:00-24:00, ulica Wiślna 5/10, tel. 12-421-2567).

Indian: **Indus Tandoor** is Kraków's oldest Indian restaurant, and the best I've tried in town. If you're ready for a break from Polish fare, this is the place (20-35-zł dishes, daily 12:00-22:00, Fri-Sat until 24:00, Sławkowska 13-15, tel. 12-423-2282).

Milk Bars

Kraków is a good place to try the cheap cafeterias called "milk bars." I've listed them by neighborhoods: north or south of the Main Market Square.

North of the Main Market Square

These two options, easy to squeeze into a busy day of sightseeing, are my favorites in Kraków.

Polskie Smaki ("Polish Flavors") is a homey little self-service cafeteria with a surprisingly elegant interior. They serve fast, inexpensive, and tasty traditional meals a block off the Square, with good borscht and *gołąbki* (stuffed cabbage rolls) at a fraction of what you'd pay elsewhere (9-13-zł main dishes, daily 10:00-22:00, ulica Św. Tomasza 5, tel. 12-422-4822).

U Babci Maliny, with a grinning Granny on the sign, is another well-established and popular upmarket milk bar (6-18-zł main dishes). One location is across the street from the National Theater building at Szpitalna 38 (daily 11:00-23:00), while another—frequented almost entirely by Krakovians—is designed for university students and staff and is tucked into an inner courtyard of the Science Academy (find the door at Sławkowska 17, Mon-Fri 11:00-21:00, Sat-Sun 12:00-21:00).

On Grodzka Street, South of the Main Market Square

Ulica Grodzka, the busy street that cuts south from the Main Market Square, has a convenient little pocket of three milk bars within a few steps of each other (all are open daily for lunch and dinner, but only until 19:00 or 20:00, sometimes later in summer). Survey all three options before you dive in. If they look full, just wait—there's a lot of turnover, so a table should free up soon.

Approaching from the Square, the first one you'll come to (just after the modern copper-colored Wyspiański Pavilion, on the left) is the most modern and trendy of the three, more popular with students than with their grandparents: **Kwandras Lunch Bar** ("Quarter"—as in, you can eat here in a quarter-hour; pierogi and other dishes for 9-12 zł, full dinner for 13 zł, ulica Grodzka 32, tel. 12-294-2222).

Two blocks down the street and on the right (at the corner with Senacka) is the most basic and traditional milk bar, with a sign reading simply **Bar Mleczny** ("Milk Bar"; a low-profile sign over the door gives the eatery's name, *Restauracja "pod Temidą"*). The next best thing to a time machine to the communist era, this place has grumpy monolingual service, a mostly local clientele, and cheap but good food (8-15-zł main dishes).

A few more steps down, also on the right (just before the two churches), is **Bar Grodzki,** a single tight little room with shared tables. In addition to the standard milk-bar fare, Bar Grodzki specializes in tasty potato pancake dishes *(placki ziemniaczane).* Order high on the menu and try the rich and hearty "Hunter's Delight"— potato pancake with sausage, beef, melted cheese, and spicy sauce for 20 zł. The English menu posted by the counter makes ordering easy. Order, sit, and wait to be called to fetch your food (most main dishes 9-20 zł).

Splurging on the Main Market Square

You'll find plenty of relatively expensive, tourist-oriented restaurants on the Square. While all of these places have rich interiors, there's not much point in paying a premium to dine here unless you're sitting outside on the Square (one exception is Pod Krzyżkiem at #39, with a surrealistic interior that boldly attempts to one-up Eastern Europe's top square). While tourists go for ye olde places, natives hang out at pizza joints (like Sphinx, part of a wildly popular Poland-wide chain). Poles generally afford this zone on their meager incomes by just having a drink on the Square after eating at home. If any place on the Square is a cut above, it's probably **Wierzynek**—the most famous restaurant on the Square (and maybe in all of Poland)—with a heritage dating back to 1364 and a guest list of notables ranging from heads of state to movie stars. It lives up to its big reputation with good food at not-too-outrageous prices in two dining zones (both with seating either indoors, or out on the Square—if dining outside, be clear on which area you want). The fancier restaurant serves sophisticated Polish fare (22-35-zł starters, 60-85-zł main dishes, daily 13:00-23:00), while the simpler café is a good budget alternative, with salads for under 30 zł and 20-40-zł Polish traditional classics (daily 10:00-23:00; both at #15, tel. 12-424-9600).

And for Dessert: **Słodki Wentzl** ("Sweets") is a local favorite for enjoying dessert on the Square. Consider dining more cheaply elsewhere, then finishing up with coffee, ice cream, or cake here (12-25-zł desserts, daily 11:00-23:00, at #19).

In Kazimierz

The entire district is bursting with lively cafés and bars—it's a happening night scene. Jewish food is the specialty here, but in general the neighborhood offers more diversity than the Old Town. The non-Jewish places I've listed are fast, cheap, and convenient.

Klezmer Concerts and Jewish Food

Kazimierz is a hub of Jewish restaurants, featuring cuisine and music that honors the neighborhood's Jewish heritage (and caters to its Jewish visitors). On a balmy summer night, the air is filled with the sound of klezmer music—traditional Jewish music from 19th-century Poland, generally with violin, string bass, clarinet, and accordion. Skilled klezmer musicians can make their instruments weep or laugh like human voices. Several places on ulica Szeroka (Kazimierz's main square) offer klezmer concerts around 20:00. All of these have several rooms, which the musicians move between as the evening goes on. While most places claim to do concerts nightly year-round, in reality they can be canceled anytime it's slow (especially off-season). For this reason—and because these places fill up—it's important to reserve ahead. (If you're in Kazimierz for some daytime sightseeing, visit several places, pick your favorite, and reserve dinner.) Each restaurant has a similar menu, with main dishes for 20-55 zł. Sometimes you'll need to order sides and starches separately. You'll pay an additional cover charge just for the music (about 25 zł/person). Don't expect great cuisine—you're here for the music.

Arka Noego ("Noah's Ark") has a good reputation for its music and its food (slightly cheaper food than the others, daily 10:00-2:00 in the morning, Izaaka 7, tel. 12-429-1528, mobile 669-635-106).

At **Klezmer-Hois,** which fills a venerable former Jewish ritual bathhouse, you'll feel like you're dining in a rich grandparent's home (daily 8:00-22:00, at #6, tel. 12-411-1245).

Ariel is popular but has gone downhill in recent years, and receives mixed reviews for its food (daily 10:00-24:00, music in up to six different rooms, best upstairs in the larger dining hall, at #18, tel. 12-421-7920).

Awiw is the poor man's option for live klezmer music. Each evening from 18:00 to 23:00, they have live music outside on their patio on ulica Szeroka with no cover charge. (You can also hear it just fine sitting at other restaurants and bars facing the square.) They also serve a menu of affordable Jewish and Polish food (30-50-zł main dishes, daily 10:00-23:00, Szeroka 13, tel. 12-341-4279).

Fast and Cheap

Bagelmama, run by an American named Nava (who has worked as a private chef for US tennis star John McEnroe), is a casual bagel shop that's understandably popular with expats. Nava and his staff serve up a wide range of sandwiches, soups, salads, burritos, desserts, and good espresso drinks. The bagels come dressed with a wide variety of spreads, from simple cream cheese or peanut butter to lox, tuna, or curried chicken. You can eat in or get it to go (most items 10-17 zł, 16-21-zł salads, selection of "bagel tapas" with various toppings for 18.50 zł/person for 2 people, daily 9:00-18:00, possibly later in summer, ulica Dajwór 10, tel. 12-346-1646).

Restauracja Samoobsługowa Polakowski is a glorified milk bar with country-kitchen decor, and cheap and tasty Polish fare. Curt service...cute hats (9-12-zł main dishes, borrow the English menu and/or point to what you want, daily 9:00-22:00, just behind the top of ulica Szeroka at ulica Miodowa 39).

The **plac Nowy market** offers a fully authentic, very cheap, blue-collar Polish experience—join the workers on their lunch break at the little food windows on Kazimierz's market square. This area is particularly known for its *zapiekanki*—the uniquely Polish fast food of a toasted baguette with cheese, ketchup, and other toppings (Bar Endzior is well-regarded). More recently, a wide range of trendy restaurants and bars has sprung up around the square. Survey your options and choose your favorite.

Dining in Kazimierz

For a good-quality sit-down meal, consider these options.

Starka has romantic, dark-red decor and walls hung with sketches from a circa 1910 Berlin cartoonist. In addition to good Polish cuisine, they have 16 types of their own homemade flavored vodkas (12-18-zł starters, 30-45-zł main dishes, daily 12:00-23:00, Józefa 14, tel. 12-430-6538).

Szara is a well-respected Kraków institution (with another location near the Main Market Square). This popular spot—a bit more upscale and dressy than the tired klezmer joints—provides refined food at reasonable prices (20-30-zł starters, 35-60-zł main dishes, 40-zł lunch special includes soup and a main dish, open daily, Szeroka 39, tel. 12-429-1219).

Kazimierz Bars with Food

Two of my favorite atmospheric Kazimierz bars also serve food. It's not high cuisine—the food is an afterthought to the busy bar.

Kolanko No. 6 has a classic Kazimierz atmosphere. The bar up front is filled with old secondhand furniture. Walking toward the back, you discover an inviting garden with tables, and beyond that, a hall where they host events. They serve light meals, specializing in crêpes, toasted sandwiches, and salads (13-17 zł, daily 10:00-24:00, Józefa 17, tel. 12-292-0320).

Warsztat ("Workshop") is littered with musical instruments: The bar is a piano, and the tight interior is crammed with other instruments and rakishly crooked lampshades. The menu is an odd hybrid of Italian, Middle Eastern, and Polish cuisine (15-25-zł salads, pizzas, and pastas, 30-45-zł meat dishes, daily 9:00-24:00, Izaaka 3, tel. 12-430-1451).

Kraków Connections

From Kraków by Train to: Warsaw (hourly, 2.75-3.25 hours, requires seat reservation, see below), **Gdańsk** (4/day direct, 2 more with change in Warsaw, 8.5 hours—shorter after new rail line completed; plus 2 night trains, 10.5-11.5 hours), **Toruń** (3/day direct, 7.75-9 hours; better to transfer at Warsaw's Zachodnia station: 10/day, 6-6.75 hours), **Prague** (1 early-morning direct train/day, 7.5 hours; 4/day with 1-2 changes, 8.25 hours; 1 night train, 9.5 hours), **Berlin** (1/day direct, 10 hours; otherwise transfer in Warsaw, 8.25-8.5 hours; plus 2 night trains, 10.5-11.5 hours), **Budapest** (3/day, 9.5-11 hours, transfer in Katowice, Poland, and Břeclav, Czech Republic; plus 1 night train/day, 10.75 hours; faster by infrequent Orange Ways bus: 5/week, 6.5 hours, www.orange ways.com), and **Vienna** (1/night direct, 8.5 hours; 3 decent daytime options, 7.75-8.75 hours with 1-3 changes).

The express train to **Warsaw**—which requires a reservation, even if you have a railpass—is particularly pleasant: A speedy 2.75 to 3.25 hours without stopping, from city center to city center. You'll be offered a free drink and snack to nibble on as you enjoy the pastoral scenery.

Night Trains to Hungary: If your next stop is Hungary, it can be convenient to sleep your way there on a night train. A night train from Kraków to **Budapest** runs nightly year-round (10.75 hours). If you'd rather head for **Eger,** in the summer (late June-late Aug) it may be possible to take a night train to Füzesabony, Hungary, where you can change to an Eger-bound train. However, this service has been in flux in recent years. If it's not running, ride the night train from Kraków to Budapest, then connect to Eger (either right away, or as a side-trip later). To research the latest schedules, see www.bahn.com.

By Bus: While train connections are typically faster, buses can be less expensive and make sense for some trips. Polski Bus prides itself on offering new buses with Wi-Fi and electrical outlets (www.polskibus.com).

AUSCHWITZ-BIRKENAU

The unassuming regional capital of Oświęcim (ohsh-VEENCH-im) was the site of one of humanity's most unspeakably horrifying tragedies: the systematic murder of at least 1.1 million innocent people. From 1941 until 1945, Oświęcim was the home of Auschwitz, the biggest, most notorious concentration camp in the Nazi system. Today, Auschwitz is the most poignant memorial anywhere to the victims of the Holocaust.

A visit here is obligatory for Polish 14-year-olds; students usually come again during their last year of school, as well. You'll often see Israeli high school groups walking through the grounds waving their Star of David flags. Many visitors, including Germans, leave flowers and messages. One of the messages reads, "Nations who forget their own history are sentenced to live it again."

Orientation to Auschwitz

"Auschwitz" (OWSH-vits) actually refers to a series of several camps in Poland—most importantly Auschwitz I, in the village of Oświęcim (50 miles, or a 1.25-hour drive, west of Kraków), and Auschwitz II, a.k.a. Birkenau (about 2 miles west of Oświęcim). Those visiting Auschwitz generally see both parts. **Auschwitz I,** where public transportation from Kraków arrives, has the main museum building, the *Arbeit Macht Frei* gate, and indoor museum exhibits in former prison buildings. Then a brief shuttle-bus ride takes visitors to **Birkenau** (BEER-keh-now)—on a much bigger scale and mostly outdoors, with the famous guard tower (and another bookshop and more WCs), a vast field with ruins of barracks, a few tourable rough barracks, the notorious "dividing

platform," a giant monument flanked by remains of destroyed crematoria, and a prisoner processing facility called "the Sauna."

Begin at Auschwitz I. The museum's main building has ticket
booths (to pay for a tour or to make a donation), bookshops (consider the good *Guide-Book* brochure or the bigger laminated map),
exchange offices, WCs, and basic eateries. You'll also find maps of
the camp (posted on the walls) and a theater that shows a powerful
film. A helpful **information desk**—where you can ask questions,
buy tickets for the tour (see "Tours at Auschwitz," later), and find
out about bus schedules for the return trip to Kraków—is halfway down the main entrance hall on the right, in the back corner
behind the little tables.

Cost and Hours: Entrance to the camp is free, but donations
are gladly accepted. During busy times (May-Oct 10:00-15:00),
you'll pay 40 zł to join a required organized tour (private guides
also available; see "Tours at Auschwitz," later). The museum opens
every day at 8:00, and closes June-Aug at 19:00, May and Sept at
18:00, April and Oct at 17:00, March and Nov at 16:00, and Dec-
Feb at 15:00. Information: Tel. 33-844-8100, www.auschwitz.org.

Getting There: For details on getting between Kraków
and Auschwitz, see "Auschwitz Connections," at the end of this
chapter.

Getting from Auschwitz I to Birkenau: Buses shuttle visitors two miles between the camps (free, about 4/hour in peak season, less off-season, times posted at the bus stop outside the main
building of each site, timed to correspond with tours). Taxis are
also standing by (about 15 zł). Many visitors, rather than wait for
the next bus, decide to walk the 20 minutes between the camps—

Why Visit Auschwitz?

Why visit a notorious concentration camp on your vacation? Auschwitz-Birkenau is one of the most moving sights in Europe, and certainly the most important of all the Holocaust memorials. Seeing the camp can be difficult: Many visitors are overwhelmed by a combination of sadness and anger over the tragedy, as well as inspiration at the remarkable stories of survival. Auschwitz survivors and victims' families want tourists to come here and experience the scale  and the monstrosity of the place. In their minds, a steady flow of visitors will ensure that the Holocaust is always remembered—so nothing like it will ever happen again.

Auschwitz isn't for everyone. But I've never met anyone who toured Auschwitz and regretted it. For many, it's a profoundly life-altering experience—and at the very least, it will forever affect the way you think about the Holocaust.

offering a much-needed chance for reflection. Along the way, you'll pass the Judenrampe, an old train car like the ones used to transport prisoners, explained by an informational sign.

Film: The 17-minute movie (too graphic for children) was shot by Ukrainian troops days after the Red Army liberated the camp (3.50 zł, buy ticket on arrival; always in English at 10:00, 11:00, 13:00, and 15:00, sometimes more—ask when you arrive).

Photography: Because the philosophy of the camp is to spread the story of Auschwitz, taking photographs of anything outdoors is encouraged. However, to ease the movement of visitors, photography is not allowed inside certain museum buildings.

Eating: There's a café and decent cafeteria (Bar Smak) at the main Auschwitz building. More options are in the commercial complex across the street.

Etiquette: The camp encourages visitors to remember that Auschwitz is the place where more than a million people lost their lives; behave here as you would at a cemetery.

Tours at Auschwitz

Visiting Auschwitz on your own works well, given the abundance of English descriptions (and this chapter's self-guided tour). However, due to crowd-control issues, from May to October individual visitors are not allowed to enter the Auschwitz I part of

Auschwitz Renovation

The International Auschwitz Council is planning to renovate the site over the next several years. The museum at Auschwitz I, widely considered the oldest Holocaust exhibit in the world, has remained largely unchanged in the more than 50 years since it opened. Now the museum displays will be modernized and better organized to accommodate the growing number of visitors. The key elements described in this chapter (such as the displays of human hair, eyeglasses, and suitcases) will still be part of the exhibit, but will likely be spread into more buildings (mostly on the ground floor, to avoid congestion on stairways). At Birkenau, restorers will build retaining walls to prevent the remains of the huge crematoria—key evidence of Nazi crimes—from slowly sinking into the ground.

Because of the renovation, be aware that the information in this chapter (especially the locations of exhibits on the self-guided tour) is subject to change. Ask about recent developments when you arrive at the camp.

the complex on their own between the peak times of 10:00 and 15:00. Instead, you're required to either join one of the museum's organized tours, or reserve your own private museum guide (both options are explained below). Note that even during these busy times, individuals may enter the Auschwitz II/Birkenau part of the complex without a guide.

Organized Museum Tours

The Auschwitz Museum's network of excellent guides are serious and frank, and feel a strong sense of responsibility about sharing the story of the camp. Appropriately, these well-trained guides are more historians than entertainers. The regularly scheduled 3.5-hour English tour covers Auschwitz, Birkenau, and the film (40 zł, buy ticket halfway down the main entry hall, on the right, in the back corner behind the tables). Most of the year, there are generally at least four English tours scheduled each day. You'll watch the film first, and the actual tour begins 30 minutes later (film at 10:00, 11:00, 13:00, and 15:00; possibly more with demand—as soon as 10 English-speakers gather, ask for a tour; in winter generally at 10:00, 11:00, 12:00, and 13:00). Try to arrive at least 20-30 minutes ahead, because if the tour's full, you might have to wait until the next one.

Private Official Museum Guides

If you have a special interest, a small group, or just want a more personalized visit, it's affordable and worthwhile to hire one of the museum's guides for a private tour. Choose between the basic 3.5-hour tour of the camp (250 zł), or a longer "study tour" (320 zł/4 hours, 400 zł/6 hours, 500 zł/8 hours spread over 2 days). Because English-speaking guides are limited, it's essential to reserve as far ahead as possible—at least two weeks in advance (fill out the online form at www.auschwitz.org, or call 33-844-8099 or 33-844-8100). At busy times, individuals might not be able to reserve a private guide between 10:00 and 14:00, when they're needed for bigger groups.

Tours from Kraków

Various Kraków-based companies sell round-trip tours from Kraków to Auschwitz (generally around 130 zł). While these take care of transportation for you and include a guided tour, you'll pay triple and have to adhere to a strict schedule, and the tours tend to be impersonal.

Local Guides and Drivers from Kraków

For hassle-free transportation to the camp, you can hire a Kraków-based local guide or driver to bring you to Auschwitz. However, since these people are not officially registered museum guides, they technically aren't allowed to show you around the site. Instead, they will most likely arrange a private museum guide to join you, or time your visit so you can join an organized English tour (both options described earlier). While it's pricey, some travelers consider hiring a driver/guide to be a worthwhile splurge, since you'll have door-to-door service to the camp and three hours in the car with a local expert.

Self-Guided Tour

Auschwitz I

Before World War II, this camp was a base for the Polish army. When Hitler occupied Poland, he took over these barracks and turned it into a concentration camp for his Polish political ene-mies. The location was ideal, with a nearby rail junction and riv-ers providing natural protective boundaries. In 1942, Auschwitz became a death camp for the extermination of European Jews and others whom Hitler consid-ered "undesirable." By the time  the camp was liberated in 1945, at least 1.1 million people had been murdered here—approximately 960,000 of them Jewish.

As you exit the entry building's back door and go toward the camp, you see the notorious **gate** with the cruel message, *Arbeit Macht Frei* ("Work Sets You Free"). Note that the "B" was welded on upside down by belligerent inmates. On their arrival, new

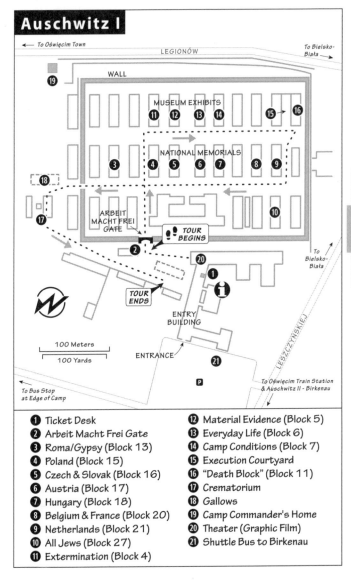

Auschwitz I

To Oświęcim Town →

LEGIONÓW

To Bielsko-Biała →

WALL

19

MUSEUM EXHIBITS

11 **12** **13** **14** **15** **16**

NATIONAL MEMORIALS

3 **4** **5** **6** **7** **8** **9**

18

17

ARBEIT MACHT FREI GATE

TOUR BEGINS

2

20

To Bielsko-Biała →

1

TOUR ENDS

10

ENTRY BUILDING

100 Meters
100 Yards

ENTRANCE

21

P

To Oświęcim Train Station & Auschwitz II - Birkenau

To Bus Stop at Edge of Camp

LESZCZYŃSKIEJ

AUSCHWITZ-BIRKENAU

1 Ticket Desk
2 Arbeit Macht Frei Gate
3 Roma/Gypsy (Block 13)
4 Poland (Block 15)
5 Czech & Slovak (Block 16)
6 Austria (Block 17)
7 Hungary (Block 18)
8 Belgium & France (Block 20)
9 Netherlands (Block 21)
10 All Jews (Block 27)
11 Extermination (Block 4)

12 Material Evidence (Block 5)
13 Everyday Life (Block 6)
14 Camp Conditions (Block 7)
15 Execution Courtyard
16 "Death Block" (Block 11)
17 Crematorium
18 Gallows
19 Camp Commander's Home
20 Theater (Graphic Film)
21 Shuttle Bus to Birkenau

prisoners were told the truth: The only way out of the camp was through the crematorium chimneys. This gate was in the news in December of 2009, when the original sign that still hung here was stolen one night, then recovered cut into three pieces two days later. While the original is now safely in the museum's possession, the sign you see here is a replica.

Just inside the gate and to the right, the camp orchestra (made up of prisoners) used to play marches; having the prisoners march made them easier to count.

The main road leads past the barracks. An average of 14,000 prisoners were kept at this camp at one time. (Birkenau could hold up to 100,000.)

The first row of barracks contains the **National Memorials,** created by the home countries of the camps' victims. As these memorials overlap with the general exhibits, and are designed for Europeans to learn more about the victims from their own home countries, most visitors skip this part of the site. But if you have time later to take a look, consider circling back here to see those that interest you. Block 13 houses the **Roma (Gypsy)** exhibit. You'll learn that the Roma, along with the Jews, were considered no better than "rats, bedbugs, and fleas," and explore elements of the so-called *Zigeunerfrage*—the "Gypsy question" about what to do with this "troublesome" population. Block 15 honors victims from **Poland,** focusing on the 1939 Nazi invasion of the country, which resulted in the immediate internment of Polish political prisoners. Exhibits explain the process of "Germanization"—such as renaming Polish streets with German names—and (upstairs) the underground resistance that fought to re-assert some control over Poland. Block 16 contains a new and well-presented exhibit about **Czech and Slovak** victims. Block 17 contains a new presentation about victims from **Austria** (but only in German and Polish). Block 18 holds a very modern, conceptual exhibit about **Hungary**'s victims, with an eerie heartbeat sound pervading the space. Block 20, a former hospital block, is shared by **Belgium** and **France.** A room near the entrance explains how some prisoners were killed by lethal injection, with portraits and biographical sketches of victims. Upstairs is the powerful Belgium exhibit, with a room featuring portraits of victims. Block 21 honors **Dutch Jews;** like Hungary's, the exhibit is experiential, with a walk-through tunnel. Finally, Block 27 is devoted to all **Jewish victims** of Auschwitz (interactive exhibit).

The most interesting part of the camp is the second row of barracks, which holds the museum exhibitions. Blocks 4 and 5 focus on how Auschwitz prisoners were killed. Blocks 6, 7, and 11 explore the conditions for prisoners who survived here a little longer than most.

Block 4 features exhibits on **extermination.** In the first room is a map showing the countries from which Auschwitz prisoners were brought—as far away as Norway and Greece. You'll also

Chilling Statistics: The Holocaust in Poland

The majority of people murdered by the Nazis during the Holocaust were killed right here in Poland. For centuries, Poland was known for its relative tolerance of Jews, and right up until the beginning of World War II, Poland had Europe's largest concentration of Jews: 3,500,000. Throughout the Holocaust, the Nazis murdered 4,500,000 Jews in Poland (many of them brought in from other countries) at camps, including Auschwitz, and in ghettos such as Warsaw's.

By the end of the war, only 300,000 Polish Jews had survived—less than 10 percent of the original population. Many of these survivors were granted "one-way passports" (read: deported) to Israel by the communist government in 1968 (following a big student demonstration with a strong Jewish presence). Today, only about 10,000 Jews live in all of Poland.

find an urn filled with ashes, a symbolic memorial to all of the camp's victims. In Room 2, a map shows how the victims were transported here from all over Europe. To prevent a riot, the Nazis claimed at first that this was only a transition camp for resettlement in Eastern Europe. Room 3 displays some of the only photos that exist of victims inside the camp—taken by arrogant SS men.

Upstairs in Room 4 is a chilling model of a Birkenau crematorium. People entered on the left, then got undressed in the underground rooms (hanging their belongings on numbered hooks and encouraged to remember their numbers to retrieve their clothes later). They then moved into the "showers" and were killed by Zyklon-B gas (hydrogen cyanide), a German-produced cleaning agent that is lethal in high doses. This efficient factory of murder took about 20 minutes to kill 8,000 people in four gas chambers. Elevators brought the bodies up to the crematorium. Members of the *Sonderkommand*—Jewish inmates who were kept isolated and forced by the Nazis to work here—removed the corpses' gold teeth and shaved off their hair (to be sold) before putting the bodies in the ovens. It wasn't unusual for a *Sonderkommand* worker to discover a wife, child, or parent among the dead. A few of these workers committed suicide by throwing themselves at electric fences; those who didn't were systematically executed by the Nazis after a two-month shift. Across from the model of the crematorium are canisters of Zyklon-B. Across the hall in Room 5 is a wall of victims' hair—4,400 pounds of it. Also displayed is cloth made of the hair, used to make Nazi uniforms.

Back downstairs in Room 6 is an exhibit on the plunder of victims' personal belongings. People being transported here were

St. Maksymilian Kolbe
(1894-1941)

Among the many inspirational stories of Auschwitz is that of a Polish priest named Maksymilian Kolbe. Before the war, Kolbe traveled as a missionary to Japan, then worked in Poland for a Catholic newspaper. While he was highly regarded for his devotion to the Church, some of his writings had an unsettling anti-Semitic sentiment. But during the Nazi occupation, Kolbe briefly ran an institution that cared for refugees—including Jews.

In 1941, Kolbe was arrested and interned at Auschwitz. When a prisoner from Kolbe's block escaped in July of that year, the Nazis punished the remaining inmates by selecting 10 of them to be put in the Starvation Cell until they died—based on the Nazi "doctrine of collective responsibility." After the selection had been made, Kolbe offered to replace a man who expressed concern about who would care for his family. The Nazis agreed. (The man Kolbe saved is said to have survived the Holocaust.)

All 10 of the men—including Kolbe—were put into Starvation Cell 18. Two weeks later, when the door was opened, only Kolbe had survived. The story spread throughout the camp, and Kolbe became an inspiration to the inmates. To squelch the hope he had given the others, Kolbe was executed by lethal injection.

In 1982, Kolbe was canonized by the Catholic Church. Some critics—mindful of his earlier anti-Semitic rhetoric—still consider Kolbe's sainthood controversial. But most Poles feel he redeemed himself for his earlier missteps through this noble act at the end of his life.

encouraged to bring luggage—and some victims had even paid in advance for houses in their new homeland. After they were killed, everything of value was sorted and stored in warehouses that prisoners named "Canada" (after a country they associated with great wealth). Although the Canada warehouses were destroyed, you can see a few of these items in the next building.

Block 5 focuses on **material evidence** of the crimes that took place here. It consists mostly of piles of the victims' goods, a tiny fraction of everything the Nazis stole. As you wander through the rooms, you'll see eyeglasses; fine Jewish prayer shawls; crutches and prosthetic limbs (the first people the Nazis exterminated were mentally and physically ill German citizens); a seemingly endless mountain of shoes; and suitcases with names of victims—many marked *Kind*, or "child." Visitors often wonder if the suitcase with the name "Frank" belonged to Anne, one of the Holocaust's most famous victims. After being discovered in Amsterdam by the

Nazis, the Frank family was transported here to Auschwitz, where they were split up. Still, it's unlikely this suitcase was theirs. Anne Frank and her sister Margot were sent to the Bergen-Belsen camp in northern Germany, where they died of typhus shortly before the war ended. Their father, Otto Frank, survived Auschwitz and was found barely alive by the Russians, who liberated the camp in January of 1945.

Although the purpose of Auschwitz was to murder its inmates, not all of them were killed immediately. After an initial evaluation, some prisoners were registered and forced to work. (This did not mean they were chosen to live—just to die later.) In Block 6, you see elements of the **everyday life** of prisoners. The halls are lined with photographs of victims. The dates of arrival *(przybył)* and death *(zmarł)* show that those registered survived here an average of two to three months. (Flowers are poignant reminders that these victims are survived by loved ones.) Room 1 displays drawings of the arrival process—sketched by survivors of the camp.

1947 2
DĄBROWSKI JAN

After the initial selection, those chosen to work were showered, shaved, and photographed. After a while, photographing each prisoner got to be too expensive, so prisoners were tattooed instead (see photographs): on the chest, on the arm, or—for children—on the leg. A display shows the symbols that prisoners had to wear to show their reason for internment—Jew, Roma (Gypsy), homosexual, political prisoner, and so on.

Room 4 shows the starvation that took place here. The 7,500 survivors that the Red Army found when the camp was liberated were essentially living skeletons (the "healthier" inmates had been forced to march to Germany). Of those liberated, 20 percent died soon after of disease and starvation. Look for a display of the prisoners' daily ration (in the glass case): a pan of tea or coffee in the morning; thin vegetable soup in the afternoon; and a piece of bread (often made with sawdust or chestnuts) for dinner. This makes it clear that Auschwitz was never intended to be a "work camp," where people were kept alive, healthy, and efficient to do work. Rather, people were meant to die here—if not in the gas chambers, then through malnutrition and overwork.

You can see scenes from the prisoner's workday (sketched by survivors after liberation) in Room 5. Prisoners worked as long as the sun shone—eight hours in winter, up to twelve hours in summer—mostly on farms or in factories. Room 6 is about Auschwitz's child inmates, 20 percent of the camp's victims. Blond, blue-eyed children—like the girl in the bottom row on the right—were either "Germanized" in special schools or, if younger, adopted by German families. Dr. Josef Mengele conducted gruesome experiments here on children, especially twins and triplets, ostensibly to find ways to increase fertility for German mothers.

Block 7 shows **living and sanitary conditions** at the camp—which you'll see in more detail later at Birkenau. Blocks 8-10 are vacant (medical experiments were carried out in Block 10).

Step into the **courtyard** between Blocks 10 and 11. The wall at the far end is where the Nazis shot several thousand political prisoners, leaders of camp resistance, and religious leaders. Notice that the windows are covered, so that nobody could witness the executions. Also take a close look at the memorial—the back of it is made of a material designed by Nazis to catch the bullets without a ricochet. Inmates were shot at short range—about three feet. The pebbles represent prayers from Jewish visitors.

The most feared place among prisoners was the **"Death Block"** (#11), from which nobody ever left alive. In Room 5, you can see how prisoners lived in these barracks—three-level bunks, with three prisoners sleeping in each bed (they had to sleep on their sides so they could fit). Death here required a trial (the room in which sham trials were held—lasting about two minutes each—is on display). In Room 6, people undressed before they were executed. In the basement, you'll see several different types of cells. The Starvation Cell (#18) held prisoners selected to starve to death when a fellow prisoner escaped; Maksymilian Kolbe spent two weeks here to save another man's life (see sidebar). In the Dark Cell (#20), which held up to 30, people had only a small window for ventilation—and if it became covered with snow, the prisoners suffocated. At the end of the hall in Cell 21, you can see where a prisoner scratched a crucifix (left) and image of Jesus (right) on the wall. In the Standing Cells (#22), four people would be forced to stand together for hours at a time (the bricks went all the way to the ceiling then). Upstairs is an exhibit on resistance within the camp.

Before you leave Auschwitz, visit the **crematorium** (from Block 11, exit straight ahead and go past the first row of barracks, then turn right and go straight on the road between the two rows of barracks; pass through the gap in the fence and look for the chimney on your left). People undressed outside, or just inside the door. Up to 700 people at a time could be gassed here. Inside the door, go into the big room on the right. Look for the vents in the ceiling—this is where the SS men dropped the Zyklon-B. Through the door is a replica of the furnace. This facility could burn 340 bodies a day—so it took two days to burn all of the bodies from one round of executions. (The Nazis didn't like this inefficiency, so they built four more huge crematoria at Birkenau.)

Shortly after the war, camp commander Rudolf Höss was tried, convicted, and sentenced to death. Survivors requested that he be executed at Auschwitz, and in 1947, he was hanged here. The **gallows** are preserved behind the crematorium (about a hundred yards from his home where his wife—who loved her years here— read stories to their children, very likely by the light of a human-skin lampshade).

Take your time with Auschwitz I. When you're ready, continue to the second stage of the camp—Birkenau.

Auschwitz II—Birkenau

In 1941, realizing that the original Auschwitz camp was too small to meet their needs, the Nazis began a second camp in some nearby farm fields. The original plan

was for a camp that could hold 200,000 people, but at its peak, Birkenau (Brzezinka) held only about 100,000. They were still adding onto it when the camp was liberated in 1945.

Train tracks lead past the main building and into the camp. The first sight that greeted prisoners was the **guard tower** (familiar to many visitors from the stirring scenes in *Schindler's List*). Climb to the top of the entry building (also houses WCs and bookstore) for an overview of the massive camp. As you look over the camp, you'll see a vast field of chimneys and a few intact wooden and brick barracks. The train tracks lead straight back to the dividing platform, and then dead-end at the ruins of the crematorium and camp monument at the far side.

Some of the barracks were destroyed by Germans. Most were dismantled to be used for fuel and building materials shortly after the war. But the first row has been reconstructed (using components from the original structures). Visit the barracks on the right.

The first of these barrack buildings was the **latrine:** The front half of the building contained washrooms, and the back was a row of toilets. There was no running water, and prisoners were in charge of keeping the latrine clean. Because of the resulting

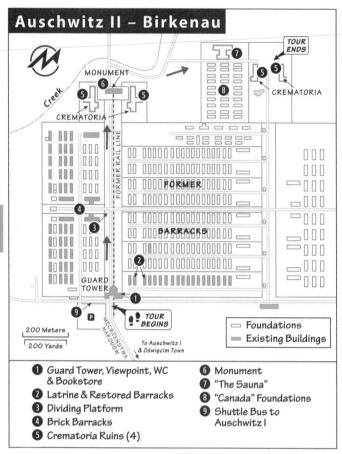

Auschwitz II – Birkenau

MONUMENT

Creek

CREMATORIA

CREMATORIA

FORMER RAIL LINE

FORMER

BARRACKS

GUARD TOWER

TOUR ENDS

CREMATORIA

P

TOUR BEGINS

200 Meters
200 Yards

MIEDZYNSKA NARODOW

To Auschwitz I
& Oświęcim Town

☐ Foundations
▬ Existing Buildings

1 Guard Tower, Viewpoint, WC
   & Bookstore
2 Latrine & Restored Barracks
3 Dividing Platform
4 Brick Barracks
5 Crematoria Ruins (4)

6 Monument
7 "The Sauna"
8 "Canada" Foundations
9 Shuttle Bus to
   Auschwitz I

unsanitary conditions and risk of disease, the Nazis were afraid to come in here—so the latrine became the heart of the black market and the inmates' resistance movement.

The fourth **barrack** was a bunk building. Each inmate had a personal number, a barrack number, and a bed number. Inside, you can see the beds (angled so that more could fit). An average of 400 prisoners—but up to 1,000—would be housed in each of these buildings. These wooden structures, designed as stables by a German company (look for the horse-tying rings on the wall), came in prefab pieces that made them cheap and convenient. Two chimneys connected by a brick duct provided a little heat. The bricks were smoothed by inmates who sat here to catch a bit of warmth.

Follow the train tracks toward the monument about a half-mile away, at the back end of Birkenau. At the intersection of these tracks and the perpendicular gravel road (halfway to the monument) was the gravel **dividing platform.** A Nazi doctor would stand facing the guard tower and evaluate each prisoner. If he pointed to the right, the prisoner was sentenced to death, and trudged—unknowingly—to the gas chamber. If he pointed to the left, the person would be registered and live a little longer. It was here that families from all over Europe were torn apart forever.

On the left-hand side of the tracks are some **brick barracks.** Go inside one of them. The supervisors lived in the two smaller rooms near the door. Farther in, most barracks still have the wooden bunks that held about 700 people per building. Four or five people slept on each bunk, including the floor—reserved for new arrivals. There were chamber pots at either end of the building. After a Nazi doctor died of typhus, sanitation improved, and these barracks got running water.

As you walk along the camp's only road, which leads along the tracks to the crematorium, imagine the horror of this place—no grass, only mud, and all the barracks packed with people, with smoke blowing in from the busy crematoria. This was an even worse place to die than Auschwitz I.

The train tracks lead to the camp memorial and crematorium. At the end of the tracks, go 50 yards to the left and climb the three concrete steps to view the ruin of the **crematorium.** This is one of four crematoria here at Birkenau, each with a capacity to cremate more than 4,400 people per day. At the far-right end of the ruins, see the stairs where people entered the rooms to undress. They were given numbered lockers, conning them into thinking they were coming back. (The Nazis didn't want a panic.) Then they piled into the "shower room"—the underground passage branching away from the memorial—and were killed. Their bodies were burned in the crematorium (on the left), giving off a scent of sweet almonds (from the Zyklon-B). Beyond the remains of the crematorium is a hole—once a gray lake where tons of ashes were dumped. This efficient factory of death was destroyed by the Nazis as the

On the Way to Auschwitz: The Polish Countryside

You'll spend about an hour gazing out the window as you drive or ride to Auschwitz. This may be your only real look at the Polish countryside. Ponder these thoughts about what you're passing...

The small houses you see are traditionally inhabited by three generations at the same time. Nineteenth-century houses (the few that survive) often sport blue stripes. Back then, parents announced that their daughters were now eligible by getting out the blue paint. Once they saw these blue lines, local boys were welcome to come a-courtin'.

Big churches mark small villages. Like in the US, tiny roadside memorials and crosses indicate places where fatal accidents have occurred.

Polish farmers traditionally had small lots that were notorious for not being very productive. These farmers somewhat miraculously survived the communist era without having to merge their farms. For years, they were Poland's sacred cows: producing little, paying almost no tax, and draining government resources. But since Poland joined the European Union in 2004, they're being forced to get up to snuff...and, in many cases, collectivize their farms after all.

Since most people don't own cars, bikes are common and public transit is excellent. There are lots of bus stops, as well as minibuses that you can flag down anywhere for a 2-zł ride. The bad roads are a legacy of communist construction, exacerbated by heavy truck use and brutal winters.

Poland has more than 2,000 counties, or districts, each with its own coat of arms; you'll pass several along the way. The forests are state-owned, and locals enjoy the right to pick berries in the summer and mushrooms in the autumn (you may see people—often young kids—selling their day's harvest by the side of the road). The mushrooms are dried and then boiled to make tasty soups in the winter.

Red Army approached, leaving the haunting ruins you see today.

When the Soviets arrived on January 27, 1945, the nightmare of Auschwitz-Birkenau was over. The Polish parliament voted to turn these grounds into a museum, so that the world would understand, and never forget, the horror of what happened here. The **monument** at the back of the camp, built in 1967 (by the communist government in its heavy "Socialist Realism" style), represents gravestones and the chimney of a crematorium. The plaques, written in each of the languages spoken by camp victims (including English, far right), explain that the memorial is "a cry of despair and a warning to humanity."

With more time, you could continue deeper into the camp—to the reception and disinfection building that prisoners called **"the Sauna"** (the long building with four tall chimneys). It was

here that prisoners would be forced to strip and be de-loused; their belongings were seized and taken to the "Canada" warehouses (described earlier) to be sorted. Walking through here (on glass floors designed to protect the original structure below), you'll see artifacts of the queasy efficiency with which prisoners were "processed"—their heads were shaved, they were tattooed with a serial number, and they were assigned uniforms and wooden clogs to wear. Portraits at the end of the building humanize those who passed through here. Look for the cart, which was used to dispose of ashes. In front of the Sauna is a field of foundations of the **"Canada" warehouses.** Nearby are the other two destroyed **crematoria.**

Auschwitz Connections

The Auschwitz Museum is in the town of Oświęcim, about 50 miles west of Kraków. By bus, minibus, or train, the journey takes around an hour and 45 minutes each way; driving shaves off about 10-20 minutes.

From Kraków to Auschwitz

The easiest way to reach Auschwitz is with a **package tour** (figure around 130 zł per person) or **private guide or driver** (300-500 zł for the carload). While the package tours are more convenient than going on your own, three people can hire their own driver for less and have a more intimate experience.

If you're using public transportation, here are your choices:

The most comfortable public-transit option is to take one of the frequent **buses,** mostly run by PKS Oświęcim (10 zł, at least hourly, 1.75 hours, get the most recent schedule at any Kraków TI, buses depart from Kraków's main bus station behind the train station). Buy a one-way ticket from the bus-station ticket office or from the driver to leave your options open for getting home. Look for buses to "Oświęcim" (not necessarily "Auschwitz"). Note that these buses can be full, and since most come from other towns, there's no way to reserve a seat—so line up early (generally about 15 minutes ahead). If you don't get on a bus, you'll have to wait for the next one (or, if there's a minibus leaving sooner, you can take one of those—described next). Once in the town of Oświęcim, buses from Kraków stop first at the train station, then continue on to one of two stops near the museum: About half of the buses go directly into the parking lot at the museum itself, while the rest use a low-profile bus stop on the edge of the Auschwitz camp grounds (you'll see a small *Muzeum Auschwitz* sign on the right just before the stop, and a blue *Oświęcim Muzeum PKS* sign at the stop itself). From this bus stop, follow the sign down the road and into the parking lot; the main museum building is across the lot on your left. Note that since some buses don't actually go into the museum's parking lot, the Auschwitz stop can be easy to miss—don't be shy about letting your driver know where you want to go: *"Muzeum?"*

Several **minibuses** from Kraków head for Auschwitz (10 zł, sporadic departures—generally 1-2/hour, 1.75 hours). Like the buses, some go directly to the museum, while others use the bus stop at the edge of camp (see above). These generally depart from the lower platform of the main bus station (but confirm the departure point at the TI). Some of my readers report that the minibuses are a bit more cramped than the buses and, while intended for local commuters, can be crammed with tourists. But they work fine in a pinch.

You could ride the **train** to Oświęcim, but it's less convenient than the bus because it leaves you at the train station, farther from the museum (15/day, less Sat-Sun, 1.5 hours, 14 zł). If you do wind up at the Oświęcim train station, it's about a 20-minute walk to the camp (turn right out of station, go straight, then turn left at roundabout, camp is several blocks ahead on left). Or you can take a taxi (around 15 zł).

Returning from Auschwitz to Kraków

Upon arrival at Auschwitz I, plan your departure by visiting the information window inside the main building (halfway down the main entry hall, on the right, in the back corner behind the tables). They can give you a schedule of departures and explain where the bus or minibus leaves from. (If you'll be staying late into the afternoon, make a point of figuring out the last possible bus or train back to Kraków, and plan accordingly.) Remember to allow enough time to make it from Birkenau back to Auschwitz I to catch your bus.

Although most minibuses and a few buses back to Kraków leave from the camp parking lot itself, if you're taking the bus, you'll most likely catch it from the stop on the edge of the Auschwitz I grounds. To reach this bus stop, leave the Auschwitz I building through the main entry and walk straight along the parking lot, then turn right on the road near the end of the lot. At the T-intersection, cross the street to the little bus stop with the blue

Oświęcim Muzeum PKS sign. Don't be distracted by the ads for a nearby travel agency—you can buy tickets on board. Again, be aware that there's no public transportation back to Kraków from Birkenau, where most people end their tours; you'll have to take the shuttle bus back to Auschwitz I first.

WARSAW

Warszawa

Warsaw (Warszawa, vah-SHAH-vah in Polish) is Poland's capital and biggest city. It's huge, famous, and important...but not particularly romantic. If you're looking for Old World quaintness, head for Kraków. If you're tickled by spires and domes, get to Prague. But if you want to experience a truly 21st-century city, Warsaw's your place.

Stroll down revitalized boulevards that evoke the city's glory days, pausing at an outdoor café to sip coffee and nibble at a *pączek* (the classic Polish jelly doughnut). Commune with the soul of Poland through its artists (at the National Museum), its favorite composer (at the Chopin Museum), its dramatic history (at the Warsaw Historical Museum and Warsaw Uprising Museum), its dedication to the sciences (at the Copernicus Science Center), and its Jewish story (in the former Jewish Ghetto and—beginning in 2014—the brand-new Museum of the History of Polish Jews).

And ponder the wide range of Warsaw's postwar urban architecture, from dreary communist monstrosities to innovative skyscrapers designed by *the* top names in global architecture.

Warsaw is modernizing—fast. Mindful of its history, yet optimistic about its future, Warsaw has happily emerged from a long hibernation. Varsovians are embracing their role as the capital city of an influential nation in the "New Europe." The European Union has two universities aimed at educating future political leaders (or "Eurocrats"). One is in Bruges, Belgium, just down the road from the EU capital of Brussels. The other one is right here. You can almost feel Warsaw peeling back the layers of communist grime as it replaces pot-holed highways with pedestrian-friendly parks. Today's Warsaw has gleaming new office towers and street signs, stylishly dressed locals, cutting-edge shopping malls, swarms of international businesspeople, and a gourmet coffee shop on every corner. More recently, the city built a futuristic new stadium and an even more spiffed-up infrastructure to host key matches for the Euro Cup 2012 soccer championship.

Warsaw has good reason to be a city of the future: The past hasn't been very kind. Since becoming Poland's capital in 1596, Warsaw has seen wave after wave of foreign rulers and invasions—especially during the last hundred years. But in this horrific cru-cible, the enduring spirit of the Polish people was forged. As one proud Varsovian told me, "Warsaw is ugly because its history is so beautiful."

The city's darkest days came during the Nazi occupation of World War II. First, its Jewish residents were forced into a tiny ghetto. They rose up...and were slaughtered. Then, its Polish resi-dents rose up...and were slaughtered. Hitler sent word to system-atically demolish this troublesome city. At the war's end, Warsaw was devastated. An estimated 800,000 residents were dead—nearly two out of every three Varsovians.

The Poles almost gave up on what was then a pile of rubble to build a brand-new capital city elsewhere. But ultimately they decided to rebuild, creating a city of contrasts: painstakingly restored medieval lanes, crumbling communist apartment blocks (*bloki* in Polish), and sleek skyscrapers. Between the buildings, you'll find fragments of a complex, sometimes tragic, and often inspiring history.

A product of its complicated past, sprinkled with the big-city style and sophistication of its present, Warsaw remains quintessen-tially Polish. It is a place worth grappling with to understand the Poland of today...and the Europe of tomorrow.

Planning Your Time

Warsaw can easily fill two or three days, but if you're pressed for time, one full day is enough for most visitors. Get your bearings by taking a stroll through Polish history on the Royal Way, using my self-guided walk. Then enjoy the Old Town area. Visit other sights according to your interests: Polish artists, Holocaust history, the Warsaw Uprising, royalty, hands-on science gizmos, or Chopin. To slow down and take a break from the city, relax in Łazienki Park.

Orientation to Warsaw

Warsaw sprawls with 1.7 million residents. Everything is on a big scale—it seems to take forever to walk just a few "short" blocks. Get comfortable with public transportation and plan your sightseeing wisely to avoid backtracking.

Virtually everything of interest to travelers is on a mild hill on the west bank of the Vistula River. The city's central train station (Warszawa Centralna) is in the shadow of its biggest landmark: the can't-miss-it, skyscraping Palace of Culture and Science. From here, the avenue called aleja Jerozolimskie runs east toward the river, past the National Museum. It crosses the "Royal Way" boulevard, which connects the sights in the north (Old Town and New Town) with those in the south (Łazienki Park, and at the outskirts of town, Wilanów Palace). Most major sights and recommended hotels and restaurants are along or near these two thoroughfares (aleja Jerozolimskie and the Royal Way).

Another tip: You'll hear about two distinct uprisings against the Nazis during World War II. They're easy to confuse, but try to keep them straight: the **Ghetto Uprising** was staged by Warsaw's dwindling Jewish population in the spring of 1943; the **Warsaw Uprising,** a year later, was led by the (mostly non-Jewish) Polish Home Army.

Tourist Information

Warsaw's helpful, youthful TI has five offices: on the **Royal Way** (in the Kordegarda building directly across the street from Radziwiłł Palace, daily May-Aug 11:00-21:00, Sept-April 11:00-19:00), on the **Old Town Market Square** (daily May-Aug 9:00-21:00, March-April and Sept-Oct 9:00-19:00, Nov-Feb 9:00-18:00), at the **central train station** (daily 8:00-20:00), at the **Palace of Culture and Science** (daily 8:00-20:00), and at **Chopin Airport** (daily May-Aug 8:00-20:00, March-April and Sept-Oct 8:00-19:00, Nov-Feb 8:00-18:00). The general information number for all TIs is 19431 from inside Warsaw, or 22-19431 from outside Warsaw. All branches offer several free, useful materials: a city map (with key phone numbers on the back), a well-produced booklet called *Warsaw: In Short,* and a series of brochures on sights and activities ("city breaks," Jewish heritage, Chopin, mermaids, and so on, as well as info for kids, active types, and travelers with limited mobility); everything is also available online

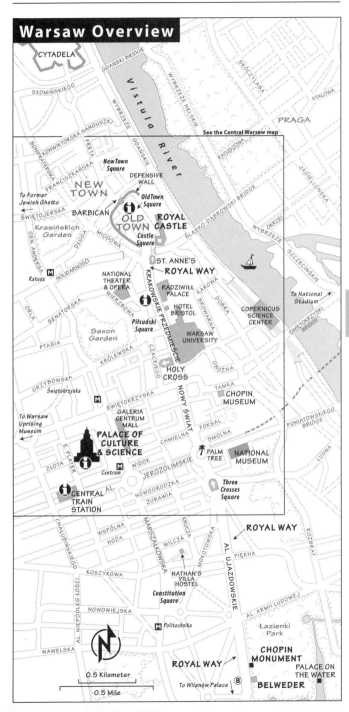

Warsaw Overview

CYTADELA

SŁOMIŃSKIEGO

GDAŃSKI BRIDGE

Vistula River

WYBRZEŻE HELSKIE

SKOCZYLASA

STALOWA

PRAGA

See the Central Warsaw map

New Town Square

DEFENSIVE WALL

NEW TOWN

To Former Jewish Ghetto

BARBICAN

Old Town Square

OLD TOWN

ROYAL CASTLE

Krasińskich Garden

Castle Square

ŚLĄSKO-DĄBROWSKI BRIDGE

ST. ANNE'S

ROYAL WAY

Ratusz

NATIONAL THEATER & OPERA

RADZIWIŁŁ PALACE

HOTEL BRISTOL

COPERNICUS SCIENCE CENTER

To National Stadium

Saxon Garden

Piłsudski Square

WARSAW UNIVERSITY

KRAKOWSKIE PRZEDMIEŚCIE

ŚWIĘTOKRZYSKI BRIDGE

HOLY CROSS

Świętokrzyska

CHOPIN MUSEUM

To Warsaw Uprising Museum

GALERIA CENTRUM MALL

PALACE OF CULTURE & SCIENCE

NOWY ŚWIAT

PALM TREE

NATIONAL MUSEUM

PONIATOWSKIEGO BRIDGE

Centrum

JEROZOLIMSKIE

Three Crosses Square

CENTRAL TRAIN STATION

ROYAL WAY

MARSZAŁKOWSKA

AL. UJAZDOWSKIE

NATHAN'S VILLA HOSTEL

Constitution Square

Politechnika

Łazienki Park

CHOPIN MONUMENT

ROYAL WAY

To Wilanów Palace

PALACE ON THE WATER

BELWEDER

0.5 Kilometer

0.5 Mile

WARSAW

(www.warsawtour.pl). The TI also has a free room-booking service.

Warsaw has a thriving live-music scene. Ask the TI for a weekly performance schedule. For light, enjoyable music events in summer, consider the Chopin concerts in Łazienki Park (only on Sun) and the organ concerts in the Cathedral of St. John the Baptist (daily except Sun).

The **Warsaw Tourist Card,** which covers public transportation and admission or discounts to nearly 30 museums, might save you some money if you're sightseeing like crazy (as the details are in flux, ask about it at the TI).

Arrival in Warsaw
By Train
Most trains arrive at the **central train station** (Warszawa Centralna), a recently renovated communist-era monstrosity next to the Palace of Culture and Science. It can be tricky to get your bearings here: Two parallel concourses run across the tracks, creating an underground maze where it's easy to get lost. The underground area includes well-signed lockers, ticket windows, and lots of shops and eateries. I'd start by heading up to the vast, open-feeling **main hall** (follow signs for *main hall/hala główna*), where you'll find a row of ticket windows, a rail customer service center, a TI (in the "Service Point" kiosk), and (from outside) views of the adjacent Palace of Culture and Science and Złota 44 skyscrapers. If you have time to kill, you can walk across the street to the super-modern **Złote Tarasy Shopping Mall**.

Getting into Town: To reach the tourist zone and most of my recommended hotels, taxis are the easiest choice, while the bus is more economical (but more challenging to find).

Taxis wait outside the main hall (many are dishonest—look for one with a company logo and telephone number, and ask for an estimate up front; the fare should be no more than about 20-30 zł for most of my recommended hotels).

From the station, **bus #175** takes you to the Royal Way and Old Town in about 10 minutes (see "Getting Around Warsaw," later). You can catch this bus—and others going in the same direction—in front of the skyscraper with the LOT airlines office and Hotel Marriott across busy aleja Jerozolimskie from the station. From the corridors under the main hall, carefully track *Al. Jerozolimskie* signs. Several different exits are marked this way, but if you hone in on *Hotel Marriott* signs, you'll reach a pedestrian underpass that pops you out next to the bus stop. **Bus #160** also goes to the Old Town (though not via the Royal Way), but it departs from the opposite side of the station: To find its stop from the main hall, go out the side door toward *ul. Emilii Plater*. Note

Warsaw Essentials

English	Polish	Pronounced
Warsaw	*Warszawa*	vah-SHAH-vah
Central Train Station	*Warszawa Centralna*	vah-SHAH-vah tsehn-TRAHL-nah
Palace of Culture and Science	*Pałac Kultury i Nauki* (or simply "*Pałac*")	PAH-wahts kool-TOO-ree ee nah-OO-kee
New Town	*Nowe Miasto*	NOH-vay mee-AH-stoh
Old Town	*Stare Miasto*	STAH-reh mee-AH-stoh
Old Town Market Square	*Rynek Starego Miasta*	REE-nehk stah-RAY-goh mee-AH-stah
Royal Way	*Szłak Królewski*	shwock kroh-LEHV-skee
Popular restaurant street on Royal Way	*Nowy Świat*	NOH-vee SHVEE-aht
Attraction-lined street on Royal Way	*Krakowskie Przedmieście*	krah-KOHV-skyeh pzhehd-MYESH-cheh
Royal Castle	*Zamek Królewski*	ZAH-mehk kroh-LEHV-skee
Castle Square	*Plac Zamkowy*	plahts zahm-KOH-vee
Piłsudski Square	*Plac Marszałka Józefa Piłsudskiego*	plahts mar-SHAW-kah yoh-ZEH-fah pew-sood-SKYAY-goh
Łazienki Park	*Park Łazienkowski*	park wah-zhehn KOV-skee
Vistula River	*Wisła*	VEES-wah

Warsaw at a Glance

▲▲**Royal Castle** Warsaw's best palace, rebuilt after World War II, but retaining its former opulence and many original furnishings. **Hours:** May-Sept Mon-Sat 10:00-18:00, Sun 11:00-18:00; Oct-April Tue-Sat 10:00-16:00, Sun 11:00-16:00, closed Mon. See page 148.

▲▲**Old Town Market Square** Re-creation of Warsaw's glory days, with lots of colorful architecture. **Hours:** Always open. See page 152.

▲▲**National Museum** Collection of mostly Polish art, with unknown but worth-discovering works by Jan Matejko and the Młoda Polska (Art Nouveau) crew. **Hours:** Tue-Sun 10:00-18:00, Thu until 21:00, closed Mon. See page 156.

▲▲**Warsaw Uprising Museum** High-tech exhibit tracing the history of the Uprising and celebrating its heroes. **Hours:** Mon, Wed, and Fri 8:00-18:00; Thu 8:00-20:00; Sat-Sun 10:00-18:00; closed Tue. See page 167.

▲▲**Copernicus Science Center** Spiffy new science museum with well-explained, hands-on exhibits in English; Warsaw's best family activity. **Hours:** Tue-Fri 9:00-18:00, Sat-Sun 10:00-19:00, closed Mon. See page 160.

▲**Castle Square** Colorful spot with whiffs of old Warsaw—Royal Castle, monuments, and a chunk of the city wall—and cafés just

that it's easiest to buy your bus ticket in the underground zone (at any kiosk marked *RUCH*) before you surface.

Buying Train Tickets: Lining one wall of the main arrival hall *(hala główna)* are 16 **ticket windows;** the two farthest to the right are designated for international tickets. A much more user-friendly **customer service center** is in the corner (daily 9:00-20:00). While it can be slower to buy tickets or make reservations here (take a number as you enter), staff members speak English and are generally more patient in helping explain your options. If you're in a hurry and the lines at the ticket windows in the main hall are way too long, you can find more ticket windows in the maze of corridors under the station. Allow yourself plenty of time to wait in line to buy tickets. Some locals bypass these lines altogether and buy their tickets on the train for an extra charge (10 zł extra; find the conductor before he finds you).

Note that even if you have a railpass, a reservation is still required on certain trains (including express trains to Kraków)—if

off the square. **Hours:** Always open. See page 147.

▲**Łazienki Park** Lovely, sprawling green space with Chopin statue, peacocks, and Neoclassical buildings. **Hours:** Always open. See page 162.

Chopin Museum Elegant old mansion features slick exhibits but not much substance about Chopin; occasional piano concerts worthwhile. **Hours:** Tue-Sun 12:00-20:00, closed Mon. See page 159.

Warsaw Historical Museum Glimpse of the city before and after World War II, with excellent movie in English. **Hours:** Museum—Tue-Thu 10:00-18:00, Fri-Sun 10:00-20:00, closed Mon; Movie—Tue-Fri at 10:00 and 12:00; Sat-Sun at 12:00 and 14:00. See page 153.

Palace of Culture and Science Huge "Stalin Gothic" skyscraper with a more impressive exterior than interior, housing theaters, multiplex cinema, observation deck, and more. **Hours:** Observation deck—daily June-Aug 9:00-20:00, until 24:00 Fri-Sat; Sept-May 9:00-18:00. See page 155.

Jewish Ghetto: Path of Remembrance Pilgrimage from Ghetto Heroes Square to the infamous Nazi "transfer spot" where Jews were sent to death camps. **Hours:** Always open. See page 166.

WARSAW

you're not sure, it's worth asking at the rail service center.

To get to your train, first find your way to the right platform (*peron*, as noted on schedules), then keep an eye on both tracks (*tor*) for your train. Train info: Tel. 19436 (22-19436 from outside Warsaw), www.rozklad-pkp.pl.

By Plane
Warsaw's **Fryderyk Chopin International Airport** (Port Lotniczy im. Fryderyk Chopina, airport code: WAW) is about six miles southwest of the center. The airport has just one terminal (Terminal A), which is divided into five check-in areas split between two zones: the old southern hall (areas A and B) and the newer northern hall (areas C, D, E). At the airport, you'll find a TI, ATMs, and exchange offices (*kantor*). Airport info: tel. 22-650-4220, www.lotnisko-chopina.pl/en.

A handy **train** zips right downtown from the airport, stopping at Centralna Station (4.40 zł, 20-30 minutes, 4/hour; operated by two different companies, SKM or KM—just take whichever is leaving first; buy ticket at any kiosk or machines at the station). Alternatively, from either hall (AB or CDE), **bus #175** runs into the city center (central train station, the Royal Way, and Old Town; 3.60 zł, buy ticket at kiosk or from driver—though sometimes drivers can't make change and require the exact amount, 4-6/hour, 30-45 minutes). Only certain **taxi** companies are authorized to pick up arriving travelers at the airport; go to the official taxi stand, and avoid random hucksters offering you a ride out front (these creeps are notorious for overcharging). The 30-minute taxi ride to the center shouldn't cost you more than 50 zł. The trip into town can take much longer during rush hour.

Modlin Airport (airport code: WMI), about 21 miles northwest of the city center, primarily serves budget airlines (especially Ryanair). The most direct option for getting to downtown Warsaw is ModlinBus, whose shuttle bus goes from the airport terminal to near the Palace of Culture and Science (price depends on how far ahead you buy ticket—typically 25-30 zł, 8-9/day, 1 hour, tel. 22-535-3381, www.modlinbus.com). A more frequent, well-coordinated bus-plus-train connection is operated by Koleje Mazowieckie (KM). You'll take a shuttle bus to Modlin's main train station, then hop on a train to Warsaw's Centralna Station (15 zł, 1-1.5 hours total, 2-3/hour, www.mazowieckie.com.pl). Airport info: www.modlinairport.pl.

By Car
Warsaw is a stressful city to drive and park in. Arrange parking with your hotel, and get around by foot or public transit.

Getting Around Warsaw
By Public Transit: In this big city, it's essential to get a handle on public transportation. The Metro will remain mostly useless to tourists until the new line opens in late 2014, but the buses and trams are great. All three systems use the same tickets. A single ticket costs 4.40 zł (called *bilet jednorazowy,* good for one trip up to 2 hours, no transfers); a one-day travelcard costs 15 zł *(bilet dobowy)*; and a three-day travelcard is 30 zł *(bilet trzydniowy).* For shorter trips, you can also buy time-limited tickets, such as the 3.40-zł "20-minute city travelcard" (*bilet 20-minutowy;* also available in 40- and 60-minute versions). Buy your ticket at any kiosk with a *RUCH* sign. Be sure to validate it as you board by inserting it in the little yellow box (one-day and three-day travelcards need only be validated the first time you ride). Some, but not all, buses have automated machines for buying tickets on board (coins only—no bills or credit cards), but it's safer to buy them in advance from a kiosk. Transit info: www.ztm.waw.pl.

Most of the city's major attractions line up on a single axis, the Royal Way, which is served by several different buses (but no trams). **Bus #175,** particularly useful on arrival, links Chopin Airport, the central train station, the Royal Way, and Old Town. Once in town, the designed-for-tourists **bus #180** conveniently connects virtually all of the significant sights and neighborhoods: the former Jewish Ghetto, Castle Square/Old Town, the Royal Way, Łazienki Park, and Wilanów Palace (south of the center). This particularly user-friendly bus lists sights in English on the posted schedule inside (other buses don't). Those two buses, as well as buses **#116, #195,** and **#222,** go along the most interesting stretch of the Royal Way (between aleja Jerozolimskie and Castle Square in the Old Town). **Bus #178** conveniently connects Castle Square to the Warsaw Uprising Museum. Bus routes beginning with "E" (and marked in red on schedules) are express, so they go long distances without stopping.

Note that on Saturdays and Sundays in summer (June-Sept), the Nowy Świat section of the Royal Way is closed to traffic, so the above routes take a detour along a parallel street.

While Warsaw's original **Metro** line is largely unhelpful to visitors (it runs roughly parallel to the Royal Way, several blocks to the west), a new Metro line is under construction that could prove very useful. Due to begin running in late 2014, this line cuts through the city from west to east, effortlessly connecting two otherwise hard-to-reach sights (Warsaw Uprising Museum and Copernicus Science Center), and also stopping at Nowy Świat (near the Copernicus Monument) and the National Stadium.

By Taxi: As in most big Eastern European cities, it's wise to use only cabs that are clearly marked with a company logo and telephone number (or call your own: Locals like MPT Radio Taxi, tel. 19191; or Ele taxi, tel. 22-811-1111). All official taxis have similar rates: 6 zł to start, then 3 zł per kilometer (4.50 zł after 22:00 or in the suburbs). The drop fee may be higher if you catch the cab in front of a fancy hotel.

Tours in Warsaw

For a big and important city, Warsaw suffers from a lack of good tour options. Each year, new companies crop up offering **walking tours** in Warsaw; as none is well-established, get the latest advice from the TI.

Various companies offer **bus tours** (which include some walking; 140 zł, 3 hours, get information at TI or your hotel). The same companies offer private, guided minivan tours to various destinations.

Two different companies offer **hop-on, hop-off bus tours.**

While City Sightseeing runs more frequently, it's still meager (1/hour); Warsaw City Tour runs even less often (every 2 hours), but has a farther-reaching route that includes more sights (such as the Jewish Quarter, not covered by City Sightseeing).

A **tourist train** does a 30-minute circuit, leaving from in front of the Royal Castle (22 zł, daily May-Oct, doesn't run Mon Nov-April).

Self-Guided Walk

Warsaw's Royal Way

The Royal Way (Szłak Królewski) is the six-mile route that the kings of Poland used to take from their main residence (at Castle Square in the Old Town) to their summer home (Wilanów Palace, south of the center and not worth visiting). In the heart of the city, the Royal Way is a busy boulevard with two different names: At the south end, hip and vibrant **Nowy Świat** offers lots of shops and restaurants, and a good glimpse of urban Warsaw; to the north, and ending at the Old Town, **Krakowskie Przedmieście** is lined with historic landmarks and better for sightseeing.

Since this spine connects most hotels, restaurants, and sights, you'll almost certainly use it—on foot or by bus—sometime during your trip (key buses are noted earlier, under "Getting Around Warsaw"). This self-guided walk should make your commute more interesting. Not counting sightseeing stops, figure about 15 minutes to walk along Nowy Świat ("Part 1"), then another 30 minutes along Krakowskie Przedmieście to the Old Town ("Part 2").

Royal Way Walk, Part 1: Nowy Świat

Begin at the head of the boulevard called Nowy Świat, at the intersection with busy **aleja Jerozolimskie** ("Jerusalem Avenue"). This street once led to a Jewish settlement called New Jerusalem. Like so much else in Warsaw, it's changed names many times.

Between the World Wars, it became "May 3rd Avenue," celebrating Poland's 1791 constitution (Europe's first). But this was too nationalistic for the occupying Nazis, who called it simply Bahnhofstrasse ("Train Station Street"). Then the communists switched it back to "Jerusalem"—strangely disregarding the religious connotations of that name. (Come on, guys—what about a good, old-fashioned "Stalin Avenue"?)

You can't miss the giant, out-of-place **palm tree** in the middle of aleja Jerozolimskie. When a local artist went to the real Jerusalem, she was struck at how many palm trees she saw there. She decided it was only appropriate that one should grace Warsaw's own little stretch of "Jerusalem." This artificial palm tree—with a trunk from France and leaves from California, where theme parks abound with such fake trees—went up years ago as a temporary installation. It was highly controversial, dividing the neighborhood. One snowy winter day, the pro-palm tree faction—who appreciated the way the tree spiced up this otherwise predictable metropolis—camped out here in bikinis and beachwear to show their support. They prevailed, and the tree still stands.

Look to the corner across the street from the palm tree, where a statue of **Charles de Gaulle** strides confidently up the street. A gift from the government of France, this celebrates the military tactician who came to Warsaw's rescue when the Red Army invaded from the USSR after World War I. The giant roundabout surrounding the palm tree is also named for de Gaulle.

As you face the palm tree, look across the street and up the block to the left to see the **National Museum**—a good place for a Polish art lesson (more interesting than it sounds—described later, under "Sights in Warsaw").

To the right of the National Museum, directly across from Nowy Świat stands a big, blocky building marked *RICOH* that used to be the **headquarters of the Communist Party.** The translation for Nowy Świat is "New World." A popular communist-era joke: What do you see when you turn your back on the Communist Party? A "New World."

Today's Poland is confidently striding into a new world...and so should we. Get marching.

Nowy Świat is a charming shopping boulevard lined with boutiques, cafés, and restaurants—the most upscale, elegant-

feeling part of the city. Before World War II, Nowy Świat was Warsaw's most popular neighborhood. And today, once again, rents are higher here than anywhere else in town. While most tourists flock into the Old Town, Varsovians and visiting businesspeople prefer this zone. The city has worked hard to revitalize this strip with new, broader, pedestrian-friendly sidewalks, flower boxes, and old-time lampposts.

Ulica Chmielna, the first street to the left, is an appealing pedestrian boutique street leading to Emil Wedel's chocolate heaven (a five-minute walk away; described later, under "Eating in Warsaw"). Between here and the Palace of Culture and Science stretches one of Warsaw's trendiest shopping neighborhoods

Central Warsaw

Accommodations

1. Hotel Le Régina
2. Novotel
3. Duval Apartments
4. Castle Inn
5. Royal Route Residence & Old Town Apts. Office
6. Zgoda Apartment Hotel
7. Hotel Harenda
8. Boutique B&B
9. Ibis Warszawa Stare Miasto
10. To Nathan's Villa Hostel
11. Oki Doki Hostel
12. Szkolne Schronisko Hostel

Eateries

13. Restauracja pod Samsonem
14. Pierogarnia na Bednarskiej
15. BrowArmia Brewpub
16. U Kucharzy Restaurant
17. U Fukiera Restaurant
18. Enoteka Polska
19. Papaya Restaurant
20. Kamahda Lwowska
21. Butchery & Wine
22. Wiking Milk Bar
23. Mleczarnia Jerozolimska

WARSAW

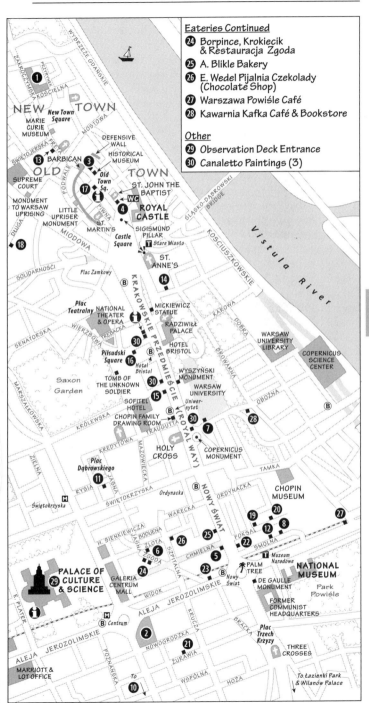

Eateries Continued

㉔ Borpince, Krokiecik & Restauracja Zgoda

㉕ A. Blikle Bakery

㉖ E. Wedel Pijalnia Czekolady (Chocolate Shop)

㉗ Warszawa Powiśle Café

㉘ Kawarnia Kafka Café & Bookstore

Other

㉙ Observation Deck Entrance

㉚ Canaletto Paintings (3)

WARSAW

(culminating at the Galleria Centrum mall, just across from the Palace).

Across the street from Chmielna (on the right) is the street called **Foksal**, one of Warsaw's most pleasant and trendy dining zones. On a balmy summer evening, this street is filled with chatty al fresco diners, sipping drinks and nibbling at plates of cutting-edge international cuisine.

A few steps down Nowy Świat, on the left, don't miss the recommended **A. Blikle** pastry shop and café—*the* place in Poland to buy sweets, especially *pączki* (rose-flavored jelly doughnuts). Or, if you're homesick for Starbucks, drop into one of the many gourmet coffee shops that line this stretch of Nowy Świat—with American-style lattes "to go."

A half-block down the street (on the left) is a rare surviving bit of pre-glitz Nowy Świat: Bar Mleczny Familijny, a classic **milk bar**—a government-subsidized cafeteria filled with locals seeking a cheap meal (an interesting cultural artifact, but not recommended for a meal). Don't be surprised if it's gone by the time you visit; in this high-rent district, it's unlikely that these few remaining holdovers from the old days will survive for much longer.

The next two blocks are more of the same. Eat and shop your way up Nowy Świat, until you reach the big Copernicus statue.

Royal Way Walk, Part 2: Krakowskie Przedmieście

The street name changes to Krakowskie Przedmieście at the big statue of **Copernicus** (by the great Danish sculptor Bertel Thorvaldsen), in front of the Polish Academy of Science. Mikołaj Kopernik (1473-1543) was born in Toruń and went to college in Kraków. The Nazis stole this statue and took it to Germany (which, like Poland, claims Copernicus as its own). Now it's back where it belongs.

Nearby, in the glass case, find a replica of a Canaletto painting of this same street scene in 1778, and compare it to today's reality. (Paintings like this were used to rebuild the city after World War II.) You may see other Canalettos like this one scattered around the city.

We'll pass many churches along this route, but the **Church of the Holy Cross** is unique (Kościół Św. Krzyża, across from Copernicus, free entry). Composer Fryderyk Chopin's heart is inside one of the pillars of the nave (first big pillar on the left, look for the marker). After two decades of exile in France, Chopin's final wish was to have his heart brought back to his native Poland after his death. During World War II, the heart was hidden away in the countryside for safety. Check out the bright gold chapel, located on the left as you face the altar, near the front of the church. It's dedicated to a saint whom Polish Catholics believe helps them with "desperate and hopeless causes." People praying here are likely dealing with some tough issues. The beads draped from the altarpieces help power their prayers, and the many

little brass plaques are messages of thanks for prayers answered. In the back-right corner (as you face the altar), behind the giant barbed wire, is a memorial to the 22,000 Polish POWs—mostly officers and prominent civilians—massacred by Soviet soldiers in 1940 near Katyń, a village in today's Russia.

Leave the church and cross the street (appreciating how pedestrian-friendly it's become in recent years). A long block up the street on the right, you'll see the gates (marked *Uniwersytet*) to the main campus of **Warsaw University,** founded in 1816. This area is a lively student district with plenty of bookstores and cafés.

The 18th century was a time of great political decline for Poland, as a series of incompetent foreign kings mishandled crises and squandered funds. But ironically, it was also Warsaw's biggest economic boom time. Along this boulevard, aristocratic families of the period built **mansions**—most of them destroyed during World War II and rebuilt since. Some have curious flourishes (just past the university on the right, look for the doorway supported by four bearded brutes admiring their overly defined abs). Over time, many of these families donated their mansions to the university. (Across the street on the corner, look for the recommended BrowArmia brewpub, with some of the best people-watching al fresco tables on the Royal Way.)

The bright-yellow church a block up from the university is the Church of the Nuns of the Visitation (Kościół Sióstr Wizytek). The monument in front commemorates **Cardinal Stefan Wyszyński,** who was the Polish primate (the head of the Polish Catholic Church) from 1948 to 1981. He took this post soon after the arrival of the communists, who opposed the Church, but also realized it would be risky for them to shut down the churches in such an ardently religious country. The Communist Party and the Catholic Church coexisted tensely in Poland, and when Wyszyński protested a Stalinist crackdown in 1953, he was arrested and imprisoned. Three years later, in a major victory for the Church, Wyszyński was released. He continued to fight the communists, becoming a great hero of the Polish people in their struggle against the regime. Across the street is another then-and-now Canaletto illustration.

Farther up (on the right) is the elegant, venerable Hotel Bristol. Leave the Royal Way briefly here to reach Piłsudski Square (a block away on the left, up the street opposite Hotel Bristol).

The vast, empty-feeling **Piłsudski Square** (Plac Marszałka Józefa Piłsudskiego) has been important Warsaw real estate for centuries, constantly changing with the times. In the 1890s, the Russians who controlled this part of Poland began construction of a huge and magnificent Orthodox cathedral on this spot. But soon after it was completed, Poland regained its independence, and anti-Russian sentiments ran hot. So in the 1920s, just over a decade after the cathedral went up, it was torn down again. During the Nazi occupation, this square took the name "Adolf-Hitler-Platz." Under the communists, it was Zwycięstwa, meaning "Victory" (of the Soviets over Hitler's fascism). When the regime imposed martial law in 1981, the people of Warsaw silently protested by filling the square with a giant cross made of flowers. The huge plaque in the ground near the road commemorates two monumental communist-era Catholic events on this square: John Paul II's first visit as pope to his homeland on June 2, 1979; and the May 31, 1981 funeral of Cardinal Stefan Wyszyński, whom we met across the street. The cross nearby also honors the 1979 papal visit, with one of his most famous and inspiring quotes to his countrymen: "Let thy spirit descend, let thy spirit descend, and renew the face of the earth—*this* earth" (meaning Poland, in a just-barely-subtle-enough dig against the communist regime that was tolerating his visit). More recently, on April 17, 2010, more than 100,000 Poles convened on this square for a more solemn occasion: a memorial service for President Lech Kaczyński, who had died in a tragic plane crash in Russia.

Stand near the giant plaque, with the Royal Way at your back, for this quick spin-tour orientation: Ahead are the Tomb of the Unknown Soldier and Saxon Garden (explained later); 90 degrees to the right is the old National Theater, eclipsed by a modern business center/parking garage; another 90 degrees to the right is a statue of Piłsudski (which you passed to get here—described later); and 90 more degrees to the right is the Sofitel—formerly the Victoria Hotel, the ultimate plush, top-of-the-top hotel where all communist-era VIPs stayed. To the right of the hotel, on the horizon, you can see Warsaw's newly emerging skyline. The imposing Palace of Culture and Science, which once stood alone over the city, is now joined by a cluster of brand-new skyscrapers, giving Warsaw a Berlin-esque vibe befitting its important role as a business center of the "New Europe."

Walk to the fragment of colonnade by the park that marks the **Tomb of the Unknown Soldier** (Grób Nieznanego Żołnierza). The colonnade was once part of a much larger palace built by the Saxon prince electors (Dresden's Augustus the Strong and his son), who became kings of Poland in the 18th century. After the palace was destroyed in World War II, this fragment was kept to memorialize Polish soldiers. The names of key battles are etched into the columns, the urns contain dirt from major Polish battlefields, and the two soldiers are pretty stiff.

Just behind the Tomb is the stately **Saxon Garden** (Ogród Saski), inhabited by genteel statues and a spurting fountain. This

park was also built by the Saxon kings of Poland. Like most foreign kings, Augustus the Strong and his son cared little for their Polish territory, building gardens like these for themselves instead of investing in more pressing needs. Poles say that foreign kings such as Augustus did nothing but "eat, drink, and loosen their belts" (it rhymes in Polish). According to Poles, these selfish absentee kings were the culprits in Poland's eventual decline.

Walk back out toward the Royal Way, stopping at the statue you passed earlier. In 1995, the square was again renamed—this

time for **Józef Piłsudski** (1867-1935), the guy with the big walrus moustache. With the help of a French captain named Charles de Gaulle (whom we met earlier), Piłsudski forced the Russian Bolsheviks out of Poland in 1920 in the so-called Miracle on the Vistula. Piłsudski is credited with creating a once-again-independent Poland after more than a century of foreign oppression, and he essentially ran Poland as a virtual dictator after World War I. Of course, under the communists, Piłsudski was swept under the rug. But since 1989, he has enjoyed a renaissance as many Poles' favorite prototype anti-communist hero (his name adorns streets, squares, and bushy-mustachioed monuments all over the country).

Return to Hotel Bristol, turn left, and continue your Royal Way walk. Next door to the hotel, you'll see the huge **Radziwiłł Palace**. The Warsaw Pact was signed here in 1955, officially uniting the Soviet satellite states in a military alliance against NATO. This building has also, from time to time, served as the Polish "White House." A **TI** is in the old guardhouse (Kordegarda) across the street.

Beyond Radziwiłł Palace, you'll reach a statue (on a pillar) of **Adam Mickiewicz,** Poland's national poet. Polish high school students have a big formal ball (like a prom) 100 days before graduation. After the ball, if students come here and hop around the statue on one leg, it's supposed to bring them good luck on their finals. Mickiewicz, for his part, looks like he's suffering from a heart attack—perhaps in response to the impressively ugly National Theater and Opera a block in front of him.

Continue to the end of the Royal Way, marked by the big

pink palace. For a scenic finale to your Royal Way stroll, climb the 150 steps of the view tower by **St. Anne's Church** (5 zł, sporadic hours but generally open daily 10:00-18:00, in summer until 21:00 or 22:00 depending on weather, closed in bad winter weather, on the right just before Castle Square). You'll be rewarded with a great view of the Old Town, river, and Warsaw's skyline.

From St. Anne's Church, it's just another block—past inviting art galleries and restaurants—to Castle Square, the TI, and the start of the Old Town.

Sights in Warsaw

The Old Town

In 1945, not a building remained standing in Warsaw's "Old" Town (Stare Miasto). Everything you see is rebuilt, mostly finished by 1956. Some think the Old Town feels artificial and phony, in a Disney World kind of way. For others, the painstaking postwar reconstruction feels just right, with Old World squares and lanes charming enough to give Kraków a run for its money. Before 1989, stifled by communist repression and choking on smog, the Old Town was an empty husk of its historic self. But now, the outdoor restaurants and market stalls have returned, and Varsovians and tourists are out strolling.

These sights are listed in order from south to north, beginning at Castle Square and ending at the entrance to the New Town. For the best route from the central train station to the Old Town, see the "Royal Way" self-guided walk, earlier.

▲Castle Square (Plac Zamkowy)

This lively square is dominated by the big, pink Royal Castle that is the historic heart of Warsaw's political power.

After the second great Polish dynasty—the Jagiellonians—died off in 1572, it was replaced by the Republic of Nobles (about 10 percent of the population), which elected various foreign kings to their throne. The guy on the 72-foot-tall **pillar** is Sigismund III, the first Polish king from the Swedish Waza family. In 1596, he relocated the capital from Kraków to Warsaw. This move made sense, since Warsaw was closer to the center of 16th-century Poland (which had expanded to the east), and because the city had gained political importance over the past 30 years as the meeting point of the Sejm, or parliament of nobles. Along the right side of the castle, notice the two previous versions of this pillar lying on a lawn. The first one, from 1644, was falling apart and had to be replaced in 1887 by a new one made of granite. In 1944, a Nazi tank broke this second pillar—a symbolic piece of Polish heritage—into the four pieces (still pockmarked with bullet holes) that you see here today. As Poland rebuilt, its citizens put Sigismund III back on his pillar. Past the pillars are great views of Warsaw's brand-new, red-and-white National Stadium across the river.

Across the square from the castle, you'll see the partially reconstructed **defensive wall**. This rampart once enclosed the entire Old Town. Warsaw—like all of Poland—has seen invasion from all sides.

Explore the café-lined lanes that branch off Castle Square. Street signs indicate the year that each lane was originally built.

The first street leading off the square is **ulica Piwna** ("Beer Street"), where you'll find **St. Martin's Church** (Kościół Św. Martina, on the left). Run by Franciscan nuns, this church has a simple, modern interior. Walk up the aisle and find the second pillar on the right. Notice the partly destroyed crucifix—it's the only church artifact that survived World War II. Across the street and closer to Castle Square, admire the carefully carved doorway of the house called *pod Gołębiami* ("Under Doves")—dedicated to the memory of an old woman who fed birds amidst the Old Town rubble after World War II.

Back on Castle Square, find the white **plaque** in the middle of the second block (by plac Zamkowy 15/19). It explains that 50 Poles were executed by Nazis on this spot on September 2, 1944. You'll see plaques like this all over the Old Town, each one commemorating victims or opponents of the Nazis. The brick planter under the plaque is often filled with fresh flowers to honor the victims.

▲▲Royal Castle (Zamek Królewski)

A castle has stood here since the Mazovian dukes built a wooden version in the 14th century. It has shifted shape with the tenor of the times, being rebuilt and remodeled by many different kings. When Warsaw became the capital in 1596, this massive building served a dual purpose: It was both the king's residence and the meeting place of the parliament (Sejm). It reached its peak under Stanisław August Poniatowski—the final Polish king—who

imported artists and architects to spiff up the interior, leaving his mark all over the place. After Luftwaffe bombs destroyed it in World War II (only one wall remained standing), rebuilding began again in the 1950s. It was not completed until the 1970s.

Warsaw's Royal Castle has a gorgeous interior—the most opulent I've seen in Poland. Many of the furnishings are original (hidden away when it became clear the city would be demolished in World War II). A visit to the castle is like perusing a great Polish history textbook. In fact, you'll likely see grade-school classes sitting cross-legged on the floors. Watching the teachers quizzing eager young history buffs, you can imagine what it's like to be a young Pole, with such a tumultuous history.

Cost and Hours: 22 zł, free on Sun, audioguide-17 zł; open May-Sept Mon-Sat 10:00-18:00, Sun 11:00-18:00; Oct-April Tue-Sat 10:00-16:00, Sun 11:00-16:00, closed Mon; last entry one hour before closing; Plac Zamkowy 4, tel. 22-355-5170, www.zamek -krolewski.pl. A public WC is on the courtyard just around the corner of the castle.

◐ Self-Guided Tour: The castle has good posted English information and a well-produced audioguide (worth the extra cost if you want the full story). For the basics, use this commentary to follow the one-way route through the castle. Because the castle visit procedure is always changing, it's possible you won't see these rooms in this exact order; if that happens, match the labels in each room to the corresponding text below.

Entering the courtyard, go to the left to buy tickets, then cross to the opposite side to tour the interior. (If you want an audio-guide, go downstairs to rent it first.) Head up the stairs and follow *Castle Route* signs.

Start in the Oval Gallery, then head into the **Council Chamber,** where a "Permanent Council" consisting of the king, 18 senators, and 18 representatives met to chart Poland's course. Next is the **Great Assembly Hall,** heavy with marble and chandeliers. The statues of Apollo and Minerva flanking the main door are modeled after King Stanisław August Poniatowski and Catherine the Great of Russia, respectively. (The king enjoyed a youthful romantic dalliance with Catherine on a trip to Russia, and never quite seemed to get over her...much to his wife's consternation, I'm sure.)

The **Knights' Hall** features the Polish Hall of Fame, with paintings of great events and busts and portraits of VIPs—Very Important Poles. The statue of Chronos—god of time, with the globe on his shoulders—is actually a functioning clock, though now it's stopped at 11:15 to commemorate the exact time in 1944 when the Nazis bombed this palace to bits. Just off this hall is the **Marble Room,** with more portraits of Polish greats ringing the top of the room. Above the fireplace is a portrait of Stanisław August Poniatowski.

Continuing back through the Knights' Hall, you'll wind up in the remarkable **Throne Room.** Notice the crowned eagle,

the symbol of Poland, decorating the banner behind the throne. The Soviets didn't allow anything royal or aristocratic, so postwar restorations came with crown-less eagles. Only after 1989 were the crowned eagles reinstated (one of the original eagles from this banner somehow turned up in the United States, and was used as a model for the ones you see here). Peek into the **Conference Rooms,** with portraits of other major European monarchs—Russia's Catherine the Great, England's George III, and France's Louis XVI—in whose esteemed company Stanisław August Poniatowski liked to consider himself.

After four more grand rooms (including the King's Bedroom, with a gorgeous silk canopy over the bed), you'll enter the **Canaletto Room,** filled with canvases of late-18th-century Warsaw painted in exquisite detail by this talented artist. (This Canaletto, also known for his panoramas of Dresden, was the nephew of another artist with the same nickname, famous for painting Venice's canals.) Paintings like these helped post-WWII restorers resurrect the city from its rubble. To the left, on the lower wall, the big canvas features the view of Warsaw from the Praga district across the river; pick out the few landmarks that are still standing (or, more precisely, have been resurrected). Notice the artist's self-portrait in the lower-left. On the right side of the room is Canaletto's depiction of the election of Stanisław August Poniatowski as king, in a field outside Warsaw (notice the empty throne in the middle of the group). Among the assembled crowd, each flag represents a different Polish province. From here, head into the **side chapel,** reserved for the king. In the box to the left of the altar is the heart of Tadeusz Kościuszko, a hero of both the American Revolution and the Polish struggle against the Partitions.

As you cross over to the other part of the castle, you'll pass through the **Four Seasons Gallery** (with some fine but faded Gobelin tapestries) before entering a few rooms occupied by the houses of parliament—a reminder that this "castle" wasn't just the king's house, but also the meeting place of the legislature. In the **Parliamentary Chambers,** notice the maps showing Poland's constantly in-flux borders—a handy visual aid for the many school groups who visit here.

After several rooms, you'll reach the grand **Senators' Chamber,** with the king's throne, surrounded by different coats of arms. Each one represents a region that was part of Poland during its Golden Age, back when it was united with Lithuania and its territory stretched from the Baltic to the Black Sea (see the map on the wall). In this room, Poland adopted its 1791 constitution  (notice the replica in the display case to the left of the throne). It was the first in Europe, written soon after America's and just months before France's. And, like the Constitution of the United States, it was very progressive, based on the ideals of the Enlightenment. But when the final Partitions followed in 1793 and 1795, Poland was divided between neighboring powers and ceased to exist as a country until 1918—so the constitution was never fully put into action.

Next, the **Crown Princes Room** features paintings by Jan Matejko that capture the excitement surrounding the adoption of this ill-fated constitution. The next room has another Matejko painting: King Stefan Batory negotiating with Ivan the Terrible's envoys to break their siege of a Russian town. Notice the hussars—

fearsome Polish soldiers wearing winged armor. Finally, you'll wind through more rooms with yet more paintings of great historical events and portraits of famous Poles.

Other Castle Sights: Consider a detour to the **Kubicki Arcades** (Arkady Kubiciego), the impressively excavated arcades

deep beneath the castle. From the entrance lobby, head downstairs to the area with the cloakroom, bathrooms, and bookshop, then find the long escalator that takes you down to the arcades. It's free to wander the long, cavernous, and newly clean and gleaming space, made elegant by grand drapes. To visit the exhibit branching off the arcade, which explains the excavation and refurbishment, you'll have to buy an 8-zł ticket (free on Sun, purchase from main ticket desk). I'd skip the exhibit and just enjoy the space.

The castle has a vast collection, which it organizes into various exhibitions—some permanent (well, as permanent as anything around here) and some temporary. The extensive **oriental carpet collection** in the "tin-roofed castle" (Pałac pod Blachą) is sparsely described and skippable for most; the same building also features seven unimpressive apartments of Prince Józef Poniatowski, the king's brother (14 zł for both, free on Sun, same hours as castle, around the right side of the castle as you face it—past the two fallen columns, buy ticket at main ticket desk). When you're buying your castle ticket, keep an eye out for **temporary exhibits** of interest.

• *After you finish touring the castle and are ready to resume exploring the Old Town, turn left at the end of the square onto...*

St. John's Street (Świętojańska)

On the plaque under the street name sign, you can guess what the dates mean, even if you don't know Polish: This building was constructed from 1433 to 1478, destroyed in 1944, and rebuilt from 1950 to 1953.

• *Partway down the street on the right, you'll come to the big brick...*

Cathedral of St. John the Baptist (Katedra Św. Jana Chrzciciela)

This cathedral-basilica is the oldest (1339) and most important church in Warsaw. Superficially unimpressive, the church's own archbishop admitted that it was "modest and poor"—but "the historical events that took place here make it magnificent." Poland's constitution was consecrated here on May 3, 1791. Much later, this church became the final battleground of the 1944 Warsaw

Uprising—when a Nazi "tracked mine" (a huge bomb on tank tracks—this one appropriately named *Goliath*) drove into the church and exploded, massacring the rebels. You can still see part of that tank's tread hanging on the outside wall of the church (through the passage on the right side, near the end of the church).

Head inside. Typical of brick churches, it has a "hall church" design, with three naves of equal height. Look for the crucifix ornamented with real human hair (chapel left of high altar). The high altar holds a copy of the Black Madonna—proclaimed "everlasting queen of Poland" after a victory over the Swedes in the 17th century. The original Black Madonna is in Częstochowa (125 miles south of Warsaw)—a mecca for Slavic Catholics, who visit in droves in hopes of a miracle. In the back-left corner, find the chapel with the tomb of Cardinal Stefan Wyszyński. The crypt (2 zł) holds graves of several important Poles, including Stanisław August Poniatowski (the last Polish king) and Nobel Prize-winning author Henryk Sienkiewicz.

Cost and Hours: Free, crypt-2 zł, good guidebook-5 zł, open to tourists daily 10:00-13:00 & 15:00-17:30, closed during services and organ concerts. The cathedral hosts organ concerts in summer—9 zł, May-late Sept Mon-Sat at 12:00, 25 minutes, no concerts Sun or late Sept-April.

• *Continue up the street and enter Warsaw's grand...*

▲▲Old Town Market Square (Rynek Starego Miasta)

Seventy-five years ago, this was one of the most happening spots in Central Europe. Sixty-five years ago, it was rubble. And today, like a phoenix from the ashes, it's risen to remind residents and tourists alike of the prewar glory of the Polish capital.

Go to the **mermaid fountain** in the middle of the square. The mermaid is an important symbol in Warsaw—you'll see her everywhere. Legend has it that a mermaid *(syrenka)* lived in the Vistula River and protected the townspeople. While this siren supposedly serenaded the town, Varsovians like her more for her strength (hence the sword). In fact, the woman who modeled for this sculpture, Krystyna Krahelska (code name: "Danuta"), served as a paramedic for the Polish Home Army during the Warsaw Uprising. On the second day of the fighting, she was shot in the chest and died, becoming a martyr for the Polish people. But life goes on in Warsaw, as it always has. I've often seen children frolicking here, oblivious to the turmoil their forebears withstood. When the fountain gurgles, the kids giggle.

Each of the square's four sides is named for a prominent 18th-century Varsovian: Kołłątaj, Dekert, Barss, and Zakrzewski. These men served as "Presidents" of Warsaw (mayors, more or less), and Kołłątaj was also a framer of Poland's 1791 constitution. Take some time to explore the square. Enjoy the colorful architecture. Notice that many of the buildings were intentionally built to lean out into the square—to simulate the higgledy-piggledy wear and tear of the original buildings.

• On the Dekert (north) side of the square is the...

Warsaw Historical Museum (Muzeum Historyczne Warszawy)

This labyrinthine museum rambles through several reconstructed buildings fronting the Old Town Market Square. They recently excavated a series of cellars that run beneath the square, which now also house museum exhibits. The English descriptions are limited, making it a bit difficult to appreciate. As you twist your way through room after room of historical bric-a-brac, keep an eye out for the model of 18th-century Warsaw, which is worth a close look. The final third of the collection, which focuses on the tumultuous 20th century, is the most updated—and the most interesting.

Cost and Hours: 8 zł, free on Sun, open Tue-Thu 10:00-18:00, Fri-Sun 10:00-20:00, closed Mon, last entry 45 minutes before closing, Rynek Starego Miasta 28/42, tel. 22-635-1625, www.mhw.pl.

Film: Unless you're fascinated by Warsaw's history, I'd skip the museum collection and just buy the separate 6-zł ticket to watch the excellent 20-minute film in English, worth ▲▲; unfortunately, it runs only twice daily (Tue-Fri at 10:00 and 12:00; Sat-Sun at 12:00 and 14:00). With somber narration and black-and-white scenes from before, during, and after the wartime devastation, this film is best appreciated after you've had a chance to see some of today's Warsaw (especially along the Royal Way). The movie ends with, "They say that there are no miracles. Then what is this city on the Vistula?" Emotionally drained, you can only respond, "Amen."

• Leave the square on Nowomiejska (at the mermaid's 2 o'clock, by the second-story niche sculpture of St. Anne). After a block, you'll reach the...

Barbican (Barbakan)

This defensive gate of the Old Town, similar to Kraków's, protected the medieval city from invaders.

• *Once you've crossed through the barbican, you're officially in Warsaw's...*

New Town (Nowe Miasto)

This 15th-century neighborhood

is "new" in name only: It was the first part of Warsaw to spring up outside of the city walls (and therefore slightly newer than the Old Town). The New Town is a fun place to wander: Only a little less charming than the Old Town, but with a more real-life feel—people live and work here. Its centerpiece is the **New Town Square** (Rynek Nowego Miasta), watched over by the distinctive green dome of St. Kazimierz Church.

Marie Skłodowska-Curie Museum

Scientists might want to pay homage at the museum (and birthplace) of Warsaw native Marie Skłodowska-Curie, a.k.a. Madame Curie (1867-1934), just off the square. This Nobel Prize winner was the world's first radiologist—discovering both radium and polonium (named for her native land) with her husband, Pierre Curie. Since she lived at a time when Warsaw was controlled by oppressive Russia, she conducted her studies in France. The museum—with photos, furniture, artifacts, and a paucity of English information—is a bit of a snoozer, best left to true fans.

Cost and Hours: Overpriced at 11 zł, Tue 8:30-16:00, Wed-Fri 9:30-16:00, Sat 10:00-16:00, Sun 10:00-15:00, closed Mon, ulica Freta 16, tel. 22/831-8092, http://muzeum-msc.pl.

From the New Town to Castle Square

You can backtrack the way you came, or, to get a look at Warsaw's back streets, consider this route from the big, round barbican gate (where the New Town meets the Old): Go back through the barbican and over the little bridge, turn right, and walk along the houses that line the inside of the wall. You'll pass a leafy garden courtyard on the left—a reminder that people actually live in the tourist zone within the Old Town walls. Just beyond the garden on the right, look for the carpet-beating rack, used to clean rugs (these are common fixtures in people's backyards). Go left into the square called Szeroki Dunaj ("Wide Danube") and look for another mermaid (over the Thai restaurant). Continue through the square and turn right at Wąski Dunaj ("Narrow Danube"). After about 100 yards, you'll pass the city wall. Just to the right (outside the wall), you'll see the monument to the **Little Upriser** of 1944, a child wearing a grown-up's helmet and too-big boots, and carrying a machine gun. Children—and especially Scouts (Harcerze)—played a key role in the resistance against the Nazis. Their job was mainly carrying messages and propaganda.

Now continue around the wall (the upper, inner part is more pleasant). Admire more public art as you head back to Castle Square.

Near the Central Train Station

These sights are near Nowy Świat, within a few blocks of the central train station.

Palace of Culture and Science
(Pałac Kultury i Nauki, or PKiN)

This massive skyscraper, dating from the early 1950s, is the tallest building between Frankfurt and Moscow (760 feet with the

spire—though several new buildings are threatening to eclipse that peak). It was a "gift" from Stalin that the people of Warsaw couldn't refuse. Varsovians call it "Stalin's Penis"...using cruder terminology than that. (There were seven such "Stalin Gothic" erections in Moscow.) Because it was to be "Soviet in substance, Polish in style," Soviet architects toured Poland to absorb local culture before starting the project. Notice the frilly decorative friezes that top each level—evocative of Poland's many Renaissance buildings (such as Kraków's Cloth Hall). The clock was added in 1999 as part of the millennium celebrations. Since the end of communism, the younger generation doesn't mind the structure so much—and some even admit to liking it for the way it enlivens the new, predictable, glass-and-steel skyline springing up around it.

Everything about the Pałac is big. It's designed to show off the strong, grand-scale Soviet aesthetic and architectural skill. The Pałac contains various theaters (the Culture), museums of evolution and technology (the Science), a congress hall, a multiplex (showing current movies), an observation deck, and lots of office space. With all of this culture and science under one roof, it's a shame that none of it makes for worthwhile sightseeing. While the interior is highly skippable, viewing the building from the outside is a quintessential Warsaw experience, worth ▲▲.

If you're killing time between trains, you could zip up to the observation deck (billed as "XXX Floor") in 20 seconds on the retrofitted Soviet elevators. Better yet, snap a photo from down below and save your money—it's overpriced and the view's a let-down. While you'll get a nice overview of Warsaw's forest of new skyscrapers, you can hardly see the Old Town, and Warsaw's most prominent big building—the Pałac itself—is missing.

Cost and Hours: Free entry, observation deck—20 zł, includes Polish-oriented special exhibitions; deck open daily June-Aug 9:00-20:00, until 24:00 Fri-Sat; Sept-May 9:00-18:00, enter through main door on east side of Pałac—opposite from central train station, tel. 22-656-7600, www.pkin.pl.

Złote Tarasy Shopping Mall

Tucked behind the central train station, "Golden Terraces" is a super-modern shopping mall with a funky, undulating glass-and-steel roof. Even though you didn't come all the way to Poland to visit a shopping mall, it's worth detouring here to get a taste of Poland's race into the future. In many ways, this—and not humble farmers munching pierogi—is the face of today's Poland.

Hours: Mon-Sat 10:00-22:00, Sun 10:00-20:00, lots of designer shops, good food court on top level, www.zlotetarasy.pl.

Złota 44

This dramatic skyscraper, rising high from the Złote Tarasy shopping mall, was designed by world-renowned architect Daniel Libeskind (who is also redeveloping the 9/11 site in New York City). Born in Poland, at a very young age Libeskind emigrated with his family to the US, returning only recently to embark on this project. Its shape evokes an eagle (a common symbol for Poland) just beginning to take flight. Of all the shiny new towers popping up in Warsaw's skyline, this is the most architecturally interesting—and offers a striking counterpoint to the Stalinist Palace of Culture and Science nearby. (For more on the building, visit www.zlota44tower.com.)

Between Nowy Świat and the River

▲▲National Museum (Muzeum Narodowe)

While short on big-name pieces, this museum interests art lovers and offers a good, accessible introduction to some talented Polish artists who are largely unknown outside their home country. A modern, state-of-the-art exhibition space allows these unsung canvases to really sing. Polish and other European artists are displayed side-by-side, as if to assert Poland's worthiness on the world artistic stage. After seeing a few of the masterpieces here, you won't disagree.

Cost and Hours: 15 zł, more for temporary exhibits, permanent collection free on Tue, open Tue-Sun 10:00-18:00, Thu until 21:00, closed Mon, last entry 45 minutes before closing, one block east of Nowy Świat at aleja Jerozolimskie 3, tel. 22-629-3093, www.mnw.art.pl.

Visiting the Museum: The collection fills several separate galleries: Ancient Art (from Greek pieces to artifacts left by early Polish tribes); Gallery Faras (highlighting the museum's fine collection of archaeological findings from that ancient Egyptian city); Medieval Art (including some of the most graphic altarpieces and crucifixes I've seen); Old European Painting (pre-19th-century canvases arranged by theme and juxtaposed to highlight the differences between southern and northern European art); Old Polish and European Portrait (as interesting as somebody else's yearbook); 19th-Century Art (Poland's strong suit, with fine works by Jan Matejko and the Młoda Polska movement—described below); 20th- and 21st-Century Art (with an impressive array of Modern and Postmodern Polish artists, including photography and film); and temporary exhibits.

If seeing Polish art is your goal—which it should be—a good place to start is in the **Gallery of 19th-Century Art.** Find your way there, then ask around to find works by Jan Matejko; ask the guards, "mah-TAY-koh?" (On the way, keep an eye out for Napoleon portraits. The Poles loved Napoleon, who bravely marched on Russia in an era when this part of Poland was occupied and oppressed by the Russians...sadly, not for the last time.)

Matejko's biggest work here—in fact, the biggest canvas in the whole building—is the enormous *Battle of Grunwald.* This epic painting commemorates one of Poland's high-water marks—the dramatic victory of a Polish-Lithuanian army over the Teutonic Knights, who had been terrorizing northern Poland for decades. On July 15, 1410, some 40,000 Poles and Lithuanians (led by the sword-waving Lithuanian in red, Grand Duke Vytautas) faced off against 27,000 Teutonic Knights (under their Grand Master, in white) in one of the medieval world's bloodiest battles. Matejko plops us right in the thick of the battle's chaos, painting life-size figures and framing off a 32-foot-long slice of the actual two-mile battle line.

In the center of the painting, the Teutonic Grand Master is about to become a shish kebab. Duke Vytautas, in red, leads the final charge. And waaaay up on a hill (in the upper right-hand corner, on horseback, wearing a silver knight's suit) is Władysław Jagiełło, the first king of the Jagiellonian dynasty...ensuring his bloodline will survive another 150 years.

Matejko spent three years covering this 450-square-foot canvas in paint. The canvas was specially made in a single seamless piece. This was such a popular work that almost as many fans turned out for its unveiling as there are figures in the painting.

From Poland's high point in the *Battle of Grunwald,* look (or

Jan Matejko
(1838-1893)

Jan Matejko (yawn mah-TAY-koh) is Poland's most important painter, period. In the mid- to late-19th century, the nation of Poland had been dissolved by foreign powers, and Polish artists struggled to make sense of their people's place in the world. Rabble-rousing Romanticism seemed to have failed (inspiring many brutally suppressed uprisings), so Polish artists and writers turned their attention to educating the people about their history, with the goal of keeping their traditions alive.

Matejko was at the forefront of this so-called "positivist" movement. Matejko saw what the tides of history had done to Poland, and was determined to make sure his countrymen learned from it. He painted two types of works: huge, grand-scale epics depicting monumental events in Polish history; and small, intimate portraits of prominent Poles. Polish schoolchildren study history from books with paintings of virtually every single Polish king—all painted by the incredibly prolific Matejko.

Matejko is admired not for his technical mastery (he's an unexceptional painter) or for the literal truth of his works—he was notorious for fudging historical details in order to give his canvases a bit more propagandistic punch. But he is revered for the emotion behind—and inspired by—his works. His paintings are utilitarian, straightforward, and dramatic enough to stir the patriot in any Pole. The intense focus on history by Matejko and other positivists is one big reason why today's Poles are still so in touch with their heritage.

You'll see Matejko's works in Warsaw's National Museum and Royal Castle, as well as in Kraków's Gallery of 19th-Century Polish Art (above the Cloth Hall). You can also visit his former residence in Kraków.

---

ask around) for another Matjeko canvas, *Stańczyk After the Loss of Smolensk*, to see how Poland's fortunes shifted drastically a century later. This smaller, more intimate portrait by Matejko depicts a popular Polish figure: the court jester Stańczyk, who's smarter than the king, but not allowed to say so. This complex character, representing the national conscience, is a favorite symbol of Matejko's. Stańczyk slumps in gloom. He's just read the news (on the table beside him) that the city of Smolensk has fallen to the Russians after a three-year siege (1512-1514). The jester had tried to warn the king to send more troops, but the king was too busy partying (behind the curtain). The painter Matejko—who may have used his own features for Stańczyk's face—also blamed the nobles of his own day for fiddling while Poland was partitioned.

Another Matejko painting depicts the tragic couple of the last Jagiellonian king, Stanisław August Poniatowski (here identified as Sigismund Augustus), and his wife, Barbara—whom the king loved deeply, even though she couldn't bear him an heir. A different painting shows the painful end to their sad tale: Barbara on her deathbed.

The generation following Matejko saw the rise of a movement called **Młoda Polska** ("Young Poland"), Poland's version of Art Nouveau. Likely displayed in the Gallery of 19th-Century Art are works by many of the leaders of the Młoda Polska movement: a self-portrait and other works by headliner **Stanisław Wyspiański;** the hypnotic *Strange Garden* by Wyspiański's friend and rival, **Józef Mehoffer;** several paintings by **Jacek Malczewski,** many of them depicting the goateed, close-cropped artist in a semi-surrealistic, Polish countryside context; and canvases by the only prominent female Polish painter, **Olga Boznańska** (past the Wyspiański room)—with a softer and more impressionistic touch than her male Młoda Polska counterparts.

Chopin Museum (Muzeum Fryderyka Chopina)

The reconstructed Ostrogski Castle houses this museum honoring Poland's most famous composer. The museum was recently overhauled for the "Year of Chopin" in 2010, when all of Poland

celebrated the composer's 200th birthday. Unfortunately, what could have been a fantastic opportunity to introduce people to Chopin instead was squandered on slick, high-tech presentations that are all style and no substance. The museum features actual Chopin artifacts (manuscripts, letters, and original handwritten compositions), video screens that delve into specific facets of his life, and listening stations for hearing his music, but completely lacks an overarching narrative of his life and any sense of who he was as a person. While Chopin devotees may find it riveting, those with only a passing familiarity with the composer leave feeling like they knew less about him than when they entered.

Cost and Hours: 22 zł, free on Tue, open Tue-Sun 12:00-20:00, closed Mon, 3 blocks east of Nowy Świat at ulica Okólnik 1, tel. 22-441-6251, www.chopin.museum.

Getting Tickets: Only 70 people can enter each hour, and because the museum is very popular, tickets can quickly sell out. While it's possible to reserve online, the system is challenging to figure out for non-Polish-speakers; instead, if your heart's set on seeing the museum, call ahead to ask what time you should arrive to ensure getting in.

Visiting the Museum: Buy your ticket at the small, adjacent building, then go up the stairs and enter the mansion that houses the exhibit. You'll be given an electronic card to wear around your neck; tap it against glowing red dots to access additional information. You'll proceed more or less chronologically through the composer's life, with various opportunities to hear his compositions. In the cellars is a virtual "Guest Book," where you can record your thoughts about Chopin to be added to the montage. Then head up into the mansion interior, with a replica of Chopin's drawing room in Paris, and his last piano, which he used for composing during the final two years of his life (1848-1849). Exhibits here trace themes of the composer's life, such as the women he knew (including his older sister Ludwika, his mother, and George Sand—the French author who took a male pseudonym in order to be published, and who was romantically linked with Chopin). The exhibit ends with Chopin's bronze death mask, featuring his distinctively Polish nose, shaped like an eagle's beak.

Concerts: In the cellar under the palace is a new **concert hall,** open for special concerts. If you're in town for one, go. There's nothing like hearing Chopin's music passionately played by a teary-eyed Pole who really feels the music (call museum to ask for concert schedule).

Other Chopin Sights: The **Chopin Family Drawing Room** is the Royal Way apartment where Chopin lived with his family, and where he wrote and premiered many of his earliest compositions (3 zł, free on Wed, open Mon-Fri 10:00-18:00, closed Sat-Sun, upstairs in the Krasiński Palace—now the Academy of Fine Arts—at Krakowskie Przedmieście 5, tel. 22-320-0275). Chopin's tourable **birth house** is in a park in Żelazowa Wola, 34 miles from Warsaw. While interesting to Chopin devotees, it's not worth the trek for most. On summer weekends, the Chopin Museum sometimes runs a handy bus to the house—ask at the museum (departs from Marszałkowska street, 30 minutes each way; 7 zł for the bus, 7 zł for the park, 23 zł for the park and birth house, 39 zł also includes museum in Warsaw; birth house open Tue-Sun 9:00-19:00, Oct-March until 17:00, closed Mon year-round, tel. 46-863-3300).

▲▲Copernicus Science Center (Centrum Nauki Kopernik)

This brand-new facility, a wonderland of completely hands-on scientific doodads that thrill kids and adults alike, is a futuristic romper room. Filling two floors of an industrial-mod, purpose-built space, this is Warsaw's best family activity. Exhibits are grouped more or less thematically and described in both Polish and English.

Cost and Hours: 25 zł, 16 zł for kids 19 and under, 66-zł family ticket for up to four people; open Tue-Fri 9:00-18:00, Sat-Sun 10:00-19:00, closed Mon, last entry one hour before closing; Wybrzeże Kościuszkowskie 20, tel. 22-596-4100, www.kopernik.org.pl.

Crowd-Beating Tips: As a relatively new attraction, the center can get crowded—especially on weekends and school holidays, when the line can be hours long. On weekdays, it's generally no problem to walk right in.

Getting There: It's an easy downhill walk from Warsaw's Royal Way, but the hike back up is fairly steep. The nearest bus stop, called Pomnik Syreny, is on a nearby corner, next to the modern bridge; from here, bus #102 goes to Nowy Świat, then up the Royal Way (Uniwersytet and Zachęta stops) before heading south to the central train station (4/hour). When the new Metro line opens (likely in late 2014), it will connect this center to the Royal Way and Warsaw Uprising Museum.

Visiting the Center: Your ticket is actually a plastic "log-in card" that you can insert into certain interactive exhibits. On the ground floor, the **"Roots of Civilization"** features working mod-

els of various tools and machines, demonstrating how humanity has mastered the mechanics of physics. By playing with a model piston, I grasped for the first time how that technology works. Other exhibits let you play archaeologist in a sandbox, listen to *Ode to Joy* while tuning into different instruments (depending on where you sit), and see a small "fire tornado" (every bit as cool as it sounds). A playroom for toddlers, called **"Buzzz!,"** has a nature theme. Meanwhile, **"RE: generation"** targets teens and adults with computer touchscreens that investigate the biological underpinnings of emotion—from what makes you laugh to what grosses you out—and examines how cultures around the world are both similar and different.

The **planetarium** requires a separate ticket (18 zł, 11 zł for kids 19 and under, in Polish with English headset, show starts at the top of each hour, ask for schedule at ticket desk).

The fun continues upstairs, where **"Humans and the Environment"** illuminates the human body (find out just how long your intestines are, identify and place the organs, and see how various joints work like hinges). One area focuses on exercise, including the engaging arena, where you can compete with various virtual animals (can you jump as high as a kangaroo or hang like a chimp?). The **"LightZone"** illustrates how light travels in waves, lets you try out an old-fashioned but still impressive camera obscura, and use prisms and lenses to play a game of "light billiards." **"On the Move"** features fascinating hands-on physics demos, including an earthquake simulator, an air cannon, and a tube that lets you harness sound waves to make water vibrate.

Nearby: The **Discovery Park** surrounding the museum was created when the busy riverfront highway was rerouted into an underground tunnel, creating this delightful people zone. From here, you have fine views of the modern Holy Cross Bridge (Most Świętokrzyski, from 2000) and the brand-new National Stadium, built to host matches for the 2012 Euro Cup and proudly wrapped in the patriotic red and white of the Polish flag.

Two short blocks inland from the science center is the architecturally innovative **Warsaw University Library** (Biblioteka Uniwersytecka w Warszawie, or BUW), with its distinctive oxidized-copper-colored facade decorated with open books from various cultures. The facade is fun to ogle, and the rooftop holds a huge and inviting garden.

South of the Center
▲Łazienki Park (Park Łazienkowski)

This huge, idyllic park is where Varsovians go to play. The park is sprinkled with fun Neoclassical buildings, strutting peacocks, and young Poles in love. It was built by Poland's very last king (before the final Partition), Stanisław August Poniatowski, to serve as his summer residence and provide a place for his citizens to relax.

On the edge of the park (along Belwederska) is a **monument to Fryderyk Chopin.** The monument, in a rose garden, is

flanked by platforms, where free summer piano **concerts** of Chopin's music are given weekly (mid-May-late Sept only, generally Sun at 12:00 and 16:00—confirm at TI). The statue shows Chopin sitting under a wind-blown willow tree. While he spent his last 20 years and wrote most of his best-known music in France, his inspiration came from wind blowing through the willow trees of his native land, Poland. The Nazis melted the original statue (from 1926) down for its metal. Today's copy was recast after World War II. Savor this spot; it's great in summer, with roses wildly in bloom, and in autumn, when the trees provide a golden backdrop for the black, romantic statue.

Venture to the center of the park, where (after a 10-minute hike) you'll find King Poniatowski's striking **Palace on the Water** (Pałac na Wodzie)—literally built in the middle of a river. Nearby, you'll spot a clever amphitheater with seating on the riverbank and the stage on an island. The king was a real man of the Enlightenment, hosting weekly dinners here for artists and intellectuals. But Poland's kings are long gone, and proud peacocks now rule this roost.

Getting There: The park is just south of the city center on the Royal Way. Buses #116, #180, and #195 run from Castle Square in the Old Town along the Royal Way directly to the park (get off at the stop called Łazienki Królewskie, by Belweder Palace—you'll see Chopin squinting through the trees on your left). Maps at park entrances locate the Chopin monument, Palace on the Water, and other park attractions.

Jewish Warsaw

After centuries of living peacefully in Poland, Warsaw's Jews suffered terribly at the hands of the Nazis. Several sights in Warsaw commemorate those who were murdered, and those who fought back. Because the Nazis leveled the ghetto, there is literally nothing left except the street plan, some monuments, and the heroic spirit of its former residents. However, a brand-new museum promises to rejuvenate the area, making it even more of a magnet for those interested in this chapter of Polish history.

Museum of the History of Polish Jews
(Muzeum Historii Żydów Polskich)

Designed by Finnish architect Rainer Mahlamäki, this striking building is pierced by a dramatically asymmetrical fracture (visible from the outside). The building, which opened in 2013, hosts cultural events and temporary exhibits. Its permanent "Core Exhibition"—opening sometime in 2014—chronologically traces the nearly millennium-long story of Jews in Poland.

Cost and Hours: Building entrance-free, 5-zł audioguide for special exhibits, permanent exhibit fee not yet determined, Wed-Mon 10:00-18:00, closed Tue, 6 Anielewicza, tel. 22-471-0300, www.jewishmuseum.org.pl.

Visiting the Museum: When the "Core Exhibition" opens, high-tech, interactive exhibits will mingle with actual artifacts to bring history to life. You'll pass through a simulated forest—evocative of legends about the Jews' arrival in Poland—to reach the **"First Encounters"** exhibit, focusing on early Jewish settlers during the Middle Ages. You'll learn about Ibrahim ibn Jakub—a Sephardic Jew who penned early travelogues about Europe—and

Warsaw's Jews and the Ghetto Uprising

From the Middle Ages until World War II, Poland was a relatively safe haven for Europe's Jews. While other kings were imprisoning and deporting Jews in the 14th century, the progressive king Kazimierz the Great welcomed Jews into Poland, even granting them special privileges (see page 39).

By the 1930s, there were more than 380,000 Jews in Warsaw—nearly a third of the population (and the largest concentration of Jews in any European city). The Nazis arrived in 1939. Within a year, they had pushed all of Warsaw's Jews into one neighborhood and surrounded it with a wall, creating a miserably overcrowded ghetto (crammed full of half a million people, including many from nearby towns). Over the next year, the Nazis brought in more Jews from throughout Poland, and the number grew by a million.

By the summer of 1942, more than a quarter of Warsaw's Jews had either died of disease, committed suicide, or been murdered. The Nazis started moving Warsaw's Jews (at the rate of 5,000 a day) into what they claimed were "resettlement camps." Most of these people were actually murdered at Treblinka or Auschwitz. After hundreds of thousands of Jews had been taken away, the waning population—now about 60,000—began to get word from concentration camp escapees about what was actually going on there. Spurred by this knowledge, Warsaw's surviving Jews staged a dramatic uprising.

On April 19, 1943, the Jews attacked Nazi strongholds and had some initial success. The overwhelming Nazi war machine—which had rolled over much of Europe—imagined they'd be able to put down the rebellion easily. Instead, they struggled for a month to finally crush the Ghetto Uprising. The ghetto's residents and structures were "liquidated." About 300 of Warsaw's Jews survived, thanks in part to a sort of "underground railroad" of courageous Varsovians.

Warsaw's Jewish sights are emotionally moving, but even more so if you know some of their stories. You may have heard of **Władysław Szpilman,** a Jewish concert pianist who survived the war with the help of Jews, Poles, and even a Nazi officer. Szpilman's life story was turned into the highly acclaimed, Oscar-winning 2002 film *The Pianist*, which powerfully depicts events in Warsaw during World War II.

Less familiar to non-Poles—but equally affecting—is the story of Henryk Goldszmit, better known by his pen name, **Janusz Korczak.** Korczak wrote imaginative children's books that are still enormously popular among Poles. He worked at an orphanage in the Warsaw ghetto. When his orphans were sent off to concentration camps, the Nazis offered the famous author a chance at freedom. Korczak turned them down, choosing to die at Treblinka with his children.

see a prayer book from 1272, with the oldest-known sentence written in Yiddish. Then, **"Paradisus Iudaeorum"** explains the ways Jewish culture flourished in tolerant Poland in the 15th and 16th centuries. An interactive model lets you explore the city of Kraków—and its Jewish quarter, Kazimierz—as it was during the golden age of Polish Jews. But with the Khmelnytsky Uprising in the mid-17th century came pogroms, anti-Semitism, and a more difficult life. **"Into the Country"** traces the spread of Jews throughout the Eastern European countryside, where they forged a unique type of settlement called a *shtetl*. The replica of a roof of a wooden synagogue from Ukraine illustrates the architecture of the time. **"Encounters with Modernity"** examines how, after the Partitions (when Polish territory was divided among neighboring powers at the end of the 18th century), Jews struggled to integrate with the respective societies of their new overlords. This was also the time of the Industrial Revolution, when Jewish businessmen were making their mark on the society. As Poland—and its Jewish population—accelerated into the modern age, it brought about changes to Jewish tradition...and saw the emergence of a hateful and aggressive new breed of anti-Semitism. **"The Street"** re-creates an early 20th-century shopping street from a Jewish community, demonstrating how Jewish culture thrived in the vibrant urban life of Poland between the World Wars. The **Holocaust** section explains the horrific events that claimed the lives of some 9 out of every 10 Polish Jews. This exhibit focuses on the Warsaw ghetto and its residents, whose daily lives and shocking fate are chronicled in a set of contemporaneous diaries and documents remarkably preserved in an underground archive. Finally, **"The Postwar Years"** follows Holocaust survivors as they navigate an unfriendly, anti-Semitic communist regime—and embrace a world of new possibility with the fall of communism.

Ghetto Walking Tour

For a quick walking tour of the former ghetto site, begin at **Ghetto Heroes Square** (plac Bohaterow Getta). To get here from the Old Town you can hop a taxi (10 zł), take a bus (to the Nalewki stop—though this stop may be renamed when the museum opens; bus #180 is particularly useful), or walk (go through barbican gate two blocks into New Town, turn left on Świętojerska, and walk straight 10 minutes—passing the new green-glass Supreme Court building—until you reach a grassy park on Zamenhofa Street). The square is in the heart of what was the Jewish ghetto—now surrounded by bland Soviet-style apartment blocks. After the uprising, the entire ghetto was reduced to dust by the Nazis, leaving the communists to rebuild to their own specifications. The district is called Muranów ("Rebuilt") today.

The **monument** in the middle of the square commemorates

those who fought and died, "for the dignity and freedom of the Jewish Nation, for a free Poland, and for the liberation of humankind." Across the street is the brand-new **Museum of the History of Polish Jews** (described earlier).

Facing the monument, head left (with the park on your left) up Zamenhofa—which, like many streets in this neighborhood, is named for a hero of the Ghetto Uprising. From the monument, you'll follow a series of three-foot-tall black stone monuments to uprising heroes—the **Path of Remembrance.** Like Stations of the Cross, each recounts an event of the uprising. Every April 19th (the day the uprising began), huge crowds follow this path. In a block, at the corner of Miła (partly obscured by some bushes), you'll find a **bunker** where organizers of the uprising hid (and where they committed suicide when the Nazis discovered them on May 8, 1943).

Continue following the black stone monuments up Zamenhofa (which becomes Dubois), then turn left at the corner (onto Stawki) and, later on that same block, cross busy Stawki street. A long block up Stawki and on the right, you'll see the **Umschlagplatz** monument—shaped like a cattle car. That's German for "transfer place," and it marks the spot where the Nazis brought Jewish families to prepare them to be loaded onto trains bound for Treblinka or Auschwitz (a harrowing scene vividly depicted in *The Pianist*). In the walls of the monument are inscribed the first names of some of the victims.

Jewish Historical Institute of Poland (Żydowski Instytut Historyczny)

For more in-depth information about Warsaw's Jewish community, including the Ghetto Uprising, visit this museum housed in the former Jewish Library building. The main floor displays well-described old photos. The 37-minute movie about life and death in the ghetto—played in English upon request—is graphic and powerful. Upstairs, you'll find more on Jewish art and culture, along with temporary exhibits.

Cost and Hours: 10 zł, Mon-Wed and Fri 9:00-16:00, Thu 11:00-18:00, Sun 10:00-18:00, closed Sat, last entry 30 minutes before closing, just north of Saxon Garden at ulica Tłomackie 3/5, tel. 22-827-9221, www.jhi.pl.

Nearby: The Peugeot building next door—appropriately dubbed "the blue tower" by locals—was built on the former site of Warsaw's biggest synagogue, destroyed by the Nazis as a victorious final kick.

Warsaw Uprising Sights

While the 1944 Warsaw Uprising is a recurring theme in virtually all Warsaw sightseeing, two sights in particular—one a monument, the other a museum—are worth a visit for anyone with a special interest. Neither is right on the main tourist trail; the monument is closer to the sightseeing action, while the museum is a tram or taxi ride away.

Warsaw Uprising Monument

The most central sight relating to the Warsaw Uprising is the monument at plac Krasińskich (intersection of ulica Długa and

Miodowa, one long block and about a five-minute walk northwest of the New Town). Larger-than-life soldiers and civilians race for the sewers in a desperate attempt to flee the Nazis. Just behind the monument is the oxidized-copper facade of Poland's Supreme Court.

▲▲Warsaw Uprising Museum (Muzeum Powstania Warszawskiego)

This museum opened on August 1, 2004—the 60th anniversary of the Warsaw Uprising. Thorough, modern, and packed with Polish field-trip groups, the museum celebrates the heroes of the uprising. It's a bit cramped, and finding your way through the exhibits can be confusing, but it thoughtfully illuminates this complicated chapter of Warsaw's history. The location is inconvenient (a 10-minute tram or bus ride west of central train station) and, because it eats up about a half-day to come here, may not be worth the trek for those with a casual interest. But for history buffs, it's Warsaw's single best museum.

Cost and Hours: 14 zł; Mon, Wed, and Fri 8:00-18:00; Thu 8:00-20:00; Sat-Sun 10:00-18:00; closed Tue; last entry 30 minutes before closing, tel. 22-539-7947, www.1944.pl.

Audioguide: The informative, two-hour audioguide is ideal if you really want to delve into the whole story (10 zł, rent it in the gift shop). A well-illustrated, 20-zł guidebook is also sold in the shop. For a quick overview, take my self-guided tour.

Getting There: It's on the western edge of downtown at ulica Przyokopowa 28; the nearest tram and bus stop is called Muzeum Powstania Warszawskiego. While it looks close on the map, it's actually a long hike through Warsaw's dullest quarter. Instead, take tram #22 or #24 from near the central train station (from the underground passageways, follow signs for *Ochota* to find the tram tracks), or across the street from the National Museum (near the start of Nowy Świat). You can also get to the museum by taking

The Warsaw Uprising

By the summer of 1944, it was becoming clear that the Nazis' days in Warsaw were numbered. The Red Army drew near, and by late July, Soviet tanks were within 25 miles of downtown Warsaw.

The Varsovians could have simply waited for the Soviets to cross the river and force the Nazis out. But they knew that Soviet "liberation" would also mean an end to Polish independence. The Polish Home Army numbered 400,000—30,000 of them in Warsaw alone—and was the biggest underground army in military history. The uprisers wanted Poland to control its own fate, and they took matters into their own hands. The resistance's symbol was an anchor made up of a *P* atop a *W* (which stands for *Polska Walcząca*, or "Poland Fighting"— you'll see this icon all around town). Over time, the Home Army had established an extensive network of underground tunnels and sewers, which allowed them to deliver messages and move around the city without drawing the Nazis' attention. These tunnels gave the Home Army the element of surprise.

On August 1, 30,000 Polish resistance fighters launched an attack on their Nazi oppressors. They poured out of the sewers and caught the Nazis off guard. The ferocity of the Polish fighters stunned the Nazis, who thought they'd put down the uprising within hours. But the Nazis regrouped, and within a few days, they had retaken several areas of the city— murdering tens of thousands of innocent civilians as they went. In one notorious incident, some 5,500 Polish soldiers and 6,000 civilians who were surrounded by Nazis in the Old Town were forced to flee through the sewers; many drowned or were shot. (This scene is depicted in the Warsaw Uprising Monument on plac Krasińskich.)

Two months after it had started, the Warsaw Uprising was over. The Home Army called a cease-fire. About 18,000 Polish uprisers had been killed, along with nearly 200,000 innocent civilians. An infuriated Hitler ordered that the city be destroyed—which it was, systematically, block by block, until virtually nothing remained.

Through all of this, the Soviets stood still, watched, and waited. When the smoke cleared and the Nazis left, the Red Army marched in and claimed the wasteland that was once called Warsaw. After the war, General Dwight D. Eisenhower said that the scale of destruction here was the worst he'd ever seen. The communists later tracked down the surviving Home Army leaders, killing or imprisoning them.

Depending on whom you talk to, the desperate uprising of Warsaw was incredibly brave, stupid, or both. As for the Poles, they remain fiercely proud of their struggle for freedom. The city of Warsaw has recently commemorated this act of bravery with the new Warsaw Uprising Museum.

bus #109 (departs in front of the central train station—from the main hall, go out the door with the bus icon). From Castle Square in the Old Town, bus #178 goes to the museum. On the Royal Way, catch bus #105 from the Uniwersytet stop (next to the university building) or the Nowy Świat stop. All of these trams and buses take you to the Muzeum Powstania Warszawskiego stop. From this stop, cross the tracks and the busy street, walk straight one short block up Grzybowska, and take a left on Przyokopowa. The museum is the big, red-brick building on the left.

When the new Metro line opens (likely in late 2014), it will connect this museum (Rondo Daszyńskiego Station) to the Royal Way and Copernicus Science Center.

❍ **Self-Guided Tour:** The museum has several parts. The beautifully restored 1905 red-brick building, once an electrical plant, houses the permanent exhibition. The more recent gray addition behind it displays temporary exhibitions. And the park stretching around the back of the complex also has some evocative sights. Buy your ticket at the little house on the left (marked *kasa*), then head into the main hall.

The high-tech **main exhibit** sprawls across three floors. It chronologically tells the story of the uprising, with a keen focus on military history. While it's easy to get turned around, look for directional signs and don't be afraid to explore. Everything is well-described in English; also look for the printed pages of English information.

The ground floor focuses on Germany's invasion and occupation of Poland. The children's area (to the right as you enter) reminds visitors that Varsovian kids played a role in the Warsaw Uprising, too. Then you'll take the elevator to the top floor (signed *2*), which features exhibits on the uprising itself. You'll meet some of the uprising's heroes, and learn about their weapons and methods. Inside the big tent is an exhibit about the Wola Massacre, during which 40,000 people were killed after the Nazis issued a take-no-prisoners decree in retribution for the uprising. Another exhibit looks at its impact on civilians and hospitals. The "Kino Palladium" movie screen shows subtitled Home Army newsreel footage from the period. To the right of the screen, you'll walk through a simulated sewer, reminiscent of the one that many Home Army soldiers and civilians used to evade the Germans. Imagine terrified troops quietly traversing a more than mile-long sewer line like this one (but with lower ceilings)—and doing it while knee-deep in liquid sewage.

The exhibit continues downstairs. If you need a break, straight ahead from the stairs are WCs and a café (past the exhibit on the USSR's role in the Warsaw Uprising, and in "liberating" and terrorizing postwar Poland). The café is oddly pleasant, serving drinks and light snacks amidst genteel ambience from prewar Warsaw.

Back in the main exhibit, one room honors the Field Postal Service, which, at great personal risk, continued mail delivery of both military communiqués and civilian correspondences. Many of these brave "mailmen" were actually Scouts who were too young to fight. The later days of the uprising are outlined, battle by battle. A chilling section describes how Warsaw became a "city of graves," with burial mounds and makeshift crosses scattered everywhere. As you learn about the uprising's aftermath, consider that the Nazis destroyed Warsaw four separate times during World War II (at the outbreak of war, to put down the Ghetto Uprising, to put down the Warsaw Uprising, and finally just to be mean).

Occupying the center of the main hall are two large-scale exhibits: a replica of an RAF Liberator B-24 J, used for airborne surveillance of wartime Warsaw;

and a giant movie screen showing more fascinating newsreels assembled by the Home Army's own propaganda unit during the uprising. Under the screen, behind the black curtains, is yet another exhibit, this one about life in Nazi-occupied Warsaw, along with another, more claustrophobic walk-through sewer.

The newest feature is the five-minute 3-D film *City of Ruins,* with aerial footage of the postwar devastation.

The **park** features several thought-provoking sights. Around the right side are several monuments, with photographs along the side wall showing the history of the museum building. Along the back is the Wall of Memory, a Vietnam War Memorial-type monument to soldiers of the Polish Home Army who were killed in action. You'll see their rank and name, followed by their code name, in quotes. The Home Army observed a strict policy of anonymity, forbidding members from calling each other by anything but their code names. The bell in the middle is dedicated to the commander of the uprising, Antoni Chruściel (code name "Monter").

Sleeping in Warsaw

Most accommodations in central Warsaw are either overpriced business-class hotels (whose rates can drop dramatically when demand is low—especially on weekends and in summer), or gloomy, impersonal communist-holdover hotels. Thankfully, there

Sleep Code

(3 zł = about $1, country code: 48)

S = Single, **D** = Double/Twin, **T** = Triple, **Q** = Quad, **b** = bathroom, **s** = shower only. Unless otherwise noted, credit cards are accepted, and breakfast is included. Everyone listed here speaks English.

To help you easily sort through these listings, I've divided the accommodations into three categories, based on the price for a double room with bath during high season:

$$$ **Higher Priced**—Most rooms 400 zł or more.
  $$ **Moderately Priced**—Most rooms between 300-400 zł.
    $ **Lower Priced**—Most rooms 300 zł or less.

Prices can change without notice; verify the hotel's current rates online or by email. For the best prices, always book direct.

WARSAW

are a few happy exceptions—such as Boutique B&B and Duval Apartments, easily the best options in Warsaw.

$$$ Hotel Le Régina is a tempting splurge buried in the quiet and charming New Town (just beyond the Old Town). From its elegant public spaces to its 61 top-notch rooms, everything here is done with class. Choose between plenty nice "standard" and "classic" rooms, or pay an extra 200 zł for bigger "superior" rooms, with hand-painted frescoes over each bed. While the official rates are ridiculously high (standard Db-1,140 zł, superior Db-1,290 zł), you'll often find amazingly lower promotional prices on their website (for a standard room in summer figure Db-550 zł on weekdays, as low as 350 zł on weekends, prices change constantly—check online for latest deals, more expensive during winter convention season, prices don't include the 90-zł breakfast—skip this very overpriced option, pricier suites, elevator, non-smoking floor, guest computer, Wi-Fi, exercise room, pool, Kościelna 12, tel. 22-531-6000, www.leregina.com, reception.leregina@mamaison.com).

$$$ Novotel, a chain hotel with 733 uninspired cookie-cutter rooms across the street from the Palace of Culture and Science, overlooks Poland's busiest intersection. Recently renovated inside and out, this is a good option for a big, business-class, downtown hotel that's handy to the central train station (official rate is Sb/Db-785 zł and possibly much higher on busy weekdays, but in slow times—especially weekends—you might pay 250-450 zł, best deals are online, optional breakfast-65 zł, non-smoking rooms, elevator; guest computer, Wi-Fi and cable Internet; Marszałkowska 94/98, tel. 22-596-0000, www.novotel.com, h3383@accor.com).

$$ Duval Apartments, named for a French woman who supposedly had an affair with the Polish king in this building, offers four beautifully appointed rooms above a restaurant (called Same Fusy) a few steps off the square in the Old Town. Each room has a different theme: traditional Polish, Japanese, glass, or retro (Sb-280 zł, Db-320 zł, Tb-400 zł, includes breakfast, lots of stairs with no elevator, some restaurant noise—light sleepers should request a quiet room, Wi-Fi, Nowomiejska 10, mobile 608-679-346, tel. 22-831-9104, www.duval.net.pl, duval@duval.net.pl). There's no reception, and the rooms aren't officially affiliated with the restaurant, so arrange a meeting time with Agnieszka (or, if she's busy, Marcin) when you reserve. On arrival, go up the stairs and ring doorbell #5; the restaurant closes at 23:00.

$$ Castle Inn, sitting right on Castle Square at the entrance to the Old Town, is the next rung up the ladder for youth hostelers who've outgrown the grungy backpacker scene. Run by the owners of Oki Doki Hostel (described later), it has 22 creative and colorful rooms, each with completely different but equally artsy decor. Youthful and funky, it provides a welcome jolt of new energy on Warsaw's hotel scene (very slushy rates depending on demand, generally Sb-255-303 zł, Db-270-360 zł, "delux" Db-350-440 zł, "delux" Tb-355-492 zł, 35 zł extra for continental breakfast—have it delivered to your room for the same price, lots of stairs and no elevator, guest computer, Wi-Fi, Świętojańska 2, tel. 22-425-0100, www.castleinn.pl, castleinn@castleinn.pl).

$$ Old Town Apartments offers 25 studio, one-bedroom, and two-bedroom apartments inside Warsaw's Old Town. The prices are good and the location is excellent, but you're pretty much on your own (no real reception, no breakfast but all have kitchens). View the apartments on their website, pick the one that looks best, and set up a meeting to get the keys at their Nowy Świat office (prices flex with demand, but figure studio-300 zł, 1-bedroom-350 zł, 2-bedroom-450 zł, some more expensive "featured" apartments on the square also available, slightly cheaper Oct-April and last-minute, tel. 22-887-9800, www.apartmentsapart.com, warsaw@bookaa.net). They also rent 15 pricey apartments on Nowy Świat, called **Royal Route Residence** (studio-400 zł, 1-bedroom-500 zł, 2-bedroom-600 zł, breakfast-25 zł, corner of Nowy Świat and Chmielna). For either place, you'll check in at the office at #3 Nowy Świat 29 (Mon-Fri 10:00-20:00, Sat-Sun 9:00-17:00, at other times arrange a meeting to get the keys). After checking in here, they'll send you in a taxi to your Old Town apartment.

$$ Zgoda Apartment Hotel is conveniently located on an urban street between the Palace of Culture and Science and the

Royal Way. With 51 classy-feeling apartments designed for business travelers, it's a comfortable home base in the city center (small Sb/Db-368 zł, studio Sb-395 zł, bigger "comfort" Sb/Db-435, twin-bedded "comfort plus" Sb/Db-455 zł, fancier rooms also available, rates are soft—especially for longer stays, extra bed-90 zł, breakfast-30 zł or use the kitchenette, air-con, elevator, guest computer, Wi-Fi, Zgoda 6, tel. 22-553-6200, www.apartamenty -zgoda.pl, apartamenty@dipservice.pl).

$$ Hotel Harenda, a reliable old standby, has 43 rooms with leather-bound doors on the second and third floors of an office building right in the middle of the Royal Way, by the Copernicus monument. The tired, communist-era rooms are crying out for a renovation, but the location is ideal, and the ground-floor pub is a popular hangout (May-June and Sept-Oct: Sb-340 zł, Db-380 zł; July-Aug and Nov-April: Sb-310 zł, Db-340 zł; breakfast-25 zł, second night is free Fri-Sun, some rowdy street noise—especially on weekends—so request a quiet room, lots of stairs with no elevator, guest computer, Wi-Fi, Krakowskie Przedmieście 4/6, tel. 22-826-0071, www.hotelharenda.com.pl, rezerwacja@hotel harenda.com.pl).

$ Boutique B&B offers more comfort and class than a hotel twice its price, in a beautifully renovated and well-located

old building near the National Museum. Jarek Chołodecki, who lived near Chicago for many years, returned to Warsaw and converted apartments into this wonderful bed-and-breakfast with 16 rooms. It's a friendly, casual, stylish place, creatively decorated and impeccably maintained. You'll feel like you're staying with your Warsaw sophisticate cousin—quirky, charismatic Jarek loves to chat with his guests, many of whom return and become his good friends. Each morning, lively conversation percolates at the big, family-style breakfast table over a morning meal made mostly from organic and locally sourced foods. A small drawing room plays host to occasional piano concerts and other convivial activities. When Jarek is out of town, his right-hand-man Paweł capably holds down the fort. Let them know what time you'll be arriving (Sb-270 zł, standard Db-300 zł, junior suite-320 zł, big suite-420 zł, these special rates are for Rick Steves readers, elevator, guest computer, Wi-Fi, ulica Smolna 14/6, tel. 22-829-4801, www.bedandbreakfast.pl, office@bedandbreakfast.pl). To make things easier, Jarek can arrange for a no-stress ride in from Chopin Airport for the same price as a taxi (45 zł, more at night,

WARSAW

request when you reserve your room).

$ Ibis Warszawa Stare Miasto, with 333 cookie-cutter rooms, is the place for predictable comfort with zero personality. This hotel, part of the popular European chain, overlooks a WWII memorial in a nondescript, businessy-feeling neighborhood a 10-minute walk north of the Old Town (Sb/Db-289 zł, or 219 zł Fri-Sun, can be higher during conventions, sometimes better deals online, breakfast-33 zł, air-con, non-smoking rooms, elevator, Muranowska 2, tel. 22-310-1000, www.ibishotel.com, h3714@accor.com).

Hostels

$ Nathan's Villa Hostel is the most appealing hostel option in Warsaw. Run by a sharp Bostonian entrepreneur with hostels all over Poland, Nathan's has 13 dorm rooms (with 95 beds) and 6 private rooms overlooking a cozy courtyard, and plenty of opportunities for backpacker bonding. The catch: It's less conveniently located than my other listings, requiring a 15-minute walk or easy bus ride south of the central train station area (dorm bed in 4-bed room-72 zł, in 6-bed room-60 zł, in 12-bed room-50 zł, D-184 zł, Db-194 zł, Db with kitchen-204 zł, Tb/Qb-234 zł, all rates about 10 zł/person less on off-season weeknights, includes basic breakfast and sheets, lockers, guest computer, Wi-Fi, laundry service-15 zł, guest kitchen, hiding behind a modern glass office building at ulica Piękna 24/26—the nearby square called plac Konstytucji has easy bus connections, tel. 22-622-2946, www.nathansvilla.com).

$ Oki Doki Hostel, on a pleasant square a few blocks in front of the Palace of Culture and Science, is colorful, creative, and easygoing. Each of its 37 rooms was designed by a different artist with a special theme—such as Van Gogh, Celtic spirals, heads of state, or Lenin. It's run by Ernest—a Pole whose parents loved Hemingway—and his wife Łucja, with help from their sometimes-jaded staff (complicated pricing structure flexes with demand: dorm bed in 4-bed room-50-67 zł, in 5- to 6-bed room-40-58 zł, in 8-bed room-40-53 zł; S-120-160 zł, D-150-180 zł, Db-192-219 zł, T-180-219 zł; prices include breakfast except for dorm-dwellers—who pay 15 zł, guest computer, Wi-Fi, laundry service-15 zł, kitchen, lots of stairs with no elevator, plac Dąbrowskiego 3, tel. 22-826-5112, 22-828-0122, www.okidoki.pl, okidoki@okidoki.pl).

$ The IYHF Szkolne Schronisko hostel, with 110 beds and lots of school groups, is institutional, well-run, bright, and clean. The downside: It's five floors up, with no elevator (nonmembers welcome, all prices per person: dorm beds-40 zł, S-70 zł, twin D-65 zł, T-60 zł, Q-50 zł, sheets-6 zł, towel-3 zł, no breakfast but members' kitchen, 10 percent cheaper for hostel members, closed 10:00-16:00, curfew at 24:00; email ahead to reserve lim-

WARSAW

ited S, D, and T rooms; good location across the street from National Museum at ulica Smolna 30, tel. 22-827-8952, www .hostelsmolna30.pl, info@hostelsmolna30.pl).

Eating in Warsaw

While the Old Town has a tourist-friendly atmosphere and traditional Polish food, Varsovians know that these days, the Nowy Świat area is where it's at—with trendy international restaurants and an enticing al fresco scene on balmy summer evenings. This is especially enticing, since Warsaw offers your best break from traditional Polish food. (Though if you do want traditional Polish, just wander along the Royal Way or the Old Town and take your

pick of the many interchangeable, ye olde options.) Most restaurants are open until the "last guest," which usually means about 23:00 (sometimes later in summer).

In or near the Old Town

Rather than spending too much to eat on the Old Town Market Square, I prefer to venture a few blocks to find a place with good food and much lower prices.

At **Restauracja pod Samsonem** ("Under Samson"), dine on affordable Jewish and Polish comfort food with well-dressed locals. The ambience is pleasant, the service is playfully opinionated, and the low prices make up for the fact that you have to pay to check your coat and use the bathroom (10-20-zł starters, most main dishes 20-35 zł, enjoyable outdoor seating in summer, daily 10:00-23:00, ulica Freta 3/5, tel. 22-831-1788).

Pierogarnia na Bednarskiej brags, "only our grandmothers make better pierogi." In addition to the classic Polish dumplings, the menu includes soups and a fun variety of drinks (from unusual fruit juices to *kvas,* the non-alcoholic, rye-flavored dark beer). Order at the counter and take a seat—they'll call you when your food's ready. With mellow country decor, wooden menus, and a loyal local crowd, this is a handy spot for a quick, cheap meal along the Royal Way (13-16-zł plates of pierogi, 18-zł combo-plate includes soup and salad, daily 12:00-20:00, hiding down a quiet street behind the statue of Adam Mickiewicz at ulica Bednarska 28/30, tel. 22-828-0392).

BrowArmia is a hit with beer lovers. This sprawling brewpub makes four different types of beer (plus special seasonal beers) and serves decent pub grub. The dark, mod, long interior fills two levels (including a fun cellar), but in good weather I'd stake out a spot on the terrace—ideal for people-watching along the Royal Way (18-32-zł starters, 30-65-zł main dishes, daily 12:00-24:00, live music or DJ in cellar on weekends, right on Krakowskie Przedmieście near Piłsudski Square at ulica Królewska 1, tel. 22-826-5455).

U Kucharzy ("By the Cooks") is the most innovative of Warsaw celebrity chef-turned-restaurateur Magda Gessler's growing empire. The kitchen of this former hotel restaurant (tucked behind the Hotel Europejski building, facing Piłsudski Square) has been converted into a dining room, with tables scattered throughout the white-tiled cooking and prep areas—so you'll get the behind-the-scenes experience of watching the chefs prepare the food. The menu is upmarket Polish classics, the ambience is dressy, and the service can be less than snappy, but it's a memorable and good-quality dining experience. Reservations are smart (25-40-zł starters, 50-70-zł main dishes, daily 12:00-24:00, live piano music in the evenings, Ossolińskich 7, tel. 22-826-7936).

On the Old Town Market Square: You'll pay triple to eat right on the square, but some visitors figure it's worth the splurge. Compare menus and views to find the spot you like best. If you want to go for the venerable old favorite—and money's no object—check out **U Fukiera.** This place offers traditional Polish and pan-European meals in a sophisticated setting with carefully designed prewar atmosphere. In summer, sit at their tables out on the square, or find your way to the cozy courtyard garden in back (30-90-zł starters, 45-105-zł main dishes, daily 12:00-24:00, at #27, tel. 22-831-1013).

Italian: **Enoteka Polska** is a dressy wine cellar serving Italian food at rustic tables squeezed between crates of wine bottles. Although the location is in the middle of nowhere (about a 10-minute walk through drab sprawl from the Old Town), the decor is nicely modern, and there's a pleasant garden in the summer. Reservations are smart (20-30-zł starters, 30-45-zł pastas, 35-50-zł main dishes, daily 12:00-23:00, Sun 13:00-21:00, Długa 23/25, tel. 22-831-3443).

On or near Nowy Świat

While most Old Town eateries are traditional and cater to tourists, locals flock to the Nowy Świat neighborhood (near the National Museum and central train station) for a fun night on the town.

Fancy Eateries on Foksal Street: Foksal—the first cross street as you go down Nowy Świat from aleja Jerozolimskie—has a thriving assortment of about a half-dozen cafés and restaurants:

Mexican, Italian, Asian, international, and more. Most have inviting outdoor seating that's ideal on a balmy summer evening. The clientele is young and sophisticated, and there's not a pierogi in sight. Find the place with the cuisine and ambience you like best. **Papaya** has tasty pan-Asian fare and a trendy, minimalist, black-and-white interior (30-60-zł main dishes plus pricier splurges, daily 12:00-24:00, at #16, tel. 22-826-1199). A block beyond this area is a far more traditional option, **Kamahda Lwowska,** named for the former Polish city that's now in Ukraine. It has a few outdoor seats and a charming, cluttered old cellar (20-25-zł starters, 30-45-zł main dishes, daily 10:00-24:00, Foksal 10, tel. 22-828-1031).

Classy Steakhouse: **Butchery & Wine,** in an unassuming location on a drab urban street, is a pocket of chic international cuisine in the heart of Warsaw. While a bit farther from the heart of Nowy Świat than the others listed here, it's worth the walk. The waiters, smartly dressed in pinstripe aprons, serve upscale comfort food (specializing in steaks) to a small, lively room of business travelers. The wine list is extensive, and reservations are smart (15-60-zł starters, 50-85-zł steaks, Mon-Sat 12:00-22:00, closed Sun, across aleja Jerozolimskie from Nowy Świat at Żurawia 22, tel. 22-502-3118).

Cheap Milk Bars: **Wiking Bar,** a colorful milk bar, serves up Polish grub right on Nowy Świat (10-15-zł main dishes, Mon-Fri 7:30-21:30, Sat 10:00-21:30, Sun 10:00-20:30, Nowy Świat 28). **Mleczarnia Jerozolimska,** just around the corner on busy aleja Jerozolimskie, is a more classic milk-bar experience (4-8-zł soups, 9-12-zł main dishes, Mon-Fri 10:00-20:00, Sat 12:00-17:00, Sun 12:00-18:00, aleja Jerozolimskie 32).

Hungarian and Polish Cuisine on Zgoda Street: **Borpince** ("Wine Cellar") is a cozy cellar serving up very authentic Hungarian fare a long block off of Nowy Świat (toward the Palace of Culture and Science). As you dive into spicy goulash and *paprikás,* you'll see just how different the cuisine can be on the other side of the Carpathians. If you won't be visiting Hungary on your trip, this is the next best way to sample Hungarian favorites. The restaurant also has a long list of Hungarian wines (15-25-zł soups including goulash, 35-60-zł main dishes, daily 12:00-23:00, closes earlier when it's slow, ulica Zgoda 1, tel. 22-828-2244). For Magyar flavors at lower prices, try **Krokiecik** ("Croquette"), the simpler self-service restaurant located next door, at street level. Choose from Polish or Hungarian food, order at the counter, then take a seat (7-12-zł soups, 12-25-zł main dishes, daily 9:00-21:00, ulica Zgoda 1, tel. 22-827-3037). **Restauracja Zgoda,** across the street and owned by the same people, has affordable, reliable Polish cuisine in an Old World setting; it's popular among traditionalists dining out (8-12-zł soups, 17-zł salads, 25-40-zł fish and meat dishes, Mon-Sat 9:00-23:00, Sun 12:00-23:00, Zgoda 4, tel. 22-827-9934).

Uniquely Polish Treats

These two places are on or close to the busy Nowy Świat boulevard.

A. Blikle, Poland's most famous pastry shop, serves a wide variety of delicious treats. This is where locals shop for cakes when they're having someone special over for coffee. The specialty: *pączki* (PONCH-kee), the quintessential Polish doughnut, filled with rose-flavored jam. You can get your goodies "to go" in the shop (2.60-zł *pączki*, Mon-Sat 9:00-19:00, Sun 10:00-18:00), or pay more to enjoy them with coffee in the swanky, classic café with indoor or outdoor seating (6-zł *pączki*, Mon-Sat 9:00-22:00, Sun 10:00-22:00; both at Nowy Świat 35, tel. 22-828-6601). While they also have a sit-down restaurant (30-50-zł main dishes), I come here only for the *pączki*.

E. Wedel Pijalnia Czekolady thrills chocoholics. Emil Wedel made Poland's favorite chocolate, and today, his former residence houses this chocolate shop and genteel café. This is the spot for delicious pastries and a *real* hot chocolate—*czekolada do picia* ("drinking chocolate"), a cup of actual melted chocolate, not just hot chocolate milk (12 zł). The menu describes it as, "True Wedel ecstasy for your mouth that will take you to a world of dreams and desires." Or, if you fancy chocolate mousse, try *pokusa* ("Wedel Temptation"). Wedel's was *the* Christmas treat for locals under communism. Cadbury bought the company when Poland privatized, but they kept the E. Wedel name, which is close to all Poles' hearts...and taste buds (Mon-Fri 8:00-22:00, Sat 10:00-22:00, Sun 10:00-21:00, between Palace of Culture and Science and Nowy Świat at ulica Szpitalna 8, tel. 22-827-2916).

Hangout Cafés near the River

If you just want to grab a drink (and possibly a light meal) and watch the world go by, Warsaw has two inviting cafés downhill, near the river, that are worth the short trip from the main tourist zone. The first one serves mostly drinks and is a hip hangout by day and by night; the second has a wider menu of food and is open only during the day.

Warszawa Powiśle occupies the old, communist-style ticket office for the suburban train station of the same name. Now it's been taken over by hipsters and converted into one of the most happening hangouts in town. Tucked picturesquely along a bike lane beneath the towering legs of a bridge, its sidewalk is jammed with cool Varsovians and in-the-know visitors living well. The building itself has some indoor seating, but it's quite small—making this a better good-weather option (light sandwiches, daily 10:00 until late, Kruczkowskiego 3B, tel. 22-474-4084). The most direct way to get here from the palm tree at the head of Nowy Świat is to walk down aleja Jerozolimskie toward the bridge, enter the rail station, go down the stairs, walk all the way along *peron* (platform) 1 to the end, then go down the stairs at the far end: You'll pop out right at the bar. Alternatively, you can walk partway across the bridge at aleja Jerozolimskie, then go down the stairs at the first tower.

Kawarnia Kafka combines a used bookstore (with books sold by weight) with a hip and creative café. You'll find comfy chairs, stay-awhile tables, and checkerboard tiles inside, while outside on the lawn across from the café, guests lounge in slingback chairs (10-12-zł sandwiches and crêpes, 20-zł pastas and salads, Wi-Fi, Mon-Fri 9:00-22:00, Sat-Sun 10:00-22:00, Oboźna 3, tel. 22-826-0822).

Warsaw Connections

Virtually all trains into and out of Warsaw go through the hulking central train station (described earlier, under "Arrival in Warsaw"; pay special attention to the "Buying Train Tickets" section). If you're heading to Gdańsk, note that the red-brick Gothic city of Toruń and the impressive Malbork Castle are on the way (though on separate train lines, so you can't do both en route; see Gdańsk and Pomerania chapters). Also be aware that express trains to many destinations—including Kraków—require seat reservations (free), even if you have a railpass.

To confirm rail journeys, check specific times online (www .rozklad-pkp.pl) or at the central train station.

From Warsaw's Central Station by Train to: Kraków (hourly, 2.75-3.25 hours, requires seat reservation), **Gdańsk** (9/day, 5-6 hours—but will drop to 3 hours when new line is finished), **Toruń** (9/day, 2.75 hours direct, longer with a transfer in Kutno), **Malbork** (6/day direct, 4.5 hours—but will drop to 2.5 hours when new line is finished), **Prague** (2/day direct, including 1 night train, more with changes, 8.5-10 hours), **Berlin** (4/day direct, 5.5-6 hours), **Budapest** (2/day direct, including 1 night train, 10.5-11.5 hours; plus 1 each per day with transfer in Győr, Hungary, or Břeclav, Czech Republic, 10 hours), **Vienna** (2/day direct, 8-8.5

hours; plus 1 night train, 9.5 hours). An overnight train leaves nightly at 20:36, splitting to reach both **Prague** (arriving at 7:45) and **Budapest** (arriving at 8:35).

By Bus: PolskiBus runs bus routes throughout Poland (www .polskibus.com).

GDAŃSK & THE TRI-CITY

Gdańsk (guh-DAYNSK) is a true find on the Baltic Coast of Poland. You may associate Gdańsk with dreary images of striking dockworkers from the nightly news in the 1980s—but there's so much more to this city than shipyards, Solidarity, and smog. It's surprisingly easy to look past the urban sprawl to find one of northern Europe's most historic and picturesque cities.

Gdańsk is second only to Kraków as Poland's most appealing destination. The gem of a Main Town boasts block after block of red-brick churches and narrow, colorful, ornately decorated Hanseatic burghers' mansions. The riverfront embankment, with its trademark medieval crane, oozes salty maritime charm. Its history is also fascinating—from its medieval Golden Age to the headlines of our own generation, big things happen here. You might even see old Lech Wałęsa still wandering the streets.

And yet, Gdańsk is also looking to its future, finally repairing some of its WWII damage after a long communist hibernation. Things picked up even more when the city was chosen to host several matches for the Euro Cup 2012 soccer championship tournament, prompting construction of a futuristic new stadium and high-speed train lines to more efficiently link Gdańsk to the rest of Poland. Newly spiffed up and excited to host hordes of European visitors, Gdańsk is poised to reclaim its former greatness as a top European city.

Gdańsk and two nearby towns (Sopot and Gdynia) together form an area known as the "Tri-City," offering several day-trip opportunities north along the coast. The once-faded, now-revitalized elegance of the seaside resort of Sopot beckons to tourists, while the modern burg of Gdynia sets the pace for today's Poland.

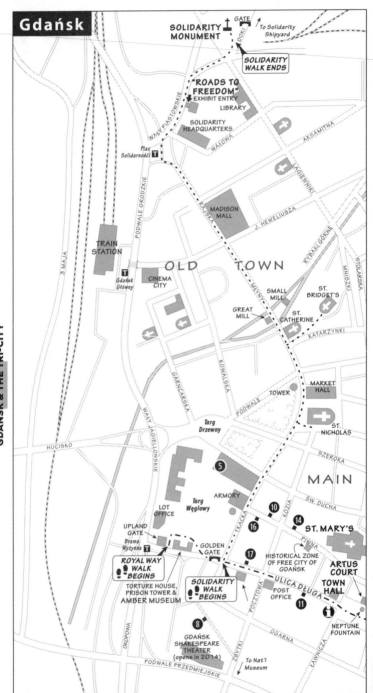

Gdańsk

SOLIDARITY MONUMENT

GATE

To Solidarity Shipyard

DOK

SOLIDARITY WALK ENDS

"ROADS TO FREEDOM" EXHIBIT ENTRY

LIBRARY

SOLIDARITY HEADQUARTERS

WAŁOWA

AKSAMITNA

WAŁY PIASTOWSKIE

Plac Solidarności

ŁAGIEWNIKI

PODWAL GRODZKIE

KLINSKA

MADISON MALL

J. HEWELIUSZA

TRAIN STATION

3 MAJA

OLD   TOWN

RYBAKI GÓRNE

STOLARSKA

Gdańsk Główny

CINEMA CITY

SMALL MILL

ST. BRIDGET'S

MŁYNSKA

MNISZKI

GREAT MILL

ST. CATHERINE

KATARZYNKI

KOWALSKA

GARNCARSKA

MARKET HALL

WAŁY JAGIELLOŃSKIE

PODWALE

TOWER

ST. NICHOLAS

HUCISKO

Targ Drzewny

SZEROKA

5

MAIN

ARMORY

Targ Węglowy

10

ŚW. DUCHA

LOT OFFICE

16

KOZIA

14

ST. MARY'S

UPLAND GATE
Brama Wyżynna

TKACKA

GOLDEN GATE

17

PIWNA

HISTORICAL ZONE OF FREE CITY OF GDAŃSK

ARTUS COURT

ROYAL WAY WALK BEGINS

SOLIDARITY WALK BEGINS

POCZTOWA

ULICA DŁUGA

POST OFFICE

TOWN HALL

TORTURE HOUSE, PRISON TOWER & AMBER MUSEUM

11

NEPTUNE FOUNTAIN

OGARNA

8

GDAŃSK SHAKESPEARE THEATER (opens in 2014)

ZBYTKI

ŁAWNICZA

OKOPOWA

PODWALE PRZEDMIEJSKIE

To Nat'l Museum

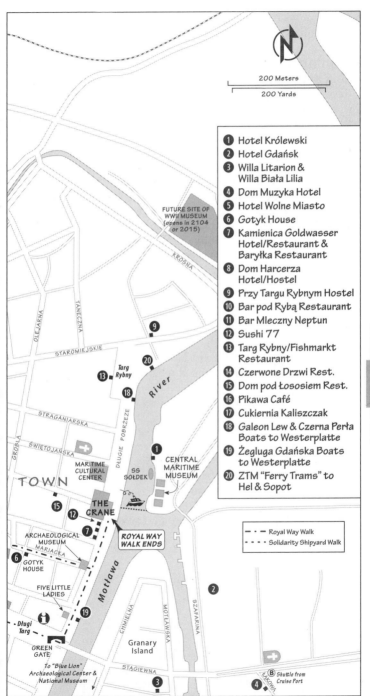

1 Hotel Królewski
2 Hotel Gdańsk
3 Willa Litarion & Willa Biała Lilia
4 Dom Muzyka Hotel
5 Hotel Wolne Miasto
6 Gotyk House
7 Kamienica Goldwasser Hotel/Restaurant & Baryłka Restaurant
8 Dom Harcerza Hotel/Hostel
9 Przy Targu Rybnym Hostel
10 Bar pod Rybą Restaurant
11 Bar Mleczny Neptun
12 Sushi 77
13 Targ Rybny/Fishmarkt Restaurant
14 Czerwone Drzwi Rest.
15 Dom pod Łososiem Rest.
16 Pikawa Café
17 Cukiernia Kaliszczak
18 Galeon Lew & Czerna Perła Boats to Westerplatte
19 Żegluga Gdańska Boats to Westerplatte
20 ZTM "Ferry Trams" to Hel & Sopot

200 Meters
200 Yards

FUTURE SITE OF WWII MUSEUM (opens in 2104 or 2015)

KROSNA

OLEJARNA
TANECZNA
STAROMIEJSKIE

Targ Rybny

River

STRAGANIARSKA

DŁUGIE POBRZEŻE

GROBLA
ŚWIĘTOJAŃSKA

MARITIME CULTURAL CENTER

TOWN

SS SOŁDEK

CENTRAL MARITIME MUSEUM

THE CRANE

ARCHAEOLOGICAL MUSEUM
MARIACKA

GOTYK HOUSE

FIVE LITTLE LADIES

Mottawa

ROYAL WAY WALK ENDS

CHMIELNA
MOTŁAWSKA
SZAFARINA

Długi Targ

GREEN GATE

To "Blue Lion" Archaeological Center & National Museum

Granary Island

STĄGIEWNA

Shuttle from Cruise Port

--- Royal Way Walk
···· Solidarity Shipyard Walk

GDAŃSK & THE TRI-CITY

Beyond the Tri-City, the sandy Hel Peninsula is a popular spot for summer sunbathing.

Planning Your Time

This region merits two days to make the trip here worthwhile. Gdańsk's major sights can be seen in a day, but a second day allows you to see everything in town at a more relaxing pace, and take your pick from among several possible side-trips.

Gdańsk sightseeing has two major components: the Royal Way (historic main drag with good museums) and the modern shipyard where Solidarity was born (with a fascinating museum). With just one day, do one of these activities in the morning, and the other in the afternoon. With two days, do one each day, and round out your time with other attractions: art lovers enjoy the National Museum (with a stunning painting by Hans Memling), history buffs make the pilgrimage to Westerplatte (where World War II began), and church fans might visit Oliwa Cathedral in Gdańsk's northern suburbs (on the way to Sopot).

If you have more time, consider the wide variety of side-trips. The most popular option is the half-day round-trip to Malbork Castle (40-50 minutes each way by train, plus two or three hours to tour the castle—see next chapter). Closer to Gdańsk, it only takes a quick visit to get a feel for the resort town of Sopot (25 minutes each way by train), but the town's beaches may tempt you to laze around longer. Consider a sprint through Gdynia to round out your take on the Tri-City. If you have a full day and great weather, and you don't mind fighting the crowds for a patch of sandy beach, go to Hel.

Gdańsk gets busy in late June, when school holidays begin, and it's downright crowded with mostly German tourists from July to mid-September—especially during St. Dominic's Fair (Jarmark Św. Dominika, three weeks in late July-mid-Aug), with market stalls, concerts, and other celebrations.

Orientation to Gdańsk

Gdańsk, with 460,000 residents, is part of the larger urban area known as the Tri-City (Trójmiasto, total population of 1 million). But the tourist's Gdańsk is compact, welcoming, and walkable—virtually anything you'll want to see is within a 20-minute stroll of everything else.

Focus on the Main Town (Główne Miasto), home to most

of the sights described, including the spectacular Royal Way main drag, ulica Długa. The Old Town (Stare Miasto) has a handful of old brick buildings and faded, tall, skinny houses—but the area is mostly drab and residential, and not worth much time. Just beyond the northern end of the Old Town (about a 20-minute walk from the heart of the Main Town) is the entrance to the Gdańsk Shipyard, with the excellent Solidarity museum. From here, shipyards sprawl for miles.

The second language in this part of Poland is German, not English. As this was a predominantly German city until the end of World War II, German tourists flock here in droves. But you'll win no Polish friends if you call the city by its more familiar German name, Danzig.

Tourist Information

Confusingly, Gdańsk has two different TI organizations. The better TI's main branch is centrally located at the bottom (river) end of the main drag, at **Długi Targ 28/29** (just to the left as you face the gate; April-Sept daily 9:00-19:00; Oct-March Mon-Sat 9:00-17:00, Sun 9:00-16:00; tel. 58-301-4355, www.gdansk4u.pl). They also have satellites at the **main train station** (in the underpass, Mon-Sat 9:00-17:00, Sun 9:00-16:00, tel. 58-721-3277) and at the **airport** (same hours as train station TI, tel. 58-348-1368). Skip the other TI, which is prominently located (in the red, high-gabled building across ulica Długa from the Town Hall) but sloppily run by the national government.

Sightseeing Card: Busy sightseers should consider the **Tourist Card,** which includes entry to 24 sights in Gdańsk, Gdynia, and Sopot, and discounts at others (such as 20 percent off admission to Malbork Castle). Check the list of what's covered (most of the biggies in town are free with the card, while the Solidarity museum is 50 percent off), and do the arithmetic. If you'll be seeing several included museums, this card could save you some money ("standard" card: 22 zł/24 hours, 35 zł/72 hours; "max" card also includes local public transit: 45 zł/24 hours, 75 zł/72 hours; sold at TIs).

Arrival in Gdańsk

By Train: Gdańsk's main train station (Gdańsk Główny) is a pretty brick palace on the western edge of the old center. (To save money, architects in Colmar, France, copied this exact design to build their city's station.) Trains to other parts of Poland (marked *PKP*) use tracks 1-3;

GDAŃSK & THE TRI-CITY

regional trains with connections to the Tri-City (marked *SKM*) use the shorter tracks 3-5.

Inside the terminal building, you'll find lockers, ATMs, and ticket windows. Outside, the pedestrian underpass by the McDonald's has a helpful TI and leads you beneath the busy road (go down the stairs and turn right; first set of exits: tram stop; end of corridor: Old Town). To reach the heart of the Main Town, you can ride the **tram** (buy tickets—*bilety*—at the *RUCH* kiosk by track 4 or at any window marked *Bilety ZKM* in pedestrian underpass; access tram stop via underpass, then board tram #2, #3, #6, #8, or #11 going to the right with your back to the station; go just one stop to Brama Wyżynna, in front of the LOT airlines office). But by the time you buy your ticket and wait for the tram, you might as well **walk** the 15 minutes to the same place (go through underpass, exit to the right, circle around the right side of Cinema City, and follow the busy road until you reach LOT airlines office, then head left toward all the brick towers). Or even easier, take a **taxi** (which shouldn't cost more than 15 zł to any of my recommended hotels).

By Plane: Gdańsk's small airport, named for Lech Wałęsa, is about five miles west of the city center (airport code: GDN, tel. 58-348-1163, www.airport.gdansk.pl). The airport has a TI desk and ATMs. Public **bus** #210 connects the airport with downtown, stopping near the main train station and at Brama Wyżynna, near the heart of the Main Town (2.80 zł if bought from TI desk, more if purchased on board, 2/hour on weekdays, 1/hour on weekends, 40 minutes, exit terminal and turn right to find bus stop). The **Airportbus shuttle** zips you directly to various points downtown, though the schedule is sporadic and it must be booked in advance (9-12 zł depending on where you go, 11/day, reserve at www.mpapo land.pl). The 25-minute **taxi** ride into town will cost you about 50 zł.

Helpful Hints

Blue Monday: In the off-season, most of Gdańsk's museums are closed Monday. In the busy summertime, the Gdańsk Historical Museum branches are open—and free—for limited hours on Monday. If museums are closed, Monday is a good day to visit churches or take a side-trip to Sopot (but not to Malbork Castle, which is also closed Mon).

Internet Access: You'll find several free Wi-Fi hotspots in major tourist zones around central Gdańsk.

Getting Around Gdańsk

If you're staying at one of my recommended hotels, everything is within easy walking distance. Public transportation is generally unnecessary for sightseers (except for reaching outlying sights such as Oliwa Cathedral, Westerplatte, Sopot, Gdynia, and Hel—transportation options for these places are described in their listings).

By Public Transportation: Gdańsk's trams and buses work on the same tickets: Choose between a single-ride ticket (3 zł), one-hour ticket (3.60 zł), and 24-hour ticket (12 zł). Buy tickets *(bilety)* at kiosks marked *RUCH* or *Bilety ZKM,* or on board (1-hour and 24-hour tickets only sold on board). In the city center, the stops worth knowing about are Plac Solidarnośći (near the shipyards), Gdańsk Główny (in front of the main train station), and Brama Wyżynna (near the heart of the tourist zone, in front of LOT airlines office). When buying tickets, don't confuse *ZKM* (the company that runs Gdańsk city transit) with *SKM* (the company that runs regional trains to outlying destinations).

By Taxi: Taxis cost about 7 zł to start, then 2 zł per kilometer (or 3 zł at night). Find a taxi stand, or call a cab (try Super Hallo Taxi, tel. 191-91).

Tours in Gdańsk

Walking Tours
In peak season, the TI sometimes offers a pricey 2.5-hour English walking tour (80 zł/person, offered with demand in July-Aug only, no set schedule—ask at TI).

Private Guide
Hiring your own local guide is an exceptional value. **Agnieszka Syroka** is bubbly and personable, and also does tours of Malbork Castle (400 zł for up to 4 hours, more for all day, mobile 502-554-584, www.tourguidegdansk.com, asyroka@interia.pl or syroka .agnieszka@gmail.com).

Self-Guided Walks

▲▲▲Gdańsk's Royal Way
In the 16th and 17th centuries, Gdańsk was Poland's wealthiest city, with gorgeous architecture (much of it in the Flemish Mannerist style) rivaling that in the two historic capitals, Kraków

and Warsaw. During this Golden Age, Polish kings would visit this city of well-to-do Hanseatic League merchants, and gawk along the same route trod by tourists today. The following walk introduces you to the best of historic Gdańsk. It only takes about 30 minutes, not counting multiple worthwhile sightseeing stops. This stroll turns tourists into poets. On my last visit, a traveler gasped to me, "It's like stepping into a Fabergé egg."

Begin at the west end of the Main Town, between the white gate and the big brick gate (near the LOT airlines office, the busy road, and the Brama Wyżynna tram stop).

City Gates: Medieval Gdańsk had an elaborate network of protection for the city, including several moats and gates—among them the white **Upland Gate** (Brama Wyżynna); the red-brick **Torture House** (Wieża Więzienna); and the taller, attached red-brick **Prison Tower** (Katownia). The three gates were all connected back then, and visitors had to pass through all of them to enter the city. The Torture House/Prison Tower complex, with walls up to 15 feet thick, now holds the fine **Amber Museum** (described later, under "Sights in Gdańsk").

Now walk around the left side of the Torture House and Prison Tower. Look to your left to see a long brick building with four gables (next to the modern theater building). This is the 16th-century **Armory** (Zbrojownia), one of the best examples of Dutch Renaissance architecture in Europe. Though this part of the building looks like four separate house facades, it's a kind of urban camouflage to hide its real purpose from potential attackers. But there's at least one clue to what it's for: Notice the exploding cannonballs at the tops of the turrets. The round, pointy-topped tower next door is the **Straw Tower** (Baszta Słomiana). Gunpowder was stored here, and the roof was straw—so if it exploded, it would blow its top without destroying the walls.

• Continue around the brick buildings until you're face-to-face with the...

Golden Gate (Złota Brama): The other gates were defensive, but this one's purely ornamental. The four women up top represent virtues that the people of Gdańsk should exhibit toward outsiders: Peace, Freedom, Prosperity, and Fame. The inscription, a psalm in medieval German, compares Gdańsk to Jerusalem: famous and important. In the middle is one of the coats of arms of Gdańsk—two white crosses under a crown on a red shield. We'll see this symbol many times today.

• Now go through the gate, entering the "Long Street"...

Ulica Długa: Look back at the gate you just came through. The women on top of this side represent virtues the people of Gdańsk should cultivate in themselves: Wisdom, Piety, Justice, and Concord (if an arrow's broken, let's take it out of the quiver and fix it).

Wander this intoxicating promenade. Gdańsk was cosmopolitan and exceptionally tolerant in the Middle Ages, attracting a wide range of people, including many who were persecuted elsewhere: Jews, Scots, Dutch, Flemish, Italians, Germans, and more. Members of each group brought with them strands of their culture, which they wove into the tapestry of this city—demonstrated by the eclectic homes along this street.

This lovely street wasn't always so lively and carefree. At the end of World War II, ulica Długa was in ruins. The city was badly damaged when the Nazis first invaded, but the worst devastation came when the Soviets arrived. This was the first traditionally German city that the Red Army reached on their march toward Berlin—and the soldiers were set loose to level the place in retaliation for all the pain the Nazis had caused. (Soviets didn't destroy nearby Gdynia—which they considered Polish, not German.) Soviet officers turned a blind eye as their soldiers raped and brutalized residents. An entire order of horrified nuns committed suicide by throwing themselves into the river. Upwards of 80 percent of this area was destroyed. It was only thanks to detailed drawings and photographs that these buildings could be so carefully reconstructed, mostly using the original brick.

During Gdańsk's Golden Age, these houses were taxed based on frontage (like the homes lining Amsterdam's canals)—so they were built skinny and deep. The widest houses belonged to the super-elite. Different as they are from the outside, every house had the same general plan inside. Each had three parts, starting with the front and moving back: First was a fancy drawing room, to show off for visitors. Then came a narrow corridor to the back rooms—often along the side of an inner courtyard. Because the houses had only a few windows facing the outer street, this courtyard provided much-needed sunlight to the rest of the house. The residential quarters were in the back, where the family actually lived: bedroom, kitchen, office. To see the interior of one of these homes, pay a visit to the very interesting **Uphagen House** (#12, on the right, a block and a half in front of

the Golden Gate; described later, under "Sights in Gdańsk").

Across the street and a little farther down are some of the most striking **facades** along ulica Długa. The blue-and-white house with the three giant heads is from the 19th century, when the hot style was eclecticism—borrowing bits and pieces from various archi-

Gdańsk History

Visitors to Gdańsk are surprised at how "un-Polish" the city's history is. In this cultural melting pot of German, Dutch, and Flemish merchants (with a smattering of Italians and Scots), Poles were only a small part of the picture until the city became exclusively Polish after World War II. However, in Gdańsk, cultural backgrounds traditionally took a back seat to the bottom line. Wealthy Gdańsk was always known for its economic pragmatism—no matter who was in charge, merchants here made money.

Gdańsk is Poland's gateway to the waters of Europe—where its main river (the Vistula) meets the Baltic Sea. The town was first mentioned in the 10th century, and was seized in 1308 by the Teutonic Knights (who called it "Danzig"; for more on the Teutonic Knights, see page 240). The Knights encouraged other Germans to settle on the Baltic coast, and gradually turned Gdańsk into a wealthy city. In 1361, Gdańsk joined the Hanseatic League, a trade federation of mostly Germanic merchant towns that provided mutual security. By the 15th century, Gdańsk was a leading member of this mighty network, which virtually dominated trade in northern Europe (and also included Toruń, Kraków, Lübeck, Hamburg, Bremen, Bruges, Bergen, Tallinn, Novgorod, and nearly a hundred other cities).

In 1454, the people of Gdańsk rose up against the Teutonic Knights, burning down their castle and forcing them out of the city. Three years later, the Polish king borrowed money from wealthy Gdańsk families to hire Czech mercenaries to take the Teutonic Knights' main castle, Malbork (described in the next chapter). In exchange, the Gdańsk merchants were granted special privileges, including exclusive export rights. Gdańsk now acted as a middleman for much of the trade passing through Polish lands, but paid only a modest annual tribute to the Polish king.

The 16th and 17th centuries were Gdańsk's Golden Age. Now a part of the Polish kingdom, the city had access to an enormous hinterland of natural resources to export—yet it maintained a privileged, semi-independent status. Like Amsterdam,

tectural eras. This was one of the few houses on the street that survived World War II.

At the next corner on the right is the huge, blocky, red **post office,** which doesn't quite fit with the skinny facades lining the rest of the street. But step inside. With doves fluttering under an airy glass atrium, the interior's a class act. (To mail postcards, take a number—category C—from the machine on the left.)

Across the street and a few doors down from the post office, notice the colorful **scenes** just overhead on the facade of the cocktail bar. These are slices of life from 17th-century Gdańsk: drink-

Gdańsk became a tolerant, progressive, and booming merchant city. Its mostly Germanic and Dutch burghers imported Dutch, Flemish, and Italian architects to give their homes an appropriately Hanseatic flourish. At a time of religious upheaval in the rest of Europe, Gdańsk became known for its tolerance—a place that opened its doors to all visitors (many Mennonites and Scottish religious refugees emigrated here). It was also a haven for great thinkers, including philosopher Arthur Schopenhauer and scientist Daniel Fahrenheit (who invented the mercury thermometer).

Gdańsk declined, along with the rest of Poland, in the late 18th century, and became a part of Prussia (today's northern Germany) during the Partitions. But the people of Gdańsk—even those of German heritage—had taken pride in their independence, and weren't enthusiastic about being ruled from Berlin. After World War I, in a unique compromise to appease its complex ethnic makeup, Gdańsk did not fall under German or Polish control, but once again became an independent city-state: the Free City of Danzig (populated by 400,000 ethnic Germans and only 15,000 Poles). The city, along with the so-called Polish Corridor connecting it to Polish lands, effectively cut off Germany from its northeastern territory. On September 1, 1939, Adolf Hitler started World War II when he invaded Gdańsk in order to bring it back into the German fold. Nearly 80 percent of the city was destroyed in the war.

After World War II, Gdańsk officially became part of Poland, and was painstakingly reconstructed (mostly replicating the buildings of its Golden Age). In 1970, and again in 1980, the shipyard of Gdańsk witnessed strikes and demonstrations that would lead to the fall of European communism. Poland's great anti-communist hero and first post-communist president—Lech Wałęsa—is Gdańsk's most famous resident, and still lives here.

A city with a recent past that's both tragic and uplifting, Gdańsk celebrated its 1,000th birthday in 1997. This occasion, and preparations for the Euro Cup 2012 soccer matches, kicked off a wave of renovation and refurbishment that has the gables of the atmospheric Hanseatic quarter gleaming once again.

ing, talking, buying, fighting, playing music. The ship is a *koga,* a typical symbol of Gdańsk.

A couple of doors down from the cocktail bar is **Neptun Cinema** (marked *KINO*). In the 1980s, this was the only movie theater in the city, and locals lined up all the way down the street to get in. Adults remember coming here with their grandparents to see a full day of cartoons. Now, as with traditional main-street cinemas in the US, this one is threatened by the rising popularity of multiplexes outside the town center.

Across the street from the theater are three houses belonging to the very influential medieval **Ferber family,** which produced many burghers, mayors, and even a bishop. On the house with the little dog over the door (#29), look for the heads in the circles. These are Caesars of Rome. At the top of the building is Mr. Ferber's answer to the constant question, "Why build such an elaborate house?"—*PRO INVIDIA,* "For the sake of envy."

A few doors down, notice the outdoor tables for Gdańsk's most popular milk bar, the recommended **Bar Mleczny Neptun.** Now you're just a few steps from the **Main Town Hall** (Ratusz Głównego Miasta). Consider climbing its observation tower and visiting its superb interior, which features ornately decorated meeting rooms for the city council (described later, under "Sights in Gdańsk"). The **TI** is across the street, on the right.

• *Just beyond the Main Town Hall, ulica Długa widens and becomes...*

Długi Targ (Long Square): The centerpiece of this square is one of Gdańsk's most important landmarks, the statue of **Neptune**—god of the sea. He's a fitting symbol for a city that dominates the maritime life of Poland. Behind him is another fine museum, the **Artus Court** (described later, under "Sights in Gdańsk"). This meeting hall for various Gdańsk brotherhoods is home to the most impressive stove you've ever seen.

As you continue down Długi targ, notice the **balconies** extending out into the square, with access to cellars underneath. These were a common feature on ulica Długa in Gdańsk's Golden Age, but were removed in the 19th century to make way for a new tram system. You can find more balconies like these on Mariacka street, which runs parallel to this one (2 blocks to the left).

• *At the end of Długi targ is the...*

Green Gate (Zielona Brama): This huge gate was actually built as a residence for visiting kings...who usually preferred to stay back by Neptune instead (maybe because the river, just on the other side of this gate, stank). It might not have been good enough for kings and queens, but it's plenty fine for a former president—Lech Wałęsa's office is upstairs (see the plaque, *Biuro Lecha Wałęsy*). Other parts of the building are used for temporary exhibitions.

Notice that these bricks are much smaller than the ones we've seen earlier on this walk, which were locally made. These, however, are Dutch: Boats from Holland would come here empty of cargo but with a load of bricks for ballast. Traders filled their ships with goods for the return trip, leaving the bricks behind to be turned into this gate.

• *Now go through the gate, and turn left along the...*

Riverfront Embankment: The Motława River—actually a side channel of the mighty Vistula—was the source of Gdańsk's phenomenal Golden Age wealth. This embankment was jam-packed in its heyday, the 14th and 15th centuries. It was so crowded with boats that you would hardly have been able to see the water, and boats had to pay a time-based tax for tying up to a post. Instead of an actual embankment (which was built later), a series of wooden piers connected the boats directly to the gates of the city. Now it's a popular place to stroll and to buy amber. Keep an eye out for old-fashioned **galleons** plying the waters here—these boats depart hourly for a fun cruise to Westerplatte and back. While kitschy, the galleons are a fun way to get out on the water.

Across the river is **Granary Island** (Spichrze), where grain was stored until it could be taken away by ships. Before World War II, there were some 400 granaries here; today the island is still in ruins. Three granaries that have been reconstructed on the next island up house exhibits for the Central Maritime Museum (described later, under "Sights in Gdańsk"); two others are now recommended hotels (Hotel Gdańsk and Hotel Królewski). A big international company has bought this island, and plans to develop the prime real estate into a new city-center zone of shops, restaurants, houses, and hotels.

Continue along the embankment until you see the five big, round stones on your left. These are the **five little ladies**—mysterious ancient sculptures. If you look closely, you can make out their features, especially the chubby one on the end.

In the next block, the huge red-brick fort houses the **Archaeological Museum** and a tower you can climb for a good view (described later, under "Sights in Gdańsk"). The gate in the middle of the building leads to **Mariacka street,** a calm, atmospheric drag lined with old balconies, amber shops, and imaginative gargoyles (which locals call "pukers" when it rains).

Consider taking a few minutes to window-shop your way up Mariacka street, comparison-pricing amber souvenirs. At the end of the street on the left (at #1), the recommended **Gotyk House** hotel has a characteristic little shop in the cellar that sells heavenly gingerbread from the town of Toruń. If you're not headed to Toruń (described in the next chapter), this is a good opportunity to buy some of its tasty treats. As that city was the hometown of Nicholas Copernicus—and Copernicus' former lover supposedly once lived in this very house—the shop also has a fondly presented mini-museum dedicated to the couple. Just after Gotyk House and the gingerbread shop, you're face-to-face with **St. Mary's Church** (enter around the far side; described later, under "Sights in Gdańsk").

• *Back on the embankment, head past a few tempting eateries (including the recommended Kamienica Goldwasser and Sushi 77)—consider scouting a table here for dinner later tonight—before running right into Gdańsk's number-one symbol, and our last stop...*

The Crane (Żuraw): This monstrous 15th-century crane was once used for loading ships, picking up small crafts for repairs, and uprighting masts...beginning a shipbuilding tradition that continued to the days of Lech Wałęsa. The crane mechanism was operated by several hardworking sailors scrambling around in giant hamster wheels up top (you can see the wheels if you look up). The Crane belongs to the Central Maritime Museum, as does the modern building just beyond it (the museum is described in detail under "Sights in Gdańsk," later). And along here, you might see a stand selling smoked fish.

• *Our orientation tour is over. Now get out there and enjoy Gdańsk... do it for Lech!*

From the Main Town to the Solidarity Shipyard

This lightly guided walk links Gdańsk's two most important sightseeing areas. Along the way, we'll see some historic landmarks, tour two of Gdańsk's more interesting red-brick churches, and wander through the city's best shopping district. The stroll takes about 20 minutes, not counting stops for sightseeing and shopping.

Begin at the top of ulica Długa, with your back to the Golden Gate. Head a few steps down the street and take a left on Tkacka. After one long block, on the left, you can see the back of the **Armory** building (described earlier). This pearl of Renaissance architecture recently had a striking facelift—examine the exquisite decorations.

After three short blocks, detour to the right down Świętojańska and use the side door to enter the brick **St. Nicholas Church** (Kościół Św. Mikołaja, with the ornate towers on the ends). Archaeologists have found the bodies of 3,000 Napoleonic soldiers buried here. Near the end of World War II, when the Soviet army reached Gdańsk on its march westward, they were given the order to burn all the churches. Only this one—dedicated to Russia's patron saint—was spared. As the best-preserved church in town, it has a more impressive interior than the others, with lavish black-and-gold Baroque altars.

Backtrack out to the main street and continue north. Immediately after the church (on the right) is Gdańsk's renovated

Market Hall. Look for the coat of arms of Gdańsk over each of its four doors (two white crosses on a red shield). Inside you'll find mostly local shoppers—browsing through produce, other foods, and clothing—as well as the graves of medieval Dominican monks, which were discovered in the basement when the building was refurbished. Look up to appreciate the delicate steel-and-glass canopy.

Across the street from the Market Hall is a round, red-brick **tower,** once part of the city's protective wall. This marks the end of the Main Town and the beginning of the Old Town.

Another long block up the street is the huge **St. Catherine's Church** (Kościół Św. Katarzyny, on the right). "Katy," as locals call it, is the oldest church in Gdańsk. In May of 2006, a carelessly discarded cigarette caused the church roof to burst into flames. Local people ran into the church and pulled everything outside, so nothing valuable was damaged; even the carillon bells were saved. However, the roof and wooden frame were totally destroyed. The people of Gdańsk were determined to rebuild this important symbol of the city. Within days of the fire, fund-raising concerts were held to scrape together most of the money needed to raise the roof once more.

The church hiding behind Katy—named for Catherine's daughter Bridget—has important ties to Solidarity, and is worth a quick detour. To get there, walk up ulica Katarzynki, along the side of St. Catherine's Church, and past the monument to Pope John Paul II.

St. Bridget's Church (Kościół Św. Brygidy) was the home church of Lech Wałęsa during the tense days of the 1980s. This church and its priest, Henryk Jankowski, were particularly aggressive in supporting the ideals of Solidarity. Jankowski became a mouthpiece for the movement, and Wałęsa named his youngest daughter Brygida in gratitude for the church's support. In the back corner, under the wall of wooden crosses, find the memorial to Solidarity martyr Jerzy Popiełuszko, a famously outspoken Warsaw priest who in 1984 was kidnapped, beaten, and murdered by the communist secret police. Notice that the figure's hands and feet are tied. At the front of the church, check out the enormous, unfinished altar made entirely of amber, featuring the Black Madonna of Częstochowa and a royal Polish eagle. If and when it's finished, it'll be 36 feet high, 20 feet wide, and 10 feet deep. But some locals criticize this ambitious project as an example of Father Jankowski's missteps. Despite his fame and contributions to Solidarity, Jankowski's public standing took a nosedive near the end of his life—thanks to ego-driven projects like this, as well as accusations of anti-Semitism and implications of pedophilia and corruption. Forced to retire in 2007, Jankowski died in 2010.

Gdańsk at a Gdlance

Note that several sights share the same opening times: Main Town Hall (see hours in listing, below), Artus Court, Amber Museum, and Uphagen House.

▲▲▲**Ulica Długa** Gdańsk's colorful showpiece main drag, cutting a picturesque swath through the heart of the wealthy burghers' neighborhood. **Hours:** Always open. See page 187.

▲▲▲**Solidarity Sights and Gdańsk Shipyard** Home to the beginning of the end of European communism, housing a towering monument and an excellent museum. **Hours:** Memorial and shipyard gate—always open. "Roads to Freedom" exhibit—May-Sept Tue-Sun 10:00-18:00, Oct-April Tue-Sun 10:00-17:00, closed Mon year-round. See page 206.

▲▲**Main Town Hall** Ornately decorated meeting rooms, exhibits of town artifacts, and climbable tower with sweeping views. **Hours:** Mid-June-mid-Sept Mon 9:00-13:00, Tue-Thu 9:00-16:00, Fri-Sat 10:00-18:00, Sun 10:00-16:00; mid-Sept-mid-June Tue 10:00-13:00, Wed-Sat 10:00-16:00, Thu until 18:00, Sun 11:00-16:00, closed Mon. See page 200.

▲▲**Artus Court** Grand meeting hall for guilds of Golden Age Gdańsk, boasting an over-the-top tiled stove. **Hours:** Same as Main Town Hall, above. See page 201.

▲▲**St. Mary's Church** Giant red-brick church crammed full of Gdańsk history. **Hours:** June-Sept Mon-Sat 9:00-18:30, Sun 13:00-18:30; closes progressively earlier off-season. See page 202.

▲**Amber Museum** High-tech new exhibit of valuable golden globs of petrified tree sap. **Hours:** Same as Main Town Hall, above. See page 198.

▲**Uphagen House** Tourable 18th-century interior, typical of the

Backtrack out past St. Catherine's Church to the main street. Just across from the church is a red-brick building with a lot of little windows in the roof. This is the **Great Mill** (Wielki Młyn), which has been converted into a shopping mall (daily 10:00-19:00). As you continue north and cross the stream, you'll also see the picturesque **Small Mill** (Mały Młyn) straddling the stream on your right.

After another block, on your right, is the modern **Madison shopping mall** (Mon-Sat 9:00-21:00, Sun 10:00-20:00). Two

pretty houses that line ulica Długa. **Hours:** Same as Main Town Hall. See page 200.

▲**Central Maritime Museum** Sprawling exhibit on all aspects of the nautical life, housed in several venues (including the landmark medieval Crane and a permanently moored steamship) connected by a ferry boat. **Hours:** July-Aug daily 10:00-18:00; Sept-Oct and March-June Tue-Sun 10:00-16:00, closed Mon; Nov-Feb Tue-Sun 10:00-15:00, closed Mon. See page 205.

Historical Zone of the Free City of Gdańsk Tiny museum examining Gdańsk's unique status as a "Free City" between the World Wars. **Hours:** May-Nov Tue-Sun 11:00-18:00, Dec-April Tue-Sun 13:00-17:00, closed Mon year-round. See page 204.

Archaeological Museum Decent collection of artifacts from this region's past. **Hours:** July-Aug Tue-Fri 9:00-17:00, Sat-Sun 10:00-17:00, closed Mon; Sept-June Tue and Thu-Fri 8:00-16:00, Wed 9:00-17:00, Sat-Sun 10:00-16:00, closed Mon. See page 205.

National Museum in Gdańsk Ho-hum art collection with a single blockbuster highlight: Hans Memling's remarkable *Last Judgment* altarpiece. **Hours:** June-Aug Tue-Wed and Fri-Sun 10:00-17:00, Thu 12:00-19:00; May and Sept Tue-Sun 10:00-17:00; Oct-April Tue-Fri 9:00-16:00, Sat-Sun 10:00-17:00, closed Mon year-round. See page 215.

"Blue Lion" Archaeological Education Center New, kid-friendly exhibit about medieval Gdańsk. **Hours:** May-Aug Tue-Sun 10:00-18:00, Sept-April Tue-Sun 9:00-17:00, closed Mon year-round. See page 217.

Oliwa Cathedral Suburban church with long, skinny nave and playful organ. **Hours:** Church open long hours daily; frequent organ concerts in summer. See page 217.

GDAŃSK & THE TRI-CITY

blocks to your left (up Heweliusza) are more shopping malls and the main train station.

But to get to the **shipyard,** keep heading straight up Rajska. After another long block, jog right (between the big, green-glass skyscraper and today's Solidarity headquarters) and head for the three tall crosses.

On the way, you'll see signs leading to the **"Roads to Freedom" exhibit** (the entrance to this underground museum is actually a freestanding kiosk by the side of the road).

But before you visit this museum, head to the shipyard to begin my self-guided tour there. Near the entrance to the museum are two artifacts from communist times. First, parked in front of the museum is an **armored personnel carrier,** just like the ones used by the ZOMO (riot police) to terrorize Polish citizens after martial law was declared in 1981. Nearby, watch for the two big chunks of **wall:** on the left, a piece of the Berlin Wall; and on the right, a chunk of the shipyard wall Lech Wałęsa scaled to get inside and lead the strike. The message: What happened behind one wall eventually led to the fall of the other Wall.

Sights in Gdańsk

Main Town (Główne Miasto)
The following sights are all in the Main Town, listed roughly in the order you'll see them on the self-guided walk of the Royal Way.

Gdańsk Historical Museum
The Gdańsk Historical Museum has four excellent branches: the Amber Museum, Uphagen House, Main Town Hall, and Artus Court. All have the same cost and hours, but you must buy a separate ticket for each.

Cost and Hours: 10 zł apiece, free Mon in summer and Tue off-season; hours fluctuate, but typically open mid-June–mid-Sept Mon 9:00-13:00, Tue-Thu 9:00-16:00, Fri-Sat 10:00-18:00, Sun 10:00-16:00; mid-Sept–mid-June Tue 10:00-13:00, Wed-Sat 10:00-16:00, Thu until 18:00, Sun 11:00-16:00, closed Mon; last entry 30 minutes before closing.

Information: The museums share a phone number and website (central tel. 58-767-9100, www.mhmg .gda.pl).

▲Amber Museum (Muzeum Bursztynu)
Housed in a pair of connected brick towers just outside the Main Town's Golden Gate, this museum has two oddly contradictory parts. One shows off Gdańsk's favorite local resource, amber, while the other focuses on implements of torture (cost and hours above, overpriced 1.5-hour audioguide—25 zł, enter at end facing Golden Gate).

Partially explained in English, the Amber Museum offers a good introduction to the globby yellow stuff, but you'll have to walk up several flights of stairs to see it all.

All About Amber

Poland's Baltic seaside is known as the Amber Coast. You can see amber *(bursztyn)* in Gdańsk's Amber Museum, in the collection at Malbork Castle (see next chapter)—and in shop windows everywhere. This fossilized tree resin originated here on the north coast of Poland 40 million years ago. It comes in as many different colors as Eskimos have words for snow: 300 distinct shades, from yellowish white to yellowish black, from opaque to transparent. (I didn't believe it either, until I toured Gdańsk's museum.) Darker-colored amber is generally mixed with ash and sand—making it more fragile, and generally less desirable. Lighter amber is mixed with gasses and air bubbles.

Amber has been popular since long before there were souvenir stands. Archaeologists have found Roman citizens (and their coins) buried with crosses made of amber. Almost 75 percent of the world's amber is mined in northern Poland, and it often simply washes up on the beaches after a winter storm. Some of the elaborate amber sculptures displayed at the museum are joined with "amber glue"—melted-down amber mixed with an adhesive agent. More recently, amber craftsmen are combining amber with silver to create artwork—a method dubbed the "Polish School."

In addition to being good for the economy, some Poles believe amber is good for their health. A traditional cure for arthritis pain is to pour strong vodka over amber, let it set, and then rub it on sore joints. Other remedies call for mixing amber dust with honey or rose oil. It sounds superstitious, but users claim that it works.

For a primer before you go, check out the "All About Amber" sidebar.

Climb up one flight of stairs, buy your ticket, then head up to the second floor for a scientific look at amber. View inclusions (items trapped in the resin) through a magnifying glass and microscope, and see dozens of samples showing the full rainbow of amber shades. Interactive video screens explain the creation of amber. The third-floor exhibit explains the "Amber Route" (the ancient Celtic trade road connecting Gdańsk to Italy), outlines medicinal uses of the stuff, and displays a wide range of functional items made from amber—clocks, pipe stems, candlesticks, chandeliers, jewelry boxes, and much more. The fourth floor shows off more artistic items made of amber—sculptures, candelabras, beer steins, chessboards, and a model ship with delicate sails made of amber. At the top floor, you'll find a modern gallery showing more recent amber craftsmanship, and displays about amber's role in fashion today.

On your way back down, detour along the upper level of the

courtyard to find the museum's dark side (the Torture Museum). First is a brief exhibit about the building's history, including its chapter as a prison tower. The rest of the exhibit—with sound effects, scant artifacts, and mannequins helpfully demonstrating the grisly equipment—tries hard to make medieval torture and imprisonment interesting.

▲Uphagen House (Dom Uphagena)

This interesting place at ulica Długa 12 is your chance to glimpse what's behind the colorful facades lining this street (see cost and hours above). Check out the cutaway model just inside the entry to see the three parts you'll visit: dolled-up visitors' rooms in front, a corridor along the courtyard, and private rooms in the back. As you enter, the costumed staffers will likely usher you to the top floor, which houses temporary exhibits. Back down on the middle floor, ogle the finely decorated salon, which was used to show off for guests. Most of this furniture is original (saved from WWII bombs by locals who hid it in the countryside). Passing into the dining room, note the knee-high paintings of hunting and celebrations. Along the passage to the back, each room has a theme: butterflies in the smoking room, then flowers in the next room, then birds in the music room. In the private rooms at the back, notice how much simpler the decor is. Downstairs, you'll pass through the kitchen, the pantry, and a room with photos of the house before the war, which were used to reconstruct what you see today.

▲▲Main Town Hall (Ratusz Głównego Miasta)

This landmark building contains remarkable decorations from Gdańsk's Golden Age. You can also climb to the top of the **tower** for commanding views (5 zł extra, mid-June-mid-Sept only).

Visiting the Main Town Hall: Buy your ticket down below (good gift shop), then head up the stairs and inside.

In the entry room, examine the photo showing this building at the end of World War II (you'll see more upstairs). The

ornately carved wooden **door,** which we'll pass through in a minute, also deserves a close look. Above the door are two crosses under a crown. This seal of Gdańsk is being held—as it's often depicted—by a pair of lions. The felines are stubborn and independent, just like the citizens of Gdańsk. Close the door partway to look at the carvings of crops. Around the frame of the door are mermen, reminding us that this agricultural bounty, like so many of Poland's resources, is transported on the Vistula and out through Gdańsk.

Go through the door into the **Red Hall,** where the Gdańsk city council met in the summertime. (The lavish fireplace—with another pair of lions holding the coat of arms of Gdańsk—was just for show.) City council members would sit in the seats around the room, debating city policy. The shin-level paintings depict the earth; the exquisitely detailed inlaid wood just over the seats are animals; the paintings on the wall above represent the seven virtues the burghers meeting in this room should have; and the ceiling is all about theology. Examine that ceiling. It has 25 paintings in total, with both Christian and pagan themes— meant to inspire the decision-makers in this room to make good choices. The smaller ones around the edges are scenes from mythology and the Bible. The one in the middle (from 1607) shows God's relationship to Gdańsk. In the foreground, the cit- izens of Gdańsk go about their daily lives. Above them, high atop the arch, God's hand reaches down (from within clouds of Hebrew characters) and grasps the city's steeple. The rainbow arching above also symbolizes God's connection to Gdańsk. Mirroring that is the Vistula River, which begins in the moun- tains of southern Poland (on the right), runs through the country, and exits at the sea in Gdańsk (on the left, where the rainbow ends).

Continue into the not-so-impressive Winter Hall, with another fireplace and coat of arms held by lions. Keep going through the next room, into a room with before-and-after photos of **WWII damage.** At the foot of the destroyed crucifix is a book with a bullet hole in it. The twist of wood is all that's left of the main support for the spiral staircase (today reconstructed in the room where you entered). Ponder the inspiring ability of a city to be reborn after the tragedy of war.

Upstairs are some temporary exhibits and several examples of **Gdańsk-style furniture.** These pieces are characterized by three big, round feet along the front, lots of ornamentation, and usu- ally a virtually impossible-to-find lock (sometimes hidden behind a movable decoration). You can also see a coin collection, from the days when Gdańsk had the elite privilege of minting its own currency.

▲▲Artus Court (Dwór Artusa)

In the Middle Ages, Gdańsk was home to many brotherhoods and guilds (like businessmen's clubs). For their meetings, the city pro- vided this elaborately decorated hall, named for King Arthur—a medieval symbol for prestige and power. Just as in King Arthur's Court, this was a place where powerful and important people came together. Such halls were once common in Baltic Europe, but this is the only original one that survives (dry and too-thorough audioguide-5 zł; in tall, white, triple-arched building behind Neptune statue at Długi targ 43-44).

In the grand hall, various **cupboards** line the walls. Each organization that met here had a place to keep its important documents and office supplies. Suspended from the ceiling are seven giant **model ships** that depict Baltic vessels, symbolic of the city's connection to the sea.

In the far-back corner is the museum's highlight: a gigantic **stove** decorated with 520 colorful tiles featuring the faces of kings, queens, nobles, mayors, and burghers. Half of these people were Protestant, and half were Catholic, mixed together in no particular order—a reminder of Gdańsk's religious tolerance. Virtually all the tiles are original, having survived WWII bombs. But not all of the original tiles are here: Three of them were recently discovered by a bargain-hunter wandering through a flea market in the southern part of the country, who returned them to their rightful home.

Notice the huge **paintings** on the walls above, with 3-D animals emerging from flat frames. Hunting is a popular theme in local artwork. Like minting coins, hunting was a privilege usually reserved for royalty, but extended in special circumstances to the burghers of special towns...like Gdańsk. If you look closely, it's obvious that these "paintings" are new, digitally generated reproductions of the originals, which were damaged in World War II.

The next room—actually in the next-door building—is a typical front room of the burghers' homes lining ulica Długa. Ogle the gorgeously carved wooden staircase. Upstairs (through the door to the right of the stairs) is a hall of knights—once again evoking Arthurian legend. If you've rented an audioguide, take it back up front to return it; otherwise, exit through the back, just down the street from St. Mary's Church; to get back to the main drag, go back around the block, to the left.

Other Museums and Churches in the Main Town
▲▲St. Mary's Church (Kościół Mariacki)
Gdańsk has so many striking red-brick churches, it's hard to keep track of them. But if you visit only one, make it St. Mary's. This is the biggest brick church in the world—with a footprint bigger than a football field (350 feet long and 210 feet wide), it can accommodate up to 25,000 standing worshippers. Built over 159 years in the 14th and 15th centuries, the church is an important symbol of Gdańsk.

Cost and Hours: 4 zł, June-Sept Mon-Sat 9:00-18:30, Sun 13:00-18:30, closes progressively earlier off-season, tel. 58-301-3982, www.bazylikamariacka.pl.

Visiting the Church: As you enter the church, notice all the white, empty space—unusual in a Catholic country, where frilly Baroque churches are the norm. In the Middle Ages, Gdańsk's tolerance attracted people who were suffering religious persecution. As the Protestant population grew, they needed a place to worship. St. Mary's, like most other Gdańsk churches, eventually became Protestant—leaving these churches with the blank walls you see now. Today you'll find only one Baroque church in central Gdańsk (the domed pink-and-green chapel behind St. Mary's).

Most Gothic stone churches are built in the basilica style—with a high nave in the middle, shorter aisles on the side, and flying buttresses to support the weight. (Think of Paris' Notre-Dame.) But that design doesn't work with brick. So, like all Gdańsk churches, St. Mary's is a "hall church"—with three naves the same height, and no exterior buttresses.

Also like other Gdańsk churches, St. Mary's gave refuge to the Polish people after the communist government declared martial law in 1981. When a riot broke out and violence seemed imminent, people would flood into churches for protection. The ZOMO riot police wouldn't follow them inside.

Most of the church decorations are original. A few days before World War II broke out in Gdańsk, locals hid precious items in the countryside. Take some time now to see a few of the highlights.

Head up the right nave and find the opulent family marker to the right of the main altar, high on the pillar. Look for the falling baby (under the crown). This is Constantine Ferber. As a precocious child, Constantine leaned out his window on ulica Długa to see the king's processional come through town. He slipped and fell, but landed in a salesman's barrel of fish. Constantine grew up to become the mayor of Gdańsk.

Look on the side of the same pillar for a coat of arms with three pigs' heads. It relates to another member of the illustrious Ferber clan. An enemy army that was laying siege to the town tried to starve its people out. A clever Ferber decided to load the cannons with pigs' heads to show the enemy that they had plenty of food—it worked, and the enemy left.

Circle around, past the front of the beautifully carved main altar. Behind it is the biggest stained-glass window in Poland. Below the window (behind the main altar) is a huge, empty glass case. The case was designed to hold Hans Memling's *Last Judgment* painting, which used to be on display here, but is currently being held hostage by the National Museum. To counter the museum's claim that the church wasn't a good environment for such a precious work, the priest had this display case built—but that still wasn't enough to convince the museum to give the painting back. You can see a smaller replica up by the main door of the church (in the little chapel on the right just before you exit), but true art fans will want to venture to the National Museum (described later) to see the much larger and masterful original.

Before you head back out to the mini-Memling (and the exit), venture to the far side of the altar and check out the elaborate **astronomical clock**—supposedly the biggest wooden clock in the world. Below is the circular calendar showing the saint's day, and above are zodiac signs and the time (only one hand).

Tower Climb: If you've got the energy, climb the 408 steps up the church's 270-foot-tall tower. You'll be rewarded with sweeping views of the entire city (tower climb-5 zł; July-Aug Mon-Sat 9:00-18:00, Sun 13:00-18:00; April-June and Sept-Oct Mon-Sat 9:00-17:00, Sun 13:00-17:00; closed Nov-March; entrance in back corner).

Historical Zone of the Free City of Gdańsk (Strefa Historyczna Wolne Miasto Gdańsk)

In a city so obsessed with its Golden Age and Solidarity history, this charming little collection illuminates a unique but often-overlooked chapter in the story of Gdańsk: The years between World Wars I and II, when—in an effort to find a workable compromise in this ethnically mixed city—Gdańsk was not part of Germany nor of Poland, but a self-governing "free city" *(wolne miasto)*. Like a holdover from medieval fiefdoms in modern times, the city-state of Gdańsk even issued its own currency and stamps. This modest museum earnestly shows off artifacts from the time—photos, stamps, maps, flags, promotional tourist leaflets, and other items from the free city, all marked with the Gdańsk symbol of two white crosses under a crown on a red shield. The brochure explains that four out of five people living in the free city identified themselves not as German or Poles, but as "Danzigers." While some might find the subject obscure, this endearing collection is a treat for WWII history buffs.

Cost and Hours: 5 zł, May-Nov Tue-Sun 11:00-18:00, Dec-April Tue-Sun 13:00-17:00, closed Mon year-round, a few steps in front of St. Mary's at ulica Piwna 19-21, tel. 58-320-2828, www .tpg.info.pl.

Archaeological Museum (Muzeum Archeologiczne)

This simple museum is worth a quick peek for those interested in archaeology. The ground floor has exhibits on excavated finds from Sudan, where the museum has a branch program. Upstairs, look for the distinctive urns with cute faces, which date from the Hallstatt Period and were discovered in slate graves around Gdańsk. Also upstairs are some Bronze and Iron Age tools; before-and-after photos of WWII Gdańsk; and a reconstructed 12th-century Viking-like Slavonic longboat. You can also climb the building's tower, with good views up Mariacka street toward St. Mary's Church.

Cost and Hours: Museum-8 zł (free on Sat), tower-5 zł; open July-Aug Tue-Fri 9:00-17:00, Sat-Sun 10:00-17:00, closed Mon; Sept-June Tue and Thu-Fri 8:00-16:00, Wed 9:00-17:00, Sat-Sun 10:00-16:00, closed Mon; ulica Mariacka 25-26, tel. 58-322-2100, www.archeologia.pl.

▲Central Maritime Museum (Centralne Muzeum Morskie)

Gdańsk's history and livelihood are tied to the sea. This collection, spread among several buildings on either side of the river, examines all aspects of this connection. While nautical types may get a thrill out of the creaky, sprawling museum, most visitors find it little more than a convenient way to pass some time and enjoy a cruise across the river. The museum's lack of English information is frustrating; fortunately, some exhibits have descriptions you can borrow.

Cost and Hours: Each part of the museum has its own admission (5-8 zł); a ticket for the whole shebang (including the ferry across the river) costs 28 zł. If you skip the Maritime Cultural Center, a ticket to everything *else* is just 18 zł. It's open July-Aug daily 10:00-18:00; Sept-Oct and March-June Tue-Sun 10:00-16:00, closed Mon; Nov-Feb Tue-Sun 10:00-15:00, closed Mon; ulica Ołowianka 9-13, tel. 58-301-8611, www.cmm.pl.

Visiting the Museum: The exhibit has four parts. The first two parts—the Crane and Maritime Cultural Center—are on the Main Town side of the river. The landmark medieval **Crane** (Żuraw), Gdańsk's most important symbol, houses an exhibit on living in the city during its Golden Age (16th-17th centuries). You can see models of Baltic buildings (including the Crane you're inside), plus traditional tools and costumes.

The **Maritime Cultural Center,** right next door to the Crane, is a beautiful facility with sparse exhibits. For adults, the most interesting areas are on the third floor ("Working Boats," with examples of vessels from around the world and English explanations) and the fourth floor (temporary exhibits). The second floor has a lively, kid-oriented interactive exhibition called "People-Ships-Ports," with lots of hands-on activities to get youngsters excited about seafaring. Tickets covering the interactive exhibit cost extra, and you can only enter that area at the top of each hour; it's not worth the expense or hassle for adults traveling without kids.

The rest of the museum—the Old Granaries and the *Sołdek* steamship—is across the river on Ołowianka Island, which you can reach via the little **ferry** (*prom*, 1 zł one-way, included in 28-zł museum ticket). The ferry runs about every 15 minutes in peak season (during museum hours only), but frequency declines sharply in the off-season (and it doesn't run if the river freezes). This also gives fine views back on the Crane.

Once on the island, visit the three rebuilt **Old Granaries** (Spichlerze). These make up the heart of the exhibit, tracing the history of Gdańsk—particularly as it relates to the sea—from

prehistoric days to the present. Models of the town and region help put things into perspective. Other exhibits cover underwater exploration, navigational aids, artifacts of the Polish seafaring tradition, peek-a-boo cross-sections of multilevel ships, and models of the modern-day shipyard where Solidarity was born. This place is home to more miniature ships than you ever thought you'd see, and the Nautical Gallery upstairs features endless rooms with paintings of boats.

Finally, crawl through the holds and scramble across the deck of a decommissioned steamship docked permanently across from the Crane, called the *Sołdek* (ship generally closed in winter). This was the first postwar vessel built at the Gdańsk shipyard. Below decks, you can see where they shoveled the coal; wander through a maze of pipes, gears, valves, gauges, and ladders; and visit the rooms where the sailors lived, slept, and ate. You can even play captain in the bridge.

▲▲▲Solidarity (Solidarność) and the Gdańsk Shipyard (Stocznia Gdańska)

Gdańsk's single best experience is exploring the shipyard that witnessed the beginning of the end of communism's stranglehold on Eastern Europe. Here in the former industrial wasteland that Lech Wałęsa called the "cradle of freedom," this evocative site tells the story of the brave Polish shipyard workers who took on—and ultimately defeated—an Evil Empire.

A visit to the Solidarity sights has two main parts: the memorial and gate out in front of the shipyard, and the excellent "Roads to Freedom" exhibit nearby. Begin at the towering monument—

with three anchor-adorned crosses—near the entrance gate to the shipyard, and allow two hours for the whole visit.

Getting to the Shipyard: The Solidarity monument and shipyard are at the north end of the Old Town, about a 20-minute walk from ulica Długa.

Background: After the communists took over Eastern Europe at the end of World War II, oppressed peoples throughout the Soviet Bloc rose up in different ways. The most dramatic uprisings—Hungary's 1956 Uprising and Czechoslovakia's 1968 "Prague Spring"—were brutally crushed under the treads of Soviet tanks. The formula for freedom that finally succeeded was a patient, decade-long series of strikes spearheaded by Lech Wałęsa and his trade union, called Solidarność—"Solidarity." (The movement also benefited from good timing, as it coincided with the *perestroika* and *glasnost* policies of the Soviet premier Mikhail Gorbachev.) While some American politicians might like to take credit for defeating communism, Wałęsa and his fellow workers were the ones fighting on the front lines, armed with nothing more than guts.

Monument of the Fallen Shipyard Workers

The seeds of August 1980 were sown a decade before. Since becoming part of the Soviet Bloc, the Poles staged frequent strikes, protests, and uprisings to secure their rights, all of which were put down by the regime. But the bloodiest of these took place in December of 1970—a tragic event memorialized by this monument.

The 1970 strike was prompted by price hikes. The communist government set the prices for all products. As Poland endured drastic food shortages in the 1960s and 1970s, the regime frequently announced what it called "regulation of prices." Invariably, this meant an increase in the cost of essential foodstuffs. (To be able to claim "regulation" rather than "increase," the regime would symbolically lower prices for a few select items—but these were always nonessential luxuries, such as elevators and TV sets, which nobody could afford anyway.) The regime was usually smart enough to raise prices on January 1—when the people were fat and happy after Christmas, and too hungover to complain. But on December 12, 1970, bolstered by an ego-stoking visit by West German Chancellor Willy Brandt, Polish premier Władysław Gomułka increased prices. The people of Poland—who cared more about the price of Christmas dinner than relations

Lech Wałęsa

In 1980, the world was turned on its ear by a walrus-mustachioed shipyard electrician. Within three years, this seemingly run-of-the-mill Pole had precipitated the collapse of communism, led a massive 10-million-member trade union with enormous political impact, been named *Time* magazine's Man of the Year, and won a Nobel Peace Prize.

Lech Wałęsa was born in Popowo, Poland, in 1943. After working as a car mechanic and serving two years in the army, he became an electrician at the Gdańsk Shipyard in 1967. Like many Poles, Wałęsa felt stifled by the communist government, and was infuriated that a system that was supposed to be for the workers clearly wasn't serving them.

When the shipyard massacre took place in December of 1970 (see description on page 207), Wałęsa was at the forefront of the protests. He was marked as a dissident, and in 1976, he was fired. Wałęsa hopped from job to job and was occasionally unemployed—under communism, a rock-bottom status reserved for only the most despicable derelicts. But he soldiered on, fighting for the creation of a trade union and building up quite a file with the secret police.

In August of 1980, Wałęsa heard news of the beginnings of the Gdańsk strike and raced to the shipyard. In an act that has since become the stuff of legend, Wałęsa scaled the shipyard wall to get inside.

Before long, Wałęsa's dynamic personality won him the unofficial role of the workers' leader and spokesman. He negotiated with the regime to hash out the August Agreements, becoming a rock star-type hero during the so-called 16 Months of Hope...until martial law came crashing down in December of 1981. Wałęsa was arrested and interned for 11 months in a coun-

with Germany—struck back.

A wave of strikes and sit-ins spread along the heavily industrialized north coast of Poland, most notably in Gdańsk, Gdynia, and Szczecin. Thousands of angry demonstrators poured through the gate of this shipyard, marched into town, and set fire to the Communist Party Committee building. In an attempt to quell the riots, the government-run radio implored the people to go back to work. On the morning of December 17, workers showed up at shipyard gates across northern Poland—and were greeted by the army and police. Without provocation, the Polish army opened fire on the workers. While the official death toll for the massa-

try house. After being released, he continued to struggle underground, becoming a symbol of anti-communist sentiment.

Finally, the dedication of Wałęsa and Solidarity paid off, and Polish communism dissolved—with Wałęsa rising from the ashes as the country's first post-communist president. But the skills that made Wałęsa a rousing success at leading an uprising didn't translate to the president's office. Wałęsa proved to be a stubborn, headstrong politician, frequently clashing with the parliament. He squabbled with his own party, declaring a "war at the top" of Solidarity and rotating higher-ups to prevent corruption and keep the party fresh. He also didn't choose his advisors well, enlisting several staffers who wound up immersed in scandal. His overconfidence was his Achilles' heel, and his governing style verged on authoritarian.

Unrefined and none too interested in scripted speeches, Wałęsa was a simple man who preferred playing Ping-Pong with his buddies to attending formal state functions. Though lacking a formal education, Wałęsa had unsurpassed drive and charisma... but that's not enough to lead a country—especially during an impossibly complicated, fast-changing time, when even the savviest politician would certainly have stumbled.

Wałęsa was defeated at the polls, by the Poles, in 1995, and when he ran again in 2000, he received a humiliating 1 percent of the vote. Since leaving office, Wałęsa has kept a lower profile, but still delivers speeches worldwide. Many poor Poles grumble that Lech, who started life simple like them, has forgotten the little people. But his fans point out that he gives much of his income to charity. And on his lapel, he still always wears a pin featuring the Black Madonna of Częstochowa—the symbol of Polish Catholicism.

Poles say there are at least two Lech Wałęsas: the young, working-class idealist Lech, at the forefront of the Solidarity strikes, who will always have a special place in their hearts; and the failed President Wałęsa, who got in over his head and tarnished his legacy.

cre stands at 44, others say the true number is much higher. This monument, with a trio of 140-foot-tall crosses, honors those lost to the regime that December.

Go to the middle of the wall behind the crosses, to the monument of the worker wearing a flimsy plastic work helmet, attempting to shield himself from bullets. Behind him is a list—pockmarked with symbolic bullet holes—of workers murdered on that day. *Lat* means "years old"—many teenagers were among the dead. The quote at the top of the wall is from Pope John Paul II, who was elected eight years after this tragedy. The Pope was known for his clever way with words, and this very carefully phrased quote—which served as an inspiration to the Poles during their darkest hours—skewers the regime in a way subtle enough to still be tolerated: "Let thy spirit descend, and renew the face of the earth—*this* earth" (that is, Poland). Below that is the dedication: "They gave their lives so you can live decently."

Stretching to the left of this center wall are plaques representing labor unions from around Poland—and around the world (look for the Chinese characters)—expressing solidarity with these workers. To the right is an enormous Bible verse: "May the Lord give strength to his people. May the Lord bless his people with the gift of peace" (Psalms 29:11).

More than a decade after the massacre, this monument was finally constructed. It marked the first time a communist regime ever allowed a monument to be built to honor its own victims. Wałęsa called it a harpoon in the heart of the communists. Inspired by the brave sacrifice of their true comrades, the shipyard workers rose up here in August of 1980, formulating the "21 Points" of a new union called Solidarity. The demands included the right to strike and form unions, the freeing of political prisoners, and an increase in wages. These 21 Points are listed in Polish on the panel at the far end of the right wall, marked *21 X TAK Solidarność* ("21 times yes Solidarity").

• *Now continue to the gate and peer through into the birthplace of Eastern European freedom.*

Gdańsk Shipyard (Stocznia Gdańska) Gate #2

When a Pole named Karol Wojtyła was elected Pope in 1978—and visited his homeland in 1979—he inspired his 40 million countrymen to believe that impossible dreams can come true. Prices continued to go up, and the workers continued to rise up. By the summer of 1980, it was clear that the dam was about to break.

In August, Anna Walentynowicz—a Gdańsk crane operator and known dissident—was fired unceremoniously just short of her retirement. This sparked a strike in the Gdańsk Shipyard (then called the Lenin Shipyard) on August 14, 1980. An electrician named Lech Wałęsa had been fired as an agitator years before and wasn't allowed into the yard. But on hearing news of the strike, Wałęsa went to the shipyard and climbed over the wall to get inside. The strike now had a leader.

Imagine being one of the 16,000 workers who stayed here for 18 days during the strike—hungry, cold, sleeping on sheets of

Styrofoam, inspired by the new Polish pope, excited about finally standing up to the regime...and terrified that at any moment you might be gunned down, like your friends had been a decade before. Workers, afraid to leave the shipyard, communicated with the outside world through this gate—wives and brothers showed up here and asked for a loved one, and those inside spread the word until the striker came forward. Occasionally, a truck pulled up inside the gate, with Lech Wałęsa standing atop its cab with a megaphone. Facing the thousands of people assembled outside the gate, Wałęsa gave progress reports on the negotiations and pleaded for supplies. The people of Gdańsk responded, bringing armfuls of bread and other food to keep the workers going. This truly was Solidarity.

During the strike, two items hung on the fence. One of them (which still hangs there today) was a picture of Pope John Paul II—a reminder to believe in your dreams and have faith in God. The other item was a makeshift list of the strikers' 21 Points—demands scrawled in red paint and black pencil on pieces of plywood.

• *You'll likely see construction in the area beyond the gate.*

Today's Shipyard

This part of the shipyard, long abandoned, is being redeveloped into a **"Young City"** (Młode Miasto)—envisioned as a new city center for Gdańsk, with shopping, restaurants, offices, and homes. Rusting shipbuilding equipment has been torn down, and old brick buildings are being converted into gentrified flats. Just behind the monument will be the new European Center of Solidarity (still an active union in some countries); the nearby boulevard called Nowa Wałowa will be the spine connecting this area to the rest of the city. Farther east, the harborfront will also be rejuvenated, creating a glitzy marina and extending the city's delightful waterfront people zone to the north. Fortunately, the shipyard gate, monument, and other important sites from the Solidarity strikes will stay put. Work in this area will likely be winding down in 2014 and 2015, while other parts of the development will continue for years to come. For more on this plan, see www.ycgdansk.com.

• *Walk to the right and go through the gate.*

The path leading into the shipyard passes through two huge **symbolic gateways.** The first resembles the rusted hull of a ship, representing the protest of the shipbuilders. The next gateway—a futuristic, colorful tower—is a small-scale contemporary reinterpretation of a 1,000-foot-tall monument planned in 1919 by the prominent Russian constructivist artist Vladimir Tatlin. Tatlin's unrealized design represented the optimism of the communist "utopia" before it was fatally perverted by totalitarianism.

The path leads to a low-profile, red-brick building—the **BHP Conference Hall,** where the communists sat down across the table from Lech Wałęsa and worked out a compromise. Today it houses an interesting exhibition called "There Is One Solidarity," celebrating the trade union that got its start right here (free, Tue-Sun 10:00-17:00, closed Mon, www.salabhp.pl). Less historical and impartial than the excellent "Roads to Freedom" museum (described next), this exhibition trumpets the accomplishments of the still-active Solidarity organization, which is straining to remain relevant in today's world.

Speaking of which, nearby you may notice the construction of a brand-new **headquarters for Solidarity,** which is planned to open in the summer of 2014. Eventually this will likely house the "Roads to Freedom" exhibit described next.

• *The museum where we'll learn the rest of the story is about 100 yards back toward the Main Town. With the main shipyard gate to your back, walk straight ahead, passing the green-and-yellow building on your right. Cross the street and walk toward the green skyscraper. After about a block, note the stairs leading underground, into the...*

"Roads to Freedom" Exhibit

This small but outstanding museum captures (better than any other sight in the country) the Polish reality under communism, and traces the step-by-step evolution of the Solidarity movement.

Cost and Hours: 6 zł, 2 zł on Wed; open May-Sept Tue-Sun 10:00-18:00, Oct-April Tue-Sun 10:00-17:00, closed Mon year-round; Wały Piastowskie 24, tel. 58-308-4428, museum: www.ecs.gda.pl, organization: www.fcs.org.pl.

Possible Move: When the new Solidarity headquarters inside the shipyard is completed, this exhibit will likely move there (late 2014 or early 2015). Confirm locally. If the exhibit does move, it's also possible that the details described below may change.

❍ Self-Guided Tour: Walk downstairs—startled by angry shouts from the ZOMO—and buy your ticket, which is designed to look like the communist ration coupons that all Poles had to carry and present before they could buy certain goods. Cashiers would stand with scissors at the ready, prepared to snip off a corner of your coupon after making the sale. Consider picking up a Solidarity book or other souvenir at the excellent gift shop here before moving on.

To the right of the ticket desk are some depressing reminders of the communist days. The phone booth is marked *Automat Nieczynny*—"Out of Order"—as virtually all phone booths were back then. In the humble, authentic commie WC, notice that instead of toilet paper, there's a wad of old newspapers. Actual toilet paper was cause for celebration. Notice the mannequin with several rolls on a string around her neck—time to party!

Across from the ticket desk is a typical **Polish shop** (marked *spożyw,* a truncated version of *spożywczy,* "grocery store") from the 1970s, at the worst of the food shortages. Great selection, eh? Often the only things in stock were vinegar and mustard. Milk and bread were generally available, but they were low quality— it wasn't unusual to find a cigarette butt in your loaf. The few blocks of cheese and other items in the case weren't real—they were props, placed there so the shop wouldn't look completely empty. Sometimes they'd hang a few pitiful, phony salamis from the hooks—otherwise, people might think it was a tile shop. The only real meat in here were the flies on the flypaper. Despite the meager supplies, shoppers (mostly women) would sometimes have to wait in line literally all day long just to pick over these scant choices. People didn't necessarily buy what they needed; instead, they'd buy anything that could be bartered on the black market. On the counter, notice the little jar holding clipped-off ration coupons.

Continue into the exhibit. The first room explains the **roots** of the shipyard strikes, including the famous uprisings in Hungary and Czechoslovakia, and the December 1970 riots in Poland. (Interactive computer screens tell you more about these events.) The prison cell is a reminder of Stalin's strong-arm tactics for getting the people of Eastern Europe to sign on to his new system.

Then head into the heart of the exhibit, **August 1980.** Near the plaster statue of Lenin are several tables. These were the actual tables used (in the red-brick building back in the shipyard) when the communist authorities finally agreed to negotiate after 18 days of protests. On the afternoon of August 31, 1980, the Governmental Commission and the Inter-Factory Strike Committee (MKS) came together and signed the August Agreements, which legalized Solidarity—the first time any communist government permitted a workers' union. Photos and a video show the giddy day, as the Polish Bob Dylan laments the evils of the regime. Lech Wałęsa— sitting at the big table, with his characteristic walrus moustache— signed the agreement with a big, red, souvenir-type pen adorned with a picture of Pope John Paul II (displayed across the room). Other union reps, sitting at smaller tables, tape-recorded the proceedings, and played them later at their own factories to prove that the unthinkable had happened. Near the end of this room are replicas of the plywood boards featuring the 21 Points, which hung on the front gate we just saw.

While the government didn't take the agreements very seriously, the Poles did...and before long, 10 million of them—one out of every four—joined Solidarity. So began the **16 Months**

of Hope—the theme of the next room. Newly legal, Solidarity continued to stage strikes and make its opposition known. Slick Solidarity posters and children's art convey the childlike enthusiasm with which the Poles seized their hard-won kernels of freedom. The poster with a baby in a Solidarity T-shirt—one year old, just like the union itself—captures the sense of hope. The communist authorities' hold on the Polish people began to slip. The rest of the Soviet Bloc looked on nervously, and the Warsaw Pact army assembled at the Polish border and glared at the uprisers. The threat of invasion hung heavy in the air.

Turn the corner to see Solidarity's progress come crashing down. On Sunday morning, December 13, 1981, the Polish head of state, General Wojciech Jaruzelski, appeared on national TV and announced the introduction of **martial law.** Solidarity was outlawed, and its leaders were arrested. Frightened Poles heard the announcement and looked out their windows to see Polish Army tanks rumbling through the snowy streets. Jaruzelski claimed that he imposed martial law to prevent the Soviets from invading. Today, many historians question whether martial law was really necessary—though Jaruzelski remains unremorseful. Martial law was a tragic, terrifying, and bleak time for the Polish people. It didn't, however, kill the Solidarity movement, which continued its fight after going underground. Notice that the movement's martial-law-era propaganda was produced with far more primitive printing equipment than their earlier posters.

In the next room, you see a clandestine print shop like those used to create that illegal propaganda. Surrounding the room are sobering displays of **ZOMO riot gear.** A film reveals the ugliness of martial law. Watch the footage of General Jaruzelski—wearing his trademark dark glasses—reading the announcement of martial law. Chilling scenes show riots, demonstrations, and crackdowns by the ZOMO police—including one in which a demonstrator is run over by a truck. An old woman is stampeded by a pack of fleeing demonstrators.

The next room shows a film tracing the whole history of **communism in Poland** (with a copy of Lech Wałęsa's Nobel Peace Prize).

For a happy ending, head into the final room, with an uplifting film about the **fall of the Iron Curtain** across Eastern Europe—right up through the 2004 "Orange Revolution" in Ukraine.

Here's how it happened in Poland: By the time the Pope visited his homeland again in 1983, martial law had finally been lifted, and Solidarity—still technically illegal—was gaining momentum, gradually pecking away at the communists. With the moral support of the Pope and the entire Western world, the brave Poles were the first European country to throw off the shackles of communism when, in the spring of 1989, the "Round Table Talks" led to the opening up of elections. The government arrogantly called for parliamentary elections, reserving 65 percent of seats for themselves. The plan backfired, as virtually every open seat went to Solidarity. This success inspired people all over Eastern Europe, and by that winter, the Berlin Wall had crumbled and the Czechs and Slovaks had staged their Velvet Revolution. Lech Wałęsa—the shipyard electrician who started it all by jumping over a wall—became the first president of post-communist Poland. And a year later, in Poland's first true elections since World War II, 29 different parties won seats in the parliament. This celebration of democracy was brought to the Polish people by the workers of Gdańsk.

North of the Main Town
World War II Museum
As if to emphasize its pivotal role in 20th-century history, Gdańsk is building this large, state-of-the-art museum just east of the Solidarity shipyard, along the river. When open, it promises high-tech interactive exhibits about Gdańsk's experience during the war that began on its doorstep. It's likely to open in 2014 or 2015; ask the TI for the latest details (or check www.muzeum1939.pl).

South of the Main Town
A 10- to 15-minute walk south of the Main Town, these two sights are probably not worth the trek on a short visit.

National Museum in Gdańsk
(Muzeum Narodowe w Gdańsku)
This art collection, housed in what was a 15th-century Franciscan monastery, is worth ▲▲ to art lovers for one reason: Hans Memling's glorious *Last Judgment* triptych altarpiece, one of the two most important pieces of art to be seen in Poland (the other is da Vinci's *Lady with an Ermine,* usually in Kraków's Czartoryski Museum). If you're not a purist, you can settle for seeing the much smaller replica in St. Mary's Church. But if medieval art is your bag, make the 10-minute walk here from the Main Town.

Cost and Hours: 10 zł; June-Aug Tue-Wed and Fri-Sun 10:00-17:00, Thu 12:00-19:00; May and Sept Tue-Sun 10:00-17:00; Oct-April Tue-Fri 9:00-16:00, Sat-Sun 10:00-17:00, closed Mon year-round; last entry 45 minutes before closing; walk 10 minutes due south from ulica Długa's Golden Gate, take pedestrian underpass beneath the big cross-street, then continue down the busy street until you see signs for the museum; ulica Toruńska 1, tel. 58-301-7061, www.muzeum.narodowe.gda.pl.

Visiting the Museum: From the entry, the altarpiece by Hans Memling (c. 1440-1494) is at the top of the stairs and to the right.

The history of the painting is as interesting as the work itself. It was commissioned in the mid-15th century by the Medicis' banker in Florence, Angelo di Jacopo Tani. The ship delivering the painting from Belgium to Florence was hijacked by a Gdańsk pirate, who brought the altarpiece to his hometown to be displayed in St. Mary's Church. For centuries, kings, emperors, and czars admired it from afar, until Napoleon seized it in the early 19th century and took it to Paris to hang in the Louvre. Gdańsk finally got the painting back, only to have it exiled again—this time into St. Petersburg's Hermitage Museum—after World War II. On its return to Gdańsk in 1956, this museum claimed it—though St. Mary's wants it back.

Have a close look at Memling's well-traveled work. It's the end of the world, and Christ rides in on a rainbow to judge humankind. Angels blow reveille, waking the dead, who rise from their graves. The winged archangel Michael—dressed for battle and wielding the cross like a weapon—weighs the grace in each person, sending them either to the fires of hell (right panel) or up the sparkling-crystal stairway to heaven (left).

It takes all 70 square feet of paneling to contain this awesome scene. Jam-packed with dozens of bodies, a Bible's worth of symbolism, and executed with astonishing detail, the painting can keep even a non-art-lover occupied. Notice the serene, happy expressions of the righteous, as they're greeted by St. Peter (with his giant key) and clothed by angels. And pity the condemned, their faces filled with terror and sorrow as they're tortured by grotesque devils more horrifying than anything Hollywood could devise.

Tune into the exquisite details: the angels' robes, the devils' genetic-mutant features, the portrait of the man in the scale (a Medici banker), Michael's peacock wings. Get as close as you can to the globe at Christ's feet and Michael's shining breastplate: You can just make out the whole scene in mirror reflection. Then back up and take it all in—three panels connected by a necklace of bodies that curves downward through hell, crosses the earth, then rises up to the towers of the New Jerusalem. On the back side of the triptych are reverent portraits of the painting's patron, Angelo Tani, and his new bride, Catarina.

Beyond the Memling, the remainder of the collection isn't too thrilling. The rest of the upstairs has more Flemish and Dutch art, as well as paintings from Gdańsk's Golden Age and various works by Polish artists. The ground floor features a cavernous, all-white cloister filled with Gothic altarpiece sculptures, gold and silver wares, majolica and Delft porcelain, and characteristic Gdańsk-style furniture.

Gdańsk Shakespeare Theater (Teatr Szekspirowski)

Gdańsk has a long and proud tradition of staging plays by Shakespeare. As early as the 17th century, theater troupes from England were coming to this cosmopolitan trading city to perform. In 1993, local actors revived the tradition with an annual Gdańsk Shakespeare Festival that typically takes place the first week of August (www.shakespearefestival.pl). And now the city is building a top-quality venue to honor its connection to the Bard. The state-of-the-art Gdańsk Shakespeare Theater building, due to be completed in late 2014, is designed to mingle the classic lines of red-brick Gdańsk with modern flourishes. It can be modified to create three different theater spaces (proscenium, thrust stage, and theater in the round)—and even has a retractable roof to wash the actors with direct sunlight. In addition to Polish-language productions, they also expect to stage plays in English. Supported by everyone from Kenneth Branagh to Prince Charles, this theater will instantly become a point of pride for the city. The building is on ulica Zbytki—just follow Pcztowa street south from the middle of ulica Długa. For details, see www.teatrszekspirowski.pl.

"Blue Lion" Archaeological Education Center (Centrum Edukacji Archeologicznej "Błękitny Lew")

Hiding far from the Main Town on Granary Island, this kid-friendly exhibit re-creates the atmosphere of medieval Gdańsk. Occupying a rebuilt granary called the "Blue Lion," its highlight is a full-scale replica of an atmospheric medieval street, populated by mannequins whose features are based on actual human remains. Also telling the tale are artifacts from the period, a selection of films (subtitled in English), and touchscreens that provide some background. While information is a bit sparse (especially along the medieval street), the collection tries hard not to be just another fuddy-duddy, dusty old museum, making it popular with kids on field trips.

Cost and Hours: 10 zł, May-Aug Tue-Sun 10:00-18:00, Sept-April Tue-Sun 9:00-17:00, closed Mon year-round, ulica Chmielna 53, tel. 58-320-3188, www.archeologia.pl.

Outer Gdańsk

These two sights—worthwhile only to those with a special interest—are each within the city limits of Gdańsk, but they take some serious time to see round-trip.

Oliwa Cathedral (Katedra Oliwska)

The suburb of Oliwa, at the northern edge of Gdańsk, is home to this visually striking church. The quirky, elongated facade hides a surprisingly long and skinny nave. The ornately decorated 18th-century organ over the main entrance features angels and stars that move around when the organ is played. While locals are proud of this place, it's hard to justify the effort it takes to get out here. Skip it unless you just love Polish churches or you're going to a concert.

Concerts: The animated organ performs its 20-minute show frequently, especially in summer (concerts at the top of each hour: July-Aug Mon-Fri 10:00-13:00 & 15:00-17:00, Sat 10:00-15:00, Sun 15:00-17:00; June Mon-Sat 10:00-13:00 & 15:00-16:00, Sun 15:00-17:00; May and Sept Mon-Sat 10:00-13:00, Sun at 15:00 and 16:00; 1-2/day off-season, www.archikatedraoliwa.pl). Confirm the schedule at the TI before making the trip. Note that on Sundays and holidays, there are no concerts before 15:00.

Getting There: Oliwa is about six miles northwest of central Gdańsk, on the way to Sopot and Gdynia. To get to Oliwa, you have two options: Take **tram** #6 or #12 from Gdańsk's main train station. These trams let you off right at the entrance to Oliwski Park. Go straight through to the back of the park; near the end, you can see the copper roof and two skinny, pointy spires of the cathedral on your right. Exit through the back of the park, bear right, and go one block to find the entrance to the church. Your other option is to take a **commuter SKM train** from Gdańsk's main train station 15 minutes to the "Gdańsk Oliwa" stop. From the Oliwa train station, it's a 15-minute walk or 10-zł taxi ride to the cathedral. Walk straight ahead out of the station and turn right when you get to the busy road. Cross the road at the light and enter the tree-filled Park Oliwski at the corner, then follow the directions above.

Westerplatte

World War II began on September 1, 1939, when Adolf Hitler sent the warship *Schleswig-Holstein* to attack this Polish munitions depot, which was guarding Gdańsk's harbor. Though it may interest serious WWII history buffs, most visitors will find little to see here aside from a modest museum, a towering monument, and some old bunkers. As it's surrounded by shipyard sprawl, it's not a particularly scenic trip, either.

Getting There: The most enjoyable approach is on a cruise—either on a modern boat, or on the fun old-fashioned galleons (45-50 minutes each way). You can also take **bus** #106 from Brama Wyżynna (just outside the Main Town) to the end (about 30 minutes).

Shopping in Gdańsk

The big story in Gdańsk is amber *(bursztyn)*, a fossil resin available in all shades, shapes, and sizes (see the "All About Amber" sidebar, earlier). While you'll see amber sold all over town, the best place to browse and buy is along the atmospheric ulica Mariacka (between the Motława River and St. Mary's Church). This pretty street, with old-fashioned balconies and dozens of display cases, is fun to wander even if you're not a shopper. Other good places to buy amber are along the riverfront embankment and on ulica Długa. To avoid rip-offs—such as amber that's been melted and reshaped—always buy it from a shop, not from someone standing on the street. (But note that most shops also have a display case and salesperson out front, which are perfectly legit.) Prices everywhere are about the same, so rather than seeking out a specific place, just window-shop until you see what you want. Styles range from gaudy necklaces with huge globs of amber, to tasteful smaller pendants in silver settings, to cheap trinkets. All shades of amber—from near-white to dark brown—cost about the same, but you'll pay more for inclusions (bugs or other objects stuck in the amber).

Gdańsk also has several modern shopping malls, most of them in the Old Town or near the main train station. The walk between the Main Town and the Solidarity shipyard goes past some of the best malls.

Sleeping in Gdańsk

Gdańsk's accommodations scene is booming. New hotels open every year, forcing dreary old ones to up their standards and/or lower their rates. Even with all those new rooms, many hotels are booked up (mostly with German tourists) in peak season (mid-June-mid-Sept), when prices increase—book ahead.

Across the River

These hotels are across the river from the Main Town. While that puts you a bit farther from the sightseeing action, it's a relatively short walk (no more than 10 minutes from any of these), and the rooms are a better value.

$$$ Hotel Królewski, a classy hotel in a beautifully renovated red-brick granary, offers 30 stylish rooms, good rates, and a friendly staff. It's just beyond the three granaries of the Central Maritime Museum, across the river from the Crane (Sb-380 zł, Db-470 zł, fancier suite-like Db "plus"-520 zł, pricier apartments, lower rates mid-Oct-April, 50 zł to reserve a view room—or try asking for one when you check in for no extra charge, non-smoking rooms, elevator, free Wi-Fi, good restaurant, ulica Ołowianka 1, tel. 58-326-1111, www.hotelkrolewski.pl, office@hotelkrolewski .pl). You can commute to your sightseeing by ferry (take the 1-zł boat trip across the river offered by the Maritime Museum). But the ferry runs only during the museum's opening hours, and is sporadic off-season. If the ferry isn't running, it's a scenic 10-minute walk along the river and over the bridge into the Main Town.

Sleep Code

(3 zł = about $1, country code: 48)
S = Single, **D** = Double/Twin, **T** = Triple, **Q** = Quad, **b** = bathroom,
s = shower only. Unless otherwise noted, English is spoken,
credit cards are accepted, and breakfast is included.

To help you easily sort through these listings, I've divided the accommodations into three categories, based on the price for a double room with bath during high season:

$$$ Higher Priced—Most rooms 400 zł or more.
$$ Moderately Priced—Most rooms between 300-400 zł.
$ Lower Priced—Most rooms 300 zł or less.

Prices can change without notice; verify the hotel's current rates online or by email. For the best prices, always book direct.

$$$ Hotel Gdańsk is a splurge hotel over a brewpub. Also in a rehabbed granary across the river from the embankment, it's a bit closer to the Main Town than the Królewski. The 90 elegant rooms are divided between the old granary (with tiny windows and big beams) and a modern annex (Mon-Thu: Sb-490 zł, Db-590 zł, bigger "premium" Db-630 zł; Fri-Sun: Sb-460 zł, Db-560 zł, premium Db-590 zł; cheaper Nov-March, elevator, guest computer, Wi-Fi, sauna and spa, ulica Szafarina 9, tel. 58-300-1717, www.hotelgdansk.pl, rezerwacja@hotelgdansk.pl).

On Ulica Spichrzowa: Several small, similar, relatively new hotels are on the back side of a charmingly restored row of colorful houses on the island just across the river from the main drag. While they overlook a dreary vacant lot, these places (and others on the same street) offer a good value in a convenient location. As these buildings are tall and skinny, expect plenty of stairs and no elevator. **$$ Willa Litarion** is run by the eager Owsikowski family. Each of the 13 small rooms has a totally different design, but all are artsy and mod (Sb-255 zł, Db-330 zł, bigger "deluxe" Db-360 zł, 20-25 percent cheaper Oct-April, extra bed-60 zł, cable Internet, parking garage-30 zł, ulica Spichrzowa 18, tel. 58-320-2553, www.litarion.pl, recepcja@litarion.pl). **$$ Willa Biała Lilia** ("Villa of the White Lily"), next door, has 14 uninspired but modern and comfortable rooms (Sb-260 zł, Db-340 zł, extra bed-70 zł, slightly cheaper Oct-April, free Wi-Fi, reserve ahead for parking garage-30 zł, ulica Spichrzowa 16, tel. 58-301-7074, www.bialalilia.pl, bialalilia@bialalilia.pl).

$$ Dom Muzyka rents 87 simple, tidy rooms in a nondescript residential neighborhood. The catch: It's very difficult to find, hiding in the back of the big Academy of Music building (Akademia Muzyczna). But the prices are worth the hunt, and once you're set up, it's an easy 10-minute walk to the sights. Their "deluxe" rooms, mostly twins, are bigger and overlook the quiet courtyard; most of the standard rooms face a busy street but have good windows and air-conditioning (Sb-250 zł, standard Db-340 zł, deluxe Db-360 zł, apartment-500 zł, extra bed-100 zł, cheaper Oct-April, elevator, guest computer, Wi-Fi, popular with tour groups, good restaurant, ulica Łąkowa 1-2, tel. 58-326-0600, www.dommuzyka.pl, biuro@dommuzyka.pl). From the Main Town's Green Gate, cross the two bridges, then walk a long block along the modern commercial building and turn right just before the park (on Łąkowa, across from the big brick church). Walk to the end of this block; before the busy road, go through the gate just before the big yellow-brick building on the right. Once inside the gate checkpoint, the hotel is around the back of the yellow building, the farthest door down. If you get lost, just ask people, "Hotel?"

In the Main Town

You'll pay a premium to sleep in the Main Town itself, but many find it worth the extra expense.

$$ Hotel Wolne Miasto ("Free City") offers rich, wood-carved public spaces with photos of old Gdańsk and 67 elegant, well-priced rooms on the edge of the Main Town, just two blocks from the main drag. Since it's above a popular disco that gets noisy on weekends (Thu-Sat nights), request a quieter room when you reserve (Sb-350 zł, Db-400 zł, bigger "deluxe" Db-500 zł, cheaper Oct-March, air-con in some rooms, elevator, guest computer, Wi-Fi, ulica Świętego Ducha 2, tel. 58-322-2442, www.hotelwm .pl, rezerwacja@hotelwm.pl).

$$ Gotyk House, a good value, is run with warmth and pride by the Rybicki family. Owner Andrzej is an energetic armchair historian who works hard to make his little hotel comfortable while still respecting the sanctity of what's supposedly Gdańsk's oldest house. The chimes from St. Mary's Church, next door, provide a pleasant soundtrack. The cellar houses a gingerbread museum and small shrine to Copernicus (whose longtime lover may have lived here). The seven straightforward rooms share a tiny breakfast room, so you'll have to tell them what time you'd like to eat (Sb-280 zł, Db-310 zł, cheaper Oct-April, free Wi-Fi in most rooms, tight public spaces, ulica Mariacka 1, tel. 58-301-8567, mobile 516-141-133, www.gotykhouse.eu, reservation@gotykhouse.eu).

$$ Kamienica Goldwasser, renting seven rooms over a recommended restaurant, is perfectly located, right on the river embankment next door to the Crane. Each room is different, but all are thoughtfully decorated, with windows facing both the river and the back. Three smaller rooms—similar to the bigger rooms, but with tight bathrooms, are an especially good value (small Sb-240 zł, big Sb-340 zł, small Db-340 zł, big Db-440 zł, extra bed-100 zł, lots of stairs and no elevator, free Wi-Fi, Długie Pobrzeże 22, tel. 58-301-8878, www.goldwasser.pl, kamienica @goldwasser.pl).

$ Dom Harcerza is a Polish-style budget hotel/hostel with 21 old, musty, but well-maintained rooms on the second floor of a dreary office building. This institutional-feeling place won't win any prizes for personality, and communication can be difficult, but it's cheap and nicely located in a corner of the Main Town just two blocks south of the Golden Gate (S-60 zł, D-120 zł, Db-200 zł, T-150 zł, Tb-252 zł, Q-160 zł, 25 percent cheaper Oct-April, includes sheets, breakfast-9 zł, cash only, all twin beds, ground-floor café, ulica Za Murami 2-10, tel. 58-301-3621, www.dom harcerza.pl, rezerwacje@domharcerza.pl).

$ Przy Targu Rybnym, a three-minute walk from the Crane at the north end of the embankment, is Gdańsk's most central hostel. Waldemar runs this easygoing, low-key, slightly grungy place with a spirit of fun that permeates the chummy common room. Aside from dorm beds, it offers private rooms for two to four people, most with shared bathrooms down the hall (bunk in dorm or crowded basement slumbermill-55 zł, D-200 zł, Db-250 zł, T-240 zł, Q-280 zł, cheaper Sept-April, prices include sheets and breakfast, guest computer, 20-zł laundry service, ulica Grodzka 21, tel. 58-301-5627, www.gdanskhostel.com.pl, gdanskhostel@hotmail .com).

Eating in Gdańsk

In addition to traditional Polish fare, Gdańsk has some fine Baltic seafood. Herring *(śledź)* is popular here, as is cod *(dorsz)*. Natives brag that their salmon *(łosoś)* is better than Norway's. For a stiff drink, sample *Goldwasser* (similar to Goldschlager). This sweet and strong liqueur, flecked with gold, was supposedly invented here in Gdańsk. The following options are all in the Main Town, within three blocks of ulica Długa.

Budget Restaurants in the City Center

These two places are remarkably cheap, tasty, quick, and wonderfully convenient—on or very near ulica Długa. They're worth considering even if you're not on a tight budget.

Bar pod Rybą ("Under the Fish") is nirvana for fans of baked potatoes *(pieczony ziemniak)*. They offer more than 20 varieties, piled high with a wide variety of toppings and sauces, from

Mexican beef to herring to Polish cheeses. They also serve fish dishes with salad and potatoes, making this a cheap place to sample local seafood. The tasteful decor—walls lined with old bottles, antique wooden hangers, and paintings by the owner—is squeezed into a single cozy room packed with happy eaters. In the summer, order inside, and they'll bring your food to you at an outdoor table (potatoes and fish dishes are each about 15-25 zł, daily 10:00-22:00, ulica Piwna 61/63, tel. 58-305-1307).

Bar Mleczny Neptun is your best milk-bar option in the Main Town. A hearty meal, including a drink, runs about 15-20 zł. This popular place has more charm than your typical institutional milk bar, including outdoor seating along the most scenic stretch of the main drag, and an upstairs dining room overlooking it all. Most of the items on the counter are for display—rather than take what's there, point to what you want and they'll dish it up fresh (Mon-Fri 7:30-18:00, until 20:00 in summer, Sat-Sun 10:00-17:00, free Wi-Fi, ulica Długa 33-34, tel. 58-301-4988).

On the Riverfront Embankment

Perhaps the most appealing dining zone in Gdańsk stretches along the riverfront embankment near the Crane. On a balmy summer evening, the outdoor tables here are enticing. As it's a popular area, consider scouting a table during your sightseeing, and reserve your choice for dinner later that night. While you have several good options along here, the following are particularly well-regarded.

Kamienica Goldwasser, which also rents rooms, offers high-quality Polish and international cuisine at fair prices. Choose between cozy, romantic indoor seating on several levels, or scenic outdoor seating (most main dishes 40-75 zł, daily 10:00-24:00, occasional live music, Długie Pobrzeże 22, tel. 58-301-8878).

Baryłka ("Barrel"), next door to Goldwasser, has a similar menu and outdoor seating. The elegant upstairs dining room, with windows overlooking the river, is appealing (40-65-zł main dishes, daily 9:00-24:00, Długie Pobrzeże 24, tel. 58-301-4938).

Sushi 77, serving up a wide selection of surprisingly good sushi right next to the Crane, is a refreshing break from ye olde Polish food. Choose between the outdoor tables bathed in red light, or the mod interior (30-50-zł sushi sets, daily 12:00-23:00, Długie Pobrzeże 30, tel. 58-682-1823).

Targ Rybny/Fishmarkt ("The Fish Market")—run by the

Goldwasser people—is farther up the embankment, overlooking a park and parking lot. The outdoor seating isn't too scenic, but the warm, mellow-yellow nautical ambience inside is pleasant, making this a good bad-weather option. It features classy but not stuffy service, and an emphasis on fish (most main dishes 30-50 zł, plus pricier seafood splurges, daily 10:00-23:00, ulica Targ Rybny 6C, tel. 58-320-9011).

Other Restaurants in Central Gdańsk

Czerwone Drzwi ("The Red Door") serves up tasty Polish and international cuisine in a single-room, six-table restaurant. The decor is artsy, and there's live piano music nightly at 19:00; at other times, recorded jazz sets the mood (22-28-zł pierogi, big 20-25-zł salads, 30-45-zł main dishes, daily 10:00-22:00, ulica Piwna 52/53, tel. 58-301-5764).

Dom pod Łososiem ("House Under the Salmon") is a venerable old standby with over-the-top formality. This place will make you feel like a rich burgher's family invited you over for dinner (right down to the greeting by a stiff, bow-tied maître d'). This elegant splurge restaurant has been serving guests for more than 400 years, racking up an impressive guest list (some pictured in the lobby)—and, somewhere in there, inventing *Goldwasser*. Reservations are smart for dinner (most main dishes 50-80 zł, emphasis on fish, small portions, daily 12:00-23:00, ulica Szeroka 52-54, tel. 58-301-7652).

Coffee and Sweets

Gdańsk's Main Town is full of hip cafés that lure in young people with long menus of exotic coffee drinks and tasty cakes. Here are two good options—one new, one old.

Pikawa (as in "3.14 Coffee," pronounced "pee-kah-vah") is a trendy, atmospheric café with a wide variety of coffee drinks and herbal teas, best accompanied by the delicious *szarlotka* (Polish apple cake). The decor is cozy Old World, the outdoor seating is pleasant, and the café is packed with socializing locals (8-16-zł cakes, daily 10:00-22:00, until 24:00 in summer, ulica Piwna 5-6, tel. 58-309-1444).

Cukiernia Kaliszczak, a bakery right on ulica Długa, is a no-frills throwback to the communist days. It's cheap but not cheery, with delicious 3-zł cakes and ice cream and no-nonsense service—just line up and place your order, comrade. If you want ice cream, order first at the register rather than at the display case (daily 9:00-22:00, ulica Długa 74, tel. 58-301-0895).

Gdańsk Connections

By Train

Gdańsk is well-connected to the Tri-City via the commuter SKM trains (explained later, under "Getting Around the Tri-City"). It also has frequent connections to Warsaw and handy night trains to Berlin and Kraków.

From Gdańsk by Train to: Hel (town on Hel Peninsula, 3/day direct July-Aug only, 2.25-3.25 hours; otherwise about hourly with transfer in Gdynia), **Malbork** (about 2/hour, 40-50 minutes), **Toruń** (6/day direct, 3.25-3.75 hours; at least hourly with a transfer in Bydgoszcz, 3-4 hours), **Warsaw** (9/day, 5-6 hours—but will drop to 3 hours when new line is finished), **Kraków** (4/day direct, 2 more with change in Warsaw, 8.5 hours—shorter when new rail line is complete; plus 2 night trains, 10.5-11.5 hours), **Berlin** (4/day, 7-7.5 hours, transfer in Szczecin or Poznań).

By Boat

Various boats depart from Gdańsk's embankment to nearby destinations, including **Westerplatte** (the monument marking where World War II started) and **Hel** (the beachy peninsula, described below). While boats also run sporadically to Sopot and Gdynia, the train is better for those trips (described under "Getting Around the Tri-City," later). As these boat schedules tend to change from year to year, confirm your plans carefully at the TI. All boat trips are weather permitting, especially the faster hydrofoils. In shoulder season (April-June and Sept-Oct), even though most boats stop running from Gdańsk, several routes still run between Sopot, Gdynia, and Hel. Boats generally don't run in winter (Nov-March).

To Westerplatte: To travel by boat to the monument at Westerplatte, you have two options. It's more enjoyable to ride

the replica **17th-century galleons,** either the *Galeon Lew* ("Lion Galleon") or the *Czerna Perła* ("Black Pearl"). These over-the-top, touristy boats depart hourly from near the Crane for a lazy 1.5-hour round-trip cruise to Westerplatte and back. (You can choose to get off at Westerplatte after 45 minutes and take a later boat back.) The *Czerna Perła* has English commentary; both boats often have live nautical music on the return trip (if you've ever wanted to hear "What Shall We Do with a Drunken Sailor?" in

Polish, here's your chance). It's not exactly pretty—you'll see more industry than scenery—but it's a fun excuse to set sail, even if you don't care about Westerplatte (40 zł round-trip, 27 zł one-way, the two boats take turns departing at the top of each hour 10:00-19:00 in July-Aug, fewer departures May-June and Sept, from the embankment near the Crane, mobile 501-571-383, www.rejsy turystyczne.pl). The duller alternative is to take a modern **Żegluga Gdańska** boat (45 zł round-trip, 30 zł one-way, 50 minutes each way, daily April-Oct, 3-6/day in each direction, www. zegluga.pl).

To Hel: Various boats—mostly the ZTM "ferry trams" *(tramwaj wodny)*—zip out to Hel in two hours three times a day from June through August, with a stop in Sopot (sometimes also runs on weekends in shoulder season; 20 zł each way, carefully confirm departure point, which can change but will likely be at the north end of the embankment, past the Crane).

By Cruise Ship
While many cruises advertise a stop in "Gdańsk," most actually dock in the nearby town of Gdynia.

The Tri-City (Trójmiasto)

Gdańsk is the anchor of the three-part metropolitan region known as the Tri-City (Trójmiasto). The other two parts are as different as night and day: Sopot, a once-swanky resort town, and Gdynia, a practical, nose-to-the-grindstone business center. The Tri-City as a whole is home to bustling industry and a sprawling university, with several campuses and plenty of well-dressed, English-speaking students. Beyond the Tri-City, the long, skinny Hel Peninsula—a sparsely populated strip of fishing villages and fun-loving beaches—arches dramatically into the Baltic Sea.

Sopot—boasting sandy beaches, tons of tourists, and a certain elegance—is clearly the most appealing day-trip option. Gdynia offers a glimpse into workaday Poland, but leaves most visitors cold. Hel, which requires the better part of a day to visit, is worthwhile only if you've got perfect summer weather and a desire to lie on the beach.

Getting Around the Tri-City
Gdańsk, Sopot, and Gdynia are connected by regional commuter trains (*kolejka,* operated by SKM) as well as by trains of Poland's national railway (operated by PKP). Tickets for one system can't be used on the other. While trains for the two systems chug along on

Gdańsk Day Trips

the same tracks, they use different (but nearby) platforms/stations. For example, at Gdańsk's main train station, national PKP trains use platforms 1-3, while regional SKM trains use platforms 3-5. And in Sopot, the SKM station is a few hundred feet before the PKP station.

Regional SKM trains are much more frequent—they go in each direction about every 10-15 minutes (less frequently after 19:30). In Gdańsk, buy tickets at the automated ticket machine marked *SKM Bilety* (near the head of platform 4, English instructions, 3.60 zł and 25 minutes to Sopot, or 5.40 zł and 35 minutes to Gdynia). If you buy your ticket from a machine, there's no need to validate it. But if you buy one from a kiosk, you'll need to stamp it in the easy-to-miss yellow slots under the boards with SKM information.

Each city has multiple stops. In Gdańsk, use "Gdańsk Główny" (the main station); for Sopot, use the stop called simply "Sopot" (only one word); and for Gdynia, it's "Gdynia Główna" (the main station).

The bigger PKP trains are faster, but less frequent—unless you notice one that happens to be leaving at a convenient time, I'd skip them and stick with the easy SKM trains. But note that trains to Hel are always operated by PKP.

For a more romantic—and much slower—approach, consider the boat (see "Gdańsk Connections," earlier).

Sopot

Sopot (SOH-poht), dubbed the "Nice of the North," was a celebrated haunt of beautiful people during the 1920s and 1930s, and remains a popular beach getaway to this day.

Sopot was created in the late 19th century by Napoleon's doctor, Jean Georges Haffner, who believed Baltic Sea water to be therapeutic. By the 1890s, it had become a fashionable seaside resort. This gambling center boasted enough high-roller casinos to garner comparisons to Monte Carlo.

The casinos are gone, but the health resorts remain, and you'll still see more well-dressed people here per capita than just about anywhere in the country. While it's not quite Cannes, Sopot feels relatively high class, which is unusual in otherwise unpretentious Poland. But even so, a childlike spirit of summer-vacation fun pervades this St-Tropez-on-the-Baltic, making it an all-around enjoyable place.

Planning Your Time

You can get the gist of Sopot in just a couple of hours. Zip in on the train, follow the main drag to the sea, wander the pier, get your feet wet at the beach, then head back to Gdańsk. Why not come here in the late afternoon, enjoy those last few rays of sunshine, stay for dinner, then take a twilight stroll on the pier?

Orientation to Sopot

The main pedestrian drag, Monte Cassino Heroes street (ulica Bohaterów Monte Cassino), leads to the Molo, the longest pleasure pier in Europe. From the Molo, a broad, sandy beach stretches in each direction. Running parallel to the surf is a tree-lined, people-filled path made for strolling.

Tourist Information

Sopot's helpful TI is directly in front of the PKP train station (look for blue *it* sign). Pick up the free map, info booklet, and events schedule. They also offer a free room-booking service (daily

June-mid-Sept 9:00-20:00, mid-Sept-May 10:00-18:00, ulica Dworcowa 4, tel. 58-550-3783, www.sopot.pl).

Arrival in Sopot

From the SKM station, exit to the left and walk down the street. After a block, you'll see the PKP train station on your left—detour here to find the TI (described above). Then continue on to the can't-miss-it main drag, ulica Bohaterów Monte Cassino (marked by the big red-brick church steeple). Follow it to the right, down to the seaside.

Sights in Sopot

▲Monte Cassino Heroes Street
(Ulica Bohaterów Monte Cassino)

Nicknamed "Monciak" (MOHN-chak) by locals, this in-love-with-life promenade may well be Poland's most manicured street. Especially after all the suburban and industrial dreck you passed through to get here, it's easy to be charmed by this pretty drag. The street is lined with happy tourists, trendy cafés, al fresco restaurants, movie theaters, and late-19th-century facades (known for their wooden balconies).

The most popular building along here (on the left, about half-way down) is the so-called **Crooked House** (Krzywy Domek), a trippy, Gaudí-inspired building that looks like it's melting. Hard-partying Poles prefer to call it the "Drunken House," and say that when it looks straight, it's time to stop drinking.

At the bottom of the boulevard, just before the Molo, pay 4 zł to climb to the top of the Art Nouveau lighthouse for a waterfront panorama.

Molo (Pier)

At more than 1,600 feet long, this is Europe's longest wooden entertainment pier. While you won't find any amusement-park rides, you will be surrounded by vendors, artists, and Poles having the time of their lives. Buy a *gofry* (Belgian waffle topped with whipped cream and fruit) or an oversized cloud of *wata cukrowa* (cotton candy), grab your partner's hand, and stroll with gusto (5 zł, free Oct-April, open long hours daily).

Scan the horizon for sailboats and tankers. Any pirate ships? For a jarring reality check, look over to Gdańsk. Barely visible from the Molo are two of the most important sites in 20th-century history: the towering monument at Westerplatte, where World War II started, and the cranes rising up from the Gdańsk Shipyard, where Solidarity was born and European communism began its long goodbye.

In spring and fall, the Molo is a favorite venue for pole vaulting—or is that Pole vaulting?

The Beach

Yes, Poland has beaches. Nice ones. When I heard Sopot compared to places like Nice, I'll admit that I scoffed. But when I saw those stretches of inviting sand as far as the eye can see, I wished I'd packed my swim trunks. (You could walk from Gdańsk to Gdynia on beaches like this.) The sand is finer than anything I've seen in Croatia...though the water's not exactly crystal-clear. Most of the beach is public, except for a small private stretch in front of the Grand Hotel Sopot. Year-round, it's crammed with locals. At these northern latitudes, the season for bathing is brief and crowded.

Overlooking the beach next to the Molo is the **Grand Hotel Sopot.** It was renovated to top-class status just recently, but its history goes way back. They could charge admission for room #226, a multiroom suite that has hosted the likes of Adolf Hitler, Marlene Dietrich, and Fidel Castro (but not all at the same time). With all the trappings of Sopot's belle époque—dark wood, plush upholstery, antique furniture—this room had me imagining Hitler sitting at the desk, looking out to sea, and plotting the course of World War II.

Gdynia

Compared to its flashier sister cities, straightforward Gdynia (guh-DIN-yah) has retained a more working-class vibe, still in touch with its salty, fishing-village roots. Gdynia is less historic than Gdańsk or Sopot, as it was mostly built in the 1920s to be Poland's main harbor after Gdańsk became a free city. Although nowhere as attractive as Gdańsk or Sopot, Gdynia has an authentic feel and a fine waterfront promenade (www.gdynia.pl).

Gdynia is a major business center, and—thanks to its youthful, progressive city government—has edged ahead of the rest of Poland in transitioning from communism. It enjoys one of the highest income levels in the country. Many of the crumbling downtown buildings have been renovated, and Gdynia is becoming known for its top-tier shopping—all the big designers have boutiques here. If a local woman has been shopping on Świętojańska street in Gdynia, it means that she's got some serious złoty.

Because Gdańsk's port is relatively shallow, the biggest cruise ships must put in at Gdynia...leaving confused tourists to poke around town looking for some medieval quaintness, before coming to their senses and heading for Gdańsk. Gdynia is also home to a major military harbor and an important NATO base.

To get a taste of Gdynia, take the SKM train to the "Gdynia Główna" station, follow signs to *wyjście do miasta,* cross the busy street, and walk 15 minutes down Starowiejska. When you come to the intersection with the broad Świętojańska street, turn right (in the direction the big statue is looking) and walk two blocks to the tree-lined park on the left. Head through the park to the Southern Pier (Molo Południowe). This concrete slab—nowhere near as charming as Sopot's wooden-boardwalk version—features a modern shopping mall and a smattering of sights, including an aquarium and a pair of permanently moored museum boats.

Plans are afoot to convert the big warehouse at the Nabrzeże Francuskie pier into an emigration museum, possibly as early as 2014; if and when this opens, it will offer a handy sightseeing opportunity for cruisers arriving here.

Arriving by Cruise in Gdynia

Many Northern European cruises include a stop at "Gdańsk"; most of these actually put in at Gdynia's sprawling port. And, while Gydnia's town center is relatively manicured and pleasant, its port area is the opposite—like an Eastern Bloc bodybuilder, it's muscular and hairy. Cruise ships are shuffled among hardworking industrial piers that make the area feel uninviting. Three of the port's many piers are used for cruises: **Nabrzeże Francuskie** (French Quay), where most large ships dock; **Nabrzeże Stanów Zjednoczonych** (United States Quay), farther out, a secondary option for large ships; and convenient **Nabrzeże Pomorskie** (Pomeranian Quay, part of the Southern Pier), used by small ships and located alongside Gdynia's one "fun" pier, with museums and pleasure craft (from here, it's easy to simply walk into downtown Gdynia). Port information: www.port.gdynia.pl.

Unfortunately, there are no **ATMs** or money-exchange options at or near the cruise-ship berths; but cash machines are plentiful in downtown Gdynia.

To get from your cruise ship to Gdańsk, the best option is a **shuttle bus-plus-train connection**. First, ride your cruise line's shuttle bus into downtown Gdynia (5-minute trip; price depends on the cruise line). The shuttle drops you off at Skwer Kościuski; from here, it's a 10-minute walk (gradually uphill) to the train station. Start by walking away from the water on the broad, parklike boulevard. After the street becomes ulica 10 Lutego (you'll pass the TI on your right), it curves to the right; once you're around the corner, use the crosswalk to reach the train station (marked *Dworzec Podmiejski*). From here, you can ride the handy *kolejka* commuter train into Gdansk (runs every 10-15 minutes, 35 minutes; for details on this train, see "Getting Around the Tri-City," earlier). Arrive at the Gdańsk train station ("Gdańsk Główny" stop). Returning on the train, you want the "Gdynia Główna" stop.

Taxi drivers line up to meet arriving cruise ships. Cabbies here tend to overcharge, but if they use the meter, these are the legitimate rates: 20 zł to Gdynia's train station (*Dworzec*, DVOH-zhets); 125 zł to Gdańsk's Main Town; and 60-80 zł to Sopot. Taxi drivers generally take euros, though their off-the-cuff exchange rate may not be favorable.

For more details on Gdynia's port—and several others on the Baltic, North Sea, and beyond—pick up *Rick Steves' Northern European Cruise Ports* guidebook.

Hel Peninsula (Mierzeja Helska)

Out on the edge of things, this slender peninsula juts 20 miles into the ocean, providing a sunny retreat from the big cities—even as it shelters them from Baltic winds. Trees line the peninsula, and the northern edge is one long, sandy, ever-shifting beach.

On hot summer days, Hel is a great place to frolic in the sun with Poles. Sunbathing and windsurfing are practically religions here. Small resort villages line Hel Peninsula: Władysławowo (at the base), Chałupy, Kuźnica, Jastarnia, Jurata, and—at the tip—a town also called Hel. Beaches right near the towns can be crowded in peak season, but you're never more than a short walk away from your own stretch of sand. There are few permanent residents, and the waterfront is shared by budget campgrounds, hotels hosting middle-class families, and mansions of Poland's rich and famous (former president Aleksander Kwaśniewski has a summer home here).

The easiest way to go to Hel—aside from coveting thy neighbor's wife—is by boat (see "Gdańsk Connections," earlier). Trains from Gdańsk also reach Hel (summer only), and from Gdynia, you can take a train, bus, or minibus. But overland transit is crowded and slow—especially in summer, when Hel is notorious for its hellish traffic jams.

POMERANIA

Malbork Castle • Toruń

The northwestern part of Poland—known as Pomerania (Pomorze)—has nothing to do with excitable little dogs, but it does offer plenty of attractions. Two in particular are worth singling out, both conveniently located between Gdańsk and Warsaw. Malbork, the biggest Gothic castle in Europe, is one of the most interesting castles in Eastern Europe. Farther south, the Gothic town of Toruń—the birthplace of Copernicus, and a favorite spot of every proud Pole—holds hundreds of red-brick buildings (and, it seems, even more varieties of tasty gingerbread).

Planning Your Time

Malbork works well as a side-trip from Gdańsk (frequent trains, 40-50 minutes each way), and it's also on the main train line from

Gdańsk to Warsaw. While Toruń doesn't merit a long detour, it's worth a stroll or an overnight if you want to sample a smaller Polish city. Unfortunately, Torún is on a different train line than Malbork—if you visit both in one day, it'll be a very long one. Ideally, if traveling round-trip from Warsaw, see one of these destinations coming to Gdańsk, and visit the other on the way back. (Note: Due to renovations at Malbork's train station, there may be no luggage storage; instead, you might have to take your bags with you to the castle to check them there.) Or do Malbork as a side-trip from Gdańsk, then visit Toruń on the way to Warsaw.

Malbork Castle

Malbork Castle is soaked in history. The biggest brick castle in the world, the largest castle of the Gothic period, and one of Europe's most imposing fortresses, it sits smugly on a marshy plain at the edge of the town of Malbork, 35 miles southeast of Gdańsk. This was the headquarters of the notorious Teutonic Knights, a Germanic band of ex-Crusaders who dominated northern Poland in the Middle Ages.

When the Teutonic Knights were invited to Polish lands to convert neighboring pagans in the 13th century, they found the perfect site for their new capital here, on the bank of the Nogat River. Construction began in 1274. After the Teutonic Knights conquered Gdańsk in 1308, the order moved its official headquarters from Venice to Malbork, where they remained for nearly 150 years. They called the castle Marienburg, the "Castle of Mary," in honor of the order's patron saint.

At its peak in the early 1400s, Malbork was both the imposing home of a seemingly unstoppable army and Europe's final bastion of chivalric ideals. Surrounded by swamplands, with only one gate in need of defense, it was a tough nut to crack. Malbork Castle was never taken by force in the Middle Ages, though it had to withstand various sieges by the Poles during the Thirteen Years' War (1454-1466)—including a campaign that lasted over three years. Finally, in 1457, the Polish king gained control of Malbork by buying off Czech mercenaries guarding the castle. Malbork became a Polish royal residence for 300 years. But when Poland was partitioned in the late 18th century, this region went back into German hands. The castle became a barracks, windows were sealed up, delicate vaulting was damaged, bricks were quarried for new buildings, and Malbork deteriorated.

In the late 19th century, Romantic German artists and poets rediscovered the place. An architect named Konrad Steinbrecht devoted 40 years of his life to Malbork, painstakingly restoring the palace to its medieval splendor. A half-century later, the Nazis used the castle to house POWs, and about half of it was destroyed by the Soviet army, who saw it as a symbol of long-standing German domination. But it was restored once again, and today Malbork has been returned to its Teutonic glory.

Getting There

Malbork is on the train line between Gdańsk and Warsaw. Coming by train from Gdańsk, you'll enjoy views of the castle on your right as you cross the Nogat River.

Unfortunately, due to ongoing renovation, there may be **no**

luggage storage at the Malbork train station. If you can't find anywhere to leave your bags at the station, you'll have to carry them with you to the castle, then check them at the guardhouse (the small wooden house near the castle exit, along the river).

To get from the station to the castle, consider taking a **taxi** (shouldn't cost more than 10 zł, though many corrupt cabbies charge twice that—keep asking until someone agrees to 10 zł). Or you can **walk** 15 minutes to the castle: Leave the station to the right, walk straight, and go through the pedestrian underpass beneath the busy road (by the red staircase). When you emerge on the other side, follow the busy road (noticing peek-a-boo views on your right of the castle's main tower) and take your first right turn (onto Kościuszki, the main shopping street). On Kościuszki, you'll pass the fancy pink building housing the TI on the right. Near the bottom of Kościuszki, at the fountain and the McDonald's, jog right, then bear left over two moats. Turn right and follow the castle wall to the end, where you'll find the ticket office (marked *kasa*).

Orientation to Malbork Castle

Cost and Hours: Mid-April–mid-Sept—39 zł, castle exhibits open Tue-Sun 9:00-19:00, grounds until 20:00; mid-Sept–mid-April—29 zł, castle exhibits open Tue-Sun 10:00-15:00, grounds until 16:00. Ask about slightly discounted family tickets (it's also cheaper to visit within 1.25 hours of closing). On Mondays year-round, most of the castle is closed, with only a few sparse exhibits remaining open (7 zł to enter), but there's little point in making the trip on a Monday. The ticket office opens 30 minutes before the castle. For details, see www.zamek.malbork.pl.

Tours: You are technically required to enter the castle with a three-hour tour or audioguide (Polish version included in your ticket), but most non-Polish speakers simply split off from their guide and tour the place on their own—just enter with any tour, wander off, and explore the castle using my self-guided tour (see next page). You can also rent an English audioguide for 6 zł.

In July and August, **English tours** run three times a day (likely at 11:00, 13:30, and 15:30; 8 zł extra). Otherwise, year-round, you can pay 210 zł for a private English tour (English guides are easy to arrange in summer—even on short notice—but more difficult in winter). Ideally, contact the castle a few days ahead to reserve a guide (tel. 55-647-0978, kasa@zamek .malbork.pl), or hire your own guide in Gdańsk (such as Agnieszka Syroka).

POMERANIA

Alternatively, if you show up and there's no scheduled English tour, ask if an English-speaking guide is available. Then take the initiative, play "tour organizer," and get together a group of frustrated English speakers by the cashier. On my last trip, it took me only a few minutes to gather a dozen strangers eager for some English information—bringing the per-person cost of the private tour down to less than 20 zł.

Expect Changes: Future plans may revamp the tour system and create several shorter tour routes. Restoration of the moat area may cause the relocation of the castle entrance (possibly in 2014).

Best Views: The views of massive Malbork are stunning—especially at sunset, when its red brick glows. Be sure to walk out across the bridge over the Nogat River. The most scenic part of the castle is probably the twin-turreted, riverside Bridge Gate, which used to be connected by a bridge to the opposite bank.

Sound-and-Light Show: Every night from mid-April through mid-September, there's a sound-and-light show in the castle courtyard. Though the commentary is in Polish, the show gives you a different perspective on the mighty fortress (20 zł, buy tickets at castle drawbridge, begins after dark—which can be as late as 22:00 at these northern latitudes). Don't make a special trip (or stay late) just for this show—it really only makes sense if you're spending the night (see "Sleeping at Malbork Castle," later).

Self-Guided Tour

The official tour of Malbork lasts about three hours. And, while there's plenty to see, this self-guided tour allows you to see the highlights at your own pace. (Remember, you can split off from your group at any time.) This tour also works if you're tagging along with a Polish group, since it corresponds more or less to the route most Malbork guides take. Still, every guide is a little different, exhibits tend to move around, and entrances can close unexpectedly. Use the map on the opposite page to navigate and jump around as needed. The castle complex is a bit of a maze, with various entrances and exits for each room, often behind closed (but unlocked) doors. Don't be shy about grabbing a medieval doorknob and letting yourself in.

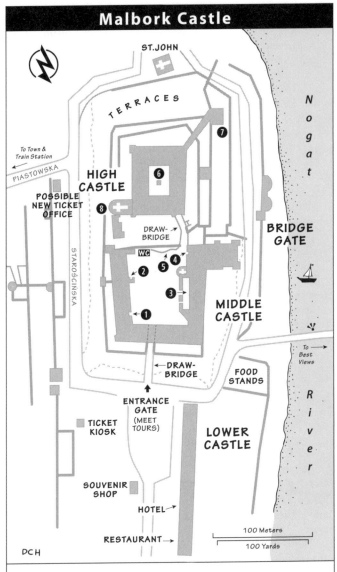

Malbork Castle

- **1** Amber Collection (downstairs)
- **2** Armory (upstairs) & Gothic Café (downstairs)
- **3** "Boiler Room" (downstairs) & Grand Refectory (upstairs)
- **4** Grand Master's Palace
- **5** Grand Master Statues
- **6** Well
- **7** Dansker Tower
- **8** St. Mary's Church

Lower Castle and Entrance Gate

Stand in front of the gate to one of Europe's most intimidating fortresses—home to the Grand Master, monks, and knights of the Teutonic Order. Across from the gate is the Lower Castle, which was an infirmary and hospital for injured knights and retirees. The end closest to you is the Chapel of St. Lawrence; farther away, former farm buildings have been converted into hotel rooms and restaurants (see "Sleeping at Malbork Castle," later).

Go up the wooden drawbridge. Above the door to the brick gate is a sculpture of St. Mary with the Baby Jesus...next to a shield and helmet. The two messages to visitors: This castle is protected by Mary, and the Teutonic Knights are here to convert pagans—by force, if necessary (or, as it turned out, even if not necessary).

Pass through this gate, into the entry area. Imagine the gate behind you closing. Look up to see wooden chutes where archers are preparing to rain arrows down on you. Your last thought: Maybe we should have left the Teutonic Knights alone, after all.

Before you're pierced by arrows, read the castle's history in its walls: The foundation is made of huge stones, which are rare in these marshy lands—they were brought from Sweden. But most of the castle, like so many other buildings in northern Poland, was built with handmade red brick. Throughout the castle, the darker-colored, rougher brick is original, and the lighter-colored, smoother brick was used during later restorations (in the 19th century, and again after World War II).

Venture through two more enclosed spaces, watching for the holes in the wall (for more guards and soldiers). The Teutonic Knights connected nearby lakes to create a system of canals, forming a moat around the castle that could be crossed only by this drawbridge. Ponder the fact that you have to go through five separate, well-defended gates to reach the...

Middle Castle (Zamek Średni)

This part of Malbork, built at an uphill incline to make it even more imposing, was designed to impress. Knights and monks lived here.

Let's get oriented: To your left is the east wing, where guests would sleep. Today this houses the Amber Collection (ground floor) and the armory (upstairs). To the right (west) as you enter the main courtyard is the Grand Refectory (closer to the entrance) and the Grand Master's Palace (the taller, squarer building at the far end).

• *Before we move on, this is a good time to read up on the history of the Teutonic Knights (see sidebar). When you're ready to continue, enter the ground floor of the building on the left (remember, don't be shy about opening closed doors), and visit the...*

Amber Collection

This exhibit will make jewelry shoppers salivate. (Even as someone with zero interest in amber, I enjoyed it.) Begin at the huge chunks of raw amber and the illuminated display of inclusions (bugs stuck in the amber, à la *Jurassic Park*). Some of the ancient amber artifacts displayed here are up to 3,000 years old. These were found in graves, put there by people who thought amber would help the deceased enter a better world. Wandering the hall, you'll see all manner of amber creations: boxes, brooches, necklaces, chess sets, pipes, miniature ships, wine glasses, and belts for skinny-waisted, fashion-conscious women. Look for two truly exquisite pieces: a small casket and an altar. Many of the finely decorated jewelry boxes and chests have ivory, silver, or shell inlays—better for contrast than gold. The portable religious shrines and altars allowed travelers to remain reverent on the road and still pack light. Find the amber crucifix. This is a small replica of a six-foot-tall amber and silver cross presented to Pope John Paul II by the people of Gdańsk. Another exhibit case contains necklaces displaying the full range of amber colors, from opaque white at the top, to transparent yellow in the middle, to virtually black at the bottom.

• *Go back outside and turn left, to the wooden staircase above the Gothic Café (worth considering for a meal, and described later, under "Eating at Malbork Castle"). Go up that staircase, and several more inside, to the top-floor...*

Armory

Browse your way through the impressive array of swords, armor, and other armaments (English descriptions). Look for the 600-year-old "hand-and-a-half" swords—too big to be held in one hand. At the end, in the display of cannons, pikes, and spears, find the giant shield. These shields could be lined up to form a portable "wall" to protect the knights.

Head downstairs to the second room of the armory, displaying suits of armor (including one for horses). On the wall behind the first suit of armor, look for some five-foot-long "two-hand swords" even bigger than the ones upstairs. Halfway down the hall on the left, find the suit of armor from the Hussars—Polish horseback knights who had wings on their armor, which created a terrifying sound when galloping.

• *Head back outside (noticing the handy WC straight ahead) and cross the main courtyard, entering the smaller courtyard through the passage*

The Teutonic Knights

The Order of the Teutonic Knights began in the Holy Land in 1191, during the Third Crusade. Officially called the "Order of the Hospital of the Blessed Virgin Mary of the German House of Jerusalem," these German monks and knights took vows of poverty, chastity, and obedience. They also built hospitals and cared for injured knights. When the Crusades ended in the 12th century, the order found itself out of a job, and went back to Europe. They set up shop in Venice and reorganized as a chivalric order of Christian mercenaries—pagan-killers for hire.

The Teutonic Knights were hired in 1226 for a gig in northern Poland, where the duke asked them to subdue a tribe of pagans who had been attacking his lands. The Teutonic Knights—claiming to be missionaries (and wearing white cloaks decorated with black crosses)—spent 60 years "saving" the pagans by turning them into serfs or brutally massacring them.

Like houseguests who didn't know when to leave, the Teutonic Knights decided they enjoyed northern Poland—and stuck around. The Knights made themselves at home, building one of Europe's biggest and most imposing fortresses: Malbork. Because they were fanatical Christians, they won the support of the pope and the Holy Roman Emperor. When the Teutonic Knights seized large parts of northern Poland in 1308, including Gdańsk—cutting off Polish access to the Baltic Sea—the Polish royals began to realize their mistake. The Teutonic Knights invited more Germans to come join them, building their numbers and tightening their grasp on the region. They grew rich from Hanseatic trade, specializing in amber, grain, and timber. The Knights conquered Estonia and Latvia, and began to threaten the Poles' pagan neighbor to the east, Lithuania. By the late 14th century, the Teutonic Knights were enjoying a Golden Age at the expense of the Poles and Lithuanians.

At about this time, Poland's long-lived Piast dynasty died out. Inspired by a mutual desire to fight back against the Teutonic

next to the dark-wood-topped tower. Find the steep steps down into the...

"Boiler Room"

The Teutonic Knights had a surprisingly sophisticated method for heating this huge complex. You see a furnace down below, and a sort of holding area for super-heated rocks above. The radiant heat given off by the rocks spread through the vents without also filling them with smoke. This is one of 11 such "boiler rooms" in the castle complex. As you tour the rest of the castle, keep an eye out for little saucer-sized vents in the floor where the heat came through.

• Head back out into the main courtyard and turn right, going uphill

Knights, the Poles and the Lithuanians decided to join their two kingdoms. In 1386, Polish Princess Jadwiga married Lithuanian Prince Władysław Jagiełło (who converted to Christianity for the occasion), uniting Poland and Lithuania and kick-starting a grand new dynasty, the Jagiellonians.

Just as every American knows the date July 4, 1776, every Pole knows the date July 15, 1410—the Battle of Grunwald. King Władysław Jagiełło and Grand Duke Vytautas the Great led a ragtag army of some 40,000 soldiers—Lithuanians, Poles, other Slavs, and even speedy Tatar horsemen—against 27,000 Teutonic Knights. At the end of the day, some 18,000 Poles and Lithuanians were dead—but so were half of the Teutonic Knights (and the other half had been captured). Poland and Lithuania were victorious. Though the Teutonic Knights remained in Poland—extending their Germanic cultural influence on the region well into the 20th century—their political power waned, they pulled out of Lithuania, and they once again allowed free trade on the Vistula. A generation later, the Thirteen Years' War (1454-1466) finally put an end to the Teutonic Knights' domination of northern Poland. The order officially dissolved in 1575, when they converted to Protestantism (though some conspiracy theorists claim the Teutonic Knights are still very much active).

The Knights' influence on Poland persists today—even beyond the striking red-brick churches and castles scattered around the northern part of the country. The Polish novelist Henryk Sienkiewicz's *The Teutonic Knights* is a cultural benchmark and a favorite work of many Poles. The 19th-century Romantics who fanned the flames of Polish patriotism turned the Teutonic Knights into a symbol of Germanic oppression. Even today, Poles—and all Slavs—think of the Teutonic Knights as murderous invaders...while the Germans see them as a mere footnote in their history.

POMERANIA

about 30 yards. At the upper part of this castle are two doors; take the one on the right, then climb up the stairs into the...

Grand Master's Palace

This was one of the grandest royal residences in medieval Europe, used in later times by Polish kings and German kaisers. (Today it's sometimes used for special exhibitions.)

• From the top of the stairs, head down the hall to the right. Notice the troughs in the ground—anyone wanting an audience with the Grand Master had to wash both his hands and his feet.

At the end of the hall, on the left, enter the elegant...

Summer Refectory: This was where the G. M. dined. With

big stained-glass windows, and all the delicate vaulting supported by a single pillar in the middle, this room was clearly not designed with defense in mind. In fact, medieval Polish armies focused their attacks on this room. On one legendary occasion, the attackers—tipped off by a spy—knew that an important meeting was going on here, and fired a cannonball into the room. It just missed the pillar. (You can see where the cannonball hit the wall, just above the fireplace.) The ceiling eventually did collapse during World War II.

As you continue into the **Winter Refectory,** notice that it has fewer windows (better insulation) and little manhole-like openings in the floor where the "central heating" entered the room.

• *Keep going, and you'll circle back around to where you came in. Go through the door just to the left of the stairs, into the...*

Private Rooms of the Grand Master: Though the Teutonic Order dictated that the monks sleep in dormitories, the Grand Master made an exception for himself. Near the entrance, you'll see his private bedroom (with rough original frescoes of four female martyrs). Exploring the rest of the Top Knight's residence, appreciate the show-off decor (including some 15th-century original frescoes of wine leaves and grapes). The Grand Master even had his own chapel, dedicated to St. Catherine.

• *You'll enter a small hall at the very end of these rooms. If it's open, go through the little door at the right end of this hall, and walk down to the...*

Grand Refectory: This enormous dining hall, damaged in World War II, recently re-opened after a decade-long restoration project. With remarkable palm vaulting and grand frescoes, the Grand Refectory hosted feasts for up to 400 people to celebrate a military victory or to impress visiting dignitaries.

• *Head outside. You're back by the boiler room. Go back out into the main courtyard and walk to the top. Look for the four...*

Grand Master Statues

These four statues came from a 19th-century Prussian monument that was mostly destroyed when the Soviets took Malbork at the end of World War II. Though this was a religious order, these powerful guys look more like kings than monks. From right to left, shake hands with Hermann von Salza (who was Grand Master when the Teutonic Knights came to Poland); Siegfried von Feuchtwangen (who actually moved the T. K. capital from Venice to Malbork, and who conquered Gdańsk for the Knights—oops, can't shake his hand, which was supposedly chopped off by Soviet troops); Winrich von Kniprode (who oversaw Malbork's Golden Age, and turned it into a castle fit for a king); and Markgraf Albrecht von Hohenzollern (the last Grand Master before the order dissolved and converted to Protestantism).

• *To the right of the statues, continue over the...*

Drawbridge

As you cross, notice the extensive system of fortifications and moats protecting the innermost part of the castle. Check out the cracks in the walls—an increasing threat to this ever-settling castle set on marshy, unstable terrain. The passage is lined with holes (for surveillance), with chutes up above (to pour scalding water or pitch on unwanted visitors). It's not quite straight—so a cannon fired here would hit the side wall of the passage, rather than entering the High Castle. Which is what you're about to do now.

High Castle (Zamek Wysoki)

This is the beating heart of the castle, and its oldest section. As much a monastery as a fortress, the High Castle was off-limits to all but 60 monks of the Teutonic Order and their servants. (The knights stayed in the Middle Castle.) Here you'll find the monks' dormitories, chapels, church, and refectory. As this was the nerve center of the Teutonic Knights—the T. K. HQ—it was also their last line of defense. They stored enormous amounts of food here in case of a siege.

In the middle of the High Castle courtyard is a **well**—an essential part of any inner castle, especially one as prone to sieges as Malbork. At the top is a sculpture of a pelican. Because this noble bird was believed to kill itself to feed its young (notice that it's piercing its own chest with its beak), it was often used in the Middle Ages as a symbol for the self-sacrifice of Jesus.

• *Take some time to explore the...*

Ground Floor

Work clockwise around the courtyard from where you entered. A door leads to the prison and torture chamber (with small "solitary confinement" cells near the entrance), behind which you'll find a long hall with a single tiny window. Along the back of the cloister is a post-WWII photo of Malbork. Beyond that, hiding in the far corner, is an exhibit on medieval stained-glass windows. Somewhere around here, you should see a demonstration of how medieval money was made. The Teutonic Knights minted their own coins—and you can buy your very own freshly minted replica today.

POMERANIA

• Continuing around the courtyard (to the right from where you entered), you'll find the most interesting exhibit on this floor, the...

Kitchen: This exhibit really gives you a feel for medieval monastery life. The monks who lived here ate three meals a day, along with lots of beer (made here) and wine (imported from France, Italy, and Hungary). A cellar under the kitchen was used as a primitive refrigerator—big chunks of ice were cut from the frozen river in winter, stored in the basement, and used to keep food cool in summer. Behind the long table, see the big dumbwaiter (with shelves), which connects this kitchen with the refectory upstairs. Step into the giant stove and look up the biggest chimney in the castle.

• Now go back out into the courtyard, and climb up the stairs near where you first entered.

Middle Floor

• From the top of the stairs, the first door on the left (with the colorfully painted arch) leads to the most important room of the High Castle, the...

Chapter Room: Monks gathered here after Mass, and it was also the site for meetings of Teutonic Knights from around the countryside. If a Grand Master was killed in battle, the new one would be elected right here. Each monk had his own seal and a name over his seat. The big chair belonged to the Grand Master. Above his chair, notice the little windows, connecting this room to St. Mary's Church next door (described later). Church music would filter in through these windows...imagine the voices of 60 monks bouncing around with these acoustics.

While monks are usually thought to pursue simple lives, the elegant vaulting in this room is anything but plain. The 14th-century frescoes (restored in the 19th century) depict Grand Masters. In the floor are more vents for the central heating.

• Leave the Chapter House and walk straight ahead, imagining the monk-filled corridors of Teutonic times. The first door on the right is the...

Treasury: As you explore the rooms of the tax collector and the house administrator, notice the wide variety of safes and other lock boxes. Near the end, look for the small bed—fit for a small medieval person.

• Continue around the cloister. At the end of the corridor, spot the little devil at the bottom of the vaulting (on the right, about eye level). He's pulling his beard and crossing his legs—pointing you down the long corridor to the...

Dansker Tower: From the devil's grimace, you might have guessed that this tower houses the latrine. For obvious sanitary (and olfactory) reasons, it's set apart from the main part of the castle. The toilets dropped straight down into the moat. The bins above them are filled with cabbage leaves, used by the T. K. as TP. This tower could also serve as a final measure of defense—it's easier to defend than the entire castle. Food was stored above, just in case.

• *Head back toward the main part of the High Castle. On the right-hand side of the long passage, a door leads into the...*

Church Exhibition: Once dormitories for the monks, these rooms today display a wide range of relics from the church (with English descriptions). The first room features various statues, including an evocative, hands-less 15th-century Christ praying in the Garden of Gethsemane. The next room displays pictures of Malbork Castle through the years, as well as some fragments of statues rescued from the destroyed St. Mary's Church. The huge, mangled crucifix dates from the mid-14th century. At the end of this exhibition is a replica of a Gothic altarpiece, with graphic paintings of the murder and dismemberment of Poland's patron saint, Adalbert.

• *Go back out into the main cloister, turn right, and continue down to the end, arriving at the...*

Golden Gate: This elaborate doorway—covered in protective glass—marks the entrance to St. Mary's Church. Ringed with

detailed carvings from the Old Testament, and symbolic messages about how monks of the Teutonic Order should live their lives, it's a marvelous example of late-13th-century art. At the bottom left end of the arch, find the five wise virgins who, having filled their lamps with oil and conserved it wisely, are headed to heaven. On the right, the five foolish virgins who overslept and used up all their oil are damned, much to their dismay.

• *Go through this door into...*

St. Mary's Church: This holy site was destroyed in World War II and sat for decades with no roof. After so much neglect, it's finally being renovated...slowly. Pictures of the original church with English descriptions explain some of the fragments.

• *Go through the narrow door next to the one where you entered the church, and hike up the tight spiral staircase to the final set of exhibits.*

Top Floor

Walk through the long hallway of temporary exhibits. At the end, go down the stairs into the monks' common room (on the left). Over the fireplace is a relief depicting the Teutonic Knights fighting the pagans. To the left of that (see the stone windows) is a balcony where musicians entertained the monks after a meal. The next, very long room, with seven pillars, is the refectory, where the monks ate in silence.

Along the right-hand wall are confessional-like, lockable storage boxes. At the end of this room, just beyond another decorated fireplace, notice the grated hole in the wall. This is where the dumbwaiter comes up from the kitchen (which we saw below). Beyond this room is an exhibit about the architectural renovation of the castle. On your way back out, you'll have the opportunity to pay 8 zł to climb the very tight and steep steps to the top of the tower for a view over the castle complex.

• Your Malbork tour ends here. When finished, you can head back the way you came. En route, you can walk around terraces lining the inner moat, between the castle walls (stairs lead down off of the drawbridge). It's hardly a must-see, but it's pleasant enough, with the Grand Master's garden, a cemetery for monks, and the remains of the small St. Anne's Chapel (with Grand Master tombs).

Sleeping at Malbork Castle

Malbork is so well-connected by rail to Gdańsk and Warsaw that there's little sense in sleeping here. If you do stay, consider the nighttime sound-and-light show in the castle courtyard.

$$ Hotel Zamek is housed in Malbork's Lower Castle, a red-brick building that was once a hospital, just across from the main part of the fortress. The 42 rooms are overpriced, dark, musty, old-feeling, and a little creepy...but, hey—you're next door to one of Europe's grandest Gothic castles (Sb-210 zł, Db-310 zł, Tb-390 zł, cheaper off-season, elevator, ulica Starościńska 14, tel. 055-272-8400, www.hotelprodus.pl, hotelprodus@hotelprodus.pl).

Eating at Malbork Castle

Several cheap food stands cluster outside the castle (by the river). For a meal inside the castle complex, your best bet is the **Gothic Café,** under the stairs to the armory in the Middle Castle. Serving traditional Polish food in a nondescript cellar setting, it's handy for its 29-zł lunch deal that includes a main dish and soup (25-40-zł main dishes, Tue-Sun 9:00-17:00 or 18:00 depending on demand, tel. 50-620-8560).

Sleep Code

(3 zł = about $1, country code: 48)
S = Single, **D** = Double/Twin, **T** = Triple, **Q** = Quad, **b** = bathroom,
s = shower only. At each place, credit cards are accepted,
breakfast is included, and English is spoken.

To help you easily sort through these listings, I've divided
the accommodations into two categories, based on the price
for a double room with bath during high season:

$$ Higher Priced—Most rooms 200 zł or more.
$ Lower Priced—Most rooms less than 200 zł.

Prices can change without notice; verify the hotel's cur-
rent rates online or by email. For the best prices, always book
direct.

Malbork Connections

From Malbork by Train to: Gdańsk (about 2/hour, 40-50 min-
utes), **Toruń** (about every 2 hours, 3 hours, transfer in Tczew),
Warsaw (6/day direct, 4.5 hours—but will drop to 2.5 hours when
new line is finished).

Toruń

Toruń (TOH-roon) is a pretty, lazy Gothic town conveniently
located about halfway between Warsaw and Gdańsk. It's worth a
couple of hours to stroll the lively streets, ogle the huge red-brick
buildings, and savor the flavor of Poland's most livable city.

With about 210,000 resi-
dents and 30,000 students (at
Copernicus University), Toruń is
a thriving burg. Locals brag that
their city is a "mini-Kraków."
But that sells both cities short.
Toruń lacks Kraków's over-the-
top romanticism, and its sights
are quickly exhausted. On the
other hand, Toruń may well be
Poland's most user-friendly city: tidy streets with a sensible grid
plan (and English signposts to keep you on track), wide pedes-
trian boulevards crammed with locals who greet each other like
they're long-lost friends, and an easygoing ambience that seems
to say, "Hey—relax." And, while it has its share of tourists, Toruń

POMERANIA

feels more off-the-beaten-path than the other Polish destinations in this book.

Toruń clings fiercely to its two claims to fame: It's the proud birthplace of the astronomer Copernicus (Mikołaj Kopernik), and home to a dizzying variety of gingerbread treats (*piernika;* pyer-NEE-kah).

Orientation to Toruń

Everything in Toruń worth seeing is in the walled Old Town, climbing up a gentle hill from the Vistula River. The broad, traffic-free main drag, ulica Szeroka (called Różana at the entrance of town) bisects the Old Town, running parallel to the river.

Arrival in Toruń

Toruń's main train station (called Toruń Główny) is about a mile away—and across the river—from the Old Town. The main hall has ticket windows, an ATM, and lockers.

To reach the Old Town, you have two options: If you go out the door from the main hall, you'll spot **taxis** waiting to take you into town (the trip costs around 15-20 zł). To take the **bus,** buy a 2.50-zł ticket from the *RUCH* kiosk overlooking the tracks near the main hall. Then follow the pedestrian underpass beneath track 4 (entrance to underpass marked with low-profile *wyjście do miasta* sign and bus icon, outside main hall and to the left). When you emerge on the other side, the bus stop for bus #22, #25, or #27 into the center is ahead and on your right. Take the bus to Plac Rapackiego, the first stop after the long bridge. To return to the station, catch bus #22, #25, or #27 across the busy road from where you got off.

Tourist Information

The TI is on the main square, behind the Old Town Hall. Pick up the free map, and get information about hotels in town and city tours (Tue-Fri 9:00-18:00, Mon and Sat 9:00-16:00; closed Sun except May-Sept, when it's open 11:00-15:00; Rynek Staromiejski 25, tel. 56-621-0931, www.it.torun.pl).

Self-Guided Walk

Welcome to Toruń

This very lightly guided introductory stroll takes you through the heart of Toruń. With no stops, you could do it in 15 minutes.

From the Plac Rapackiego bus stop, head into the town through the passageways under the colorful buildings. Within a block, you're at the bustling **Old Town Market Square** (Rynek

Staromiejski), surrounded by huge brick buildings and outdoor restaurants buzzing with lively locals. The big building in the center is the **Old Town Hall** (Ratusz Staromiejski), with a boring museum and a climbable tower. The building with the pointy spires on the right (across from the Old Town Hall) is the **Artus Court,** where the medieval town council and merchants' guilds met (sadly, unlike the similar court in Gdańsk, it's not open to the public).

The guy playing his violin in front of the Old Town Hall is a **rafter** *(retman)*—one of the medieval lumberjacks who lashed tree trunks together and floated them down the Vistula to Gdańsk. This particular rafter came to Toruń when the town was infested with frogs. He wooed them with his violin and marched them out of town. (Hmm...sounds like a certain pied piper....)

The bigger statue, at the other end of the Old Town Hall, depicts **Mikołaj Kopernik,** better known as Nicholas Copernicus (1473-1543). This Toruń-born son of aristocrats turned the world on its ear when he suggested that the sun, not the earth, is the center of the universe (an idea called the "heliocentric theory"). Toruń is serious about this local boy done good—he's the town mascot, as well as the namesake of the local university. Among its fields of study, Copernicus U. has a healthy astronomy program. There's a planetarium in the Old Town (just past the far corner of the square) and a giant radio telescope on the town outskirts. Despite all the local fuss over Copernicus, there's some dispute about his ethnicity; he was born in Toruń, all right, but at a time when it was a predominantly German town. So is he Polish or German? (For more on Copernicus, visit his birth house—now a modest museum on the astronomer—just two blocks away, and described later, under "Sights in Toruń").

What's that sweet smell in the air? For Poles, Toruń is synonymous with **gingerbread** *(piernika)*. This Toruń treat can be topped with different kinds of jams or glazes, and/or dipped in chocolate. You'll see gingerbread shops all over town, mostly selling the same stuff. The shop in the Artus Court building on the Old Town Market Square is handy and atmospheric; more are around the corner on ulica Żeglarska (toward the river; the shop on the right near the end of the block has a handy bulk system—point to what looks good and get exactly the amount and types you want).

Having satisfied your ginger tooth, head back to the square and join the human stream down the appropriately named **ulica Szeroka** ("Wide Street"), an enjoyable pedestrian promenade through the heart of town. Just before the road forks at the white Empik building, look down Przedzamcze to the right to see fragments of the town wall. This marks the border between the Old Town and the New Town (chartered only about 30 years later—both in the 13th century). While these areas are both collectively known today as the unified "Old Town," they were quite different in the Middle Ages—each with its own market square, and separated by a wall. (If you're curious to see the New Town Square and Town Hall, continue up ulica Szeroka and bear left at the fork.)

To end our walk, follow the wall to the right, down Przed-zamcze, to reach the **ruins** of a castle built by the Teutonic Knights who were so influential in northern Poland in the Middle Ages. The castle was destroyed in the 15th century by the locals—who, aside from a heap of bricks, left only the tower that housed the Teutonic toilets.

Beyond the castle ruins is the **Vistula** riverbank. The road that runs along the river here is called Bulwar Filadelfijski—for Toruń's sister city in Pennsylvania.

Sights in Toruń

Toruń is more about strolling than it is about sightseeing—the town's museums are underwhelming. Aside from its half-dozen red-brick churches (any of which are worth dropping into), the following attractions are worth considering on a rainy day.

Gingerbread Museum (Muzeum Piernika)

This fun attraction—by far Toruń's liveliest—is an actual, working gingerbread bakery of yore. Barefoot, costumed medieval bakers walk you through the traditional process of rolling, cutting out, baking, and tasting your own batch of gingerbread cookies (30-40 minutes, start to finish). After aging for 12 weeks to achieve the proper consistency, the dough bakes only 12 minutes—or, according to the medieval bakers, about 50 Hail Marys.

Cost and Hours: 11 zł, may have to wait a few minutes for an English guide to help you, daily 9:00-18:00, 2 blocks toward the river from Old Town Market Square at Rabiańska 9, tel. 56-663-6617, www.muzeumpiernika.pl.

Copernicus House (Dom Kopernika)

Filling a pair of beautiful, gabled brick buildings, this dull, over-priced little museum celebrates the hero of Toruń. As much about medieval Toruń as about the famous astronomer, and sprawling over several floors in the two buildings, the exhibits loosely explain Nicolaus Copernicus' life and achievements. While the displays—mostly copies of important documents and paintings, models of his instruments, and English descriptions—are pretty flat, it's mildly interesting to walk around the creaky interiors. The second part of the exhibit is an 18-minute "sound-and-light show" (slideshow with recorded commentary) about medieval Toruń, with a model of the city that lights up dramatically at appropriate moments (ask for English show when you enter). Finally, there's a "World of

POMERANIA

Toruń's Gingerbread" exhibit, about the city's favorite product.

Cost and Hours: Museum only-10 zł, gingerbread exhibit only-10 zł, model/slideshow only-12 zł; combo-ticket for any two-18 zł; May-Sept Tue-Sun 10:00-18:00, Oct-April Tue-Sun 10:00-16:00, closed Mon year-round; Kopernika 15/17, tel. 56-662-7038, www.muzeum.torun.pl. To get to the museum from the Old Town Market Square, head down Żeglarska and take the first right—on Kopernika, of course.

Ethnographic Park (Park Etnograficzny)

This open-air folk museum, while not ranking with Europe's best, is at least your most convenient opportunity to stroll through some traditional buildings from the region. It's in the middle of a pleasant park just outside the Old Town. Even if you're not interested in the museum, the park is a fine place to pass some time.

Cost and Hours: 14 zł; mid-April-June Tue and Thu 9:00-17:00, Wed and Fri 9:00-16:00, Sat-Sun 10:00-18:00; July-Sept Tue, Thu, and Sat-Sun 10:00-18:00, Wed and Fri 9:00-16:00; Oct-mid-April Tue-Fri 9:00-16:00, Sat-Sun 10:00-16:00; closed Mon year-round; Wały Gen. Sikorskiego 19, www.etnomuzeum.pl. To get there from the Old Town Market Square, walk up Chełmińska with the river at your back and the Old Town Hall on your left. Cross the busy road, and you're in the park.

Sleeping in Toruń

Toruń's Old Town has more than its share of good-value hotels (Db-200-300 zł). The TI has a brochure listing the options, and can help you find a room for no extra charge.

$$ Hotel Karczma "Spichrz" ("Granary") is a fresh, atmospheric hotel in a renovated old granary. Its 23 rooms and public spaces are a fun blend of old and new—with huge wooden beams around every corner, and the scent of the restaurant's wood-fired grill wafting through the halls. It's comfortable, central, well-priced, and a little kitschy (Sb-230 zł, Db-290 zł, 10-20 percent cheaper on weekends, tall people may not appreciate low ceilings and beams, elevator, a block off the main drag toward the river at ulica Mostowa 1, tel. 56-657-1140, www.spichrz.pl, hotel@spichrz .pl). The restaurant is also good (30-55-zł grilled meat dishes, daily 12:00-23:00).

$ Hotel Retman ("Rafter") has 29 older but nicely appointed rooms over a restaurant just down the street from the Gingerbread Museum (Sb-190 zł, Db-250 zł; Fri-Sun prices drop to Sb-160 zł, Db-200 zł; ulica Rabiańska 15, tel. 56-657-4460, www.hotel retman.pl, recepcja@hotelretman.pl).

Toruń Connections

Toruń is a handy stopover on the way between Warsaw and Gdańsk. It's on a different train line than Malbork—so visiting both Toruń and the mighty Teutonic castle in the same day is surprisingly time-consuming.

From Toruń by Train to: Warsaw (9/day, 2.75 hours direct, longer with a transfer in Kutno), **Gdańsk** (6/day direct, 3.25-3.75 hours; at least hourly with a transfer in Bydgoszcz, 3-4 hours), **Kraków** (2/day direct, 6.5-8 hours; better to transfer at Warsaw's Zachodnia station: 10/day, 6-6.75 hours), **Berlin** (4/day, 5.75-6 hours, transfer in Poznań).

PRACTICALITIES

This section covers just the basics on traveling in Poland (for much more information, see *Rick Steves' Eastern Europe*). You can find free advice on specific topics at www.ricksteves.com/tips.

Money

Poland uses a currency called the złoty: 3 Polish złoty (zł) = about $1. To roughly convert Polish złoty into dollars, divide by three (e.g., 30 zł = about $10, 85 zł = about $30, 150 zł = about $50).

The standard way for travelers to get złoty is to withdraw money from a cash machine (called a *bankomat* in Poland) using a debit or credit card, ideally with a Visa or MasterCard logo. Before departing, call your bank or credit-card company: Confirm that your card will work overseas, ask about international transaction fees, and alert them that you'll be making withdrawals in Europe. Also ask for the PIN number for your credit card in case it'll help you use Europe's "chip-and-PIN" payment machines (see below); allow time for your bank to mail your PIN to you. Memorizing your credit card's PIN lets you use it at some chip-and-PIN machines—just enter your PIN when prompted. To keep your valuables safe, wear a money belt.

Dealing with "Chip and PIN": While much of Europe is shifting to a "chip-and-PIN" security system for credit and debit cards, Poland still uses the old magnetic-stripe technology. (European chip-and-PIN cards are embedded with an electronic security chip, and require the purchaser to punch in a PIN rather than sign a receipt.) If you happen to encounter chip and PIN, it will probably be at payment machines, such as those at toll roads or self-serve gas pumps. On the outside chance that a machine won't take your card, find a cashier who can make your card work (they can print a receipt for you to sign), or find a machine that takes cash. But don't panic. Most travelers who are carrying only magnetic-stripe cards don't encounter problems. You can always use an ATM to withdraw cash with your magnetic-stripe card, even in countries where people predominantly use chip-and-PIN cards.

Phoning

Smart travelers use the telephone to reserve or reconfirm rooms, reserve restaurants, get directions, research transportation connections, confirm tour times, phone home, and lots more.

To call Poland from the US or Canada: Dial 011-48 and then the phone number, minus its initial zero. (The 011 is our international access code, and 48 is Poland's country code.)

To call Poland from a European country: Dial 00-48 followed by the phone number, minus its initial zero. (The 00 is Europe's international access code.)

To call within Poland: Just dial the whole number, including the initial zero.

To call from Poland to another country: Dial 00 followed by the country code (for example, 1 for the US or Canada), then the area code and number. If you're calling European countries whose phone numbers begin with 0, you'll usually have to omit that 0 when you dial.

Tips on Phoning: A mobile phone—whether an American one that works in Poland, or a European one you buy when you arrive—is handy, but can be pricey. If traveling with a smartphone, switch off data-roaming until you have free Wi-Fi. With Wi-Fi, you can use your smartphone to make free or inexpensive domestic and international calls by taking advantage of a calling app such as Skype or FaceTime.

To make calls without a mobile phone, your best bet is to buy a prepaid phone card to insert into public phone booths. Sold locally at newsstands, these are reasonable for calls within Poland; they work for international calls as well, but can be expensive. (Cheap international phone cards that work with a PIN code, which are common in many European countries, generally aren't available in Poland.)

Calling from your hotel-room phone is usually expensive—ask the rates before you dial. For more on phoning, see www.ricksteves.com/phoning.

Making Hotel Reservations

To ensure the best value, I recommend reserving rooms in advance, particularly during peak season. Email the hotelier with the following key pieces of information: number and type of rooms; number of nights; date of arrival; date of departure; and any special requests. (For a sample form, see the sidebar.) Use the European style for writing dates: day/month/year. Hoteliers typically ask for your credit-card number as a deposit.

Given the economic downturn, hoteliers may be willing to make a deal—try emailing several hotels to ask for their best price. In general, hotel prices can soften if you do any of the following: offer to pay cash, stay at least three nights, or travel off-season.

From:	rick@ricksteves.com
Sent:	Today
To:	info@hotelcentral.com
Subject:	Reservation request for 19-22 July

Dear Hotel Central,

I would like to reserve a room for 2 people for 3 nights, arriving 19 July and departing 22 July. If possible, I would like a quiet room with a double bed and a bathroom inside the room.

Please let me know if you have a room available and the price.

Thank you!
Rick Steves

Eating

Poland offers good food for relatively little money. Polish cuisine has a reputation for being heavy and hearty, with lots of pork, potatoes, and cabbage...which is true. But the food here is also delicious, with more variety than you might expect. For all the details about Polish food, see page 17. Ethnic restaurants provide a welcome change of pace. Seek out Italian, Indian, sushi, Hungarian, German, Ukrainian, and other alternatives (I've recommended several in this book).

Service: Good service is relaxed (slow to an American). You won't get the bill until you ask for it: *"Rachunek?"* (rah-KHOO-nehk). To tip at restaurants that have a waitstaff, round up the bill 5 to 10 percent if you're happy with the service.

Transportation

Public transportation is the best way to connect the cities in this book.

By Train: Poland has an extensive, if dated, rail network; you can reach most towns and cities by train. Since point-to-point tickets are affordable, a rail pass won't likely save you money (but to review your options, see www.ricksteves.com/rail). To research train schedules and fares, visit the Polish rail site, www.rozklad-pkp.pl, or Germany's excellent online timetable, www.bahn.com. While most short-haul journeys do not require a seat reservation, you must reserve on some high-speed trains (such as the Kraków-Warsaw express). It's also smart to reserve a sleeping berth if you're taking a night train. For more tips, see "Train Station Lingo" on page 6.

By Car: It's cheaper to arrange most car rentals from the US. For tips on your insurance options, see www.ricksteves.com/cdw. Bring your driver's license. It's also required to carry an International Driving Permit (IDP), available at your local AAA office ($15 plus two passport-type photos, www.aaa.com). For route planning, try www.viamichelin.com. Poland is building a network of new expressways, but they're far from complete (you'll pay tolls to take completed segments). Instead, locals travel long distances on two-lane country roads. Since each lane is about a lane and a half wide, passing is commonplace. Slower drivers should keep to the far-right of their lane, and not be surprised when faster cars zip past them. A car is a worthless headache in cities—park it safely (get tips from your hotel).

You are required to have your headlights on whenever you're driving—even in broad daylight, and it's mandatory to wear seat belts. For other rules of the Polish road, ask your car-rental company, or check the US State Department website (www.travel.state.gov, search for your country in the "Learn about your destination" box, then click on "Travel and Transportation").

By Plane: Consider covering long distances on a budget flight, which can be cheaper (and much faster) than a train. Poland's national carrier, LOT Airlines (www.lot.com), generally charges reasonable fares for short-distance trips. Or try some no-frills carriers, such as www.wizzair.com, www.easyjet.com, and www.ryanair.com. To compare several budget airlines, see www.skyscanner.com.

Helpful Hints

Emergency Help: For any emergency—whether **medical** or **police**—dial 112. If you have a minor illness, do as the locals do and go to a pharmacist for advice. Or ask at your hotel for help—they'll know of the nearest medical and emergency services. For passport problems, call the **US Embassy** in Warsaw (tel. 022-625-1401) or the **US Consulate** in Kraków (tel. 012-424-5183); or the **Canadian Embassy** in Warsaw (tel. 022-584-3100, toll-free emergency tel. 800-111-4319). For other concerns, get advice from your hotelier.

Theft or Loss: To replace a passport, you'll need to go in person to an embassy or consulate (see above). Cancel and replace your credit and debit cards by calling these 24-hour US numbers collect: Visa—tel. 303/967-1096, MasterCard—tel. 636/722-7111, American Express—tel. 336/393-1111. In Poland, to make a collect call to the US, dial 00-800-111-1111; press zero or stay on the line for an operator. File a police report either on the spot or within a day or two; it's required if you submit an insurance claim for lost or stolen rail passes or travel gear, and can help with replacing your passport or credit and debit cards. Precautionary measures can minimize the effects of loss—back up your digital photos and other files frequently. For more information, see www.ricksteves.com/help.

Time: Poland uses the 24-hour clock. It's the same through 12:00 noon, then keep going: 13:00, 14:00, and so on. Poland, like most of continental Europe, is six/nine hours ahead of the East/ West Coasts of the US.

Holidays and Festivals: Poland celebrates many holidays, which can close sights and attract crowds (book hotel rooms ahead). For information on holidays and festivals, check Poland's website: www.poland.travel. For a simple list showing major— though not all—events, see www.ricksteves.com/festivals.

Numbers and Stumblers: What Americans call the second floor of a building is the first floor in Europe. Europeans write dates as day/month/year, so Christmas is 25/12. Commas are decimal points and vice versa—a dollar and a half is 1,50, and there are 5.280 feet in a mile. Poland uses the metric system: A kilogram is 2.2 pounds; a liter is about a quart; and a kilometer is six-tenths of a mile.

Resources from Rick Steves

This Snapshot guide is excerpted from *Rick Steves' Eastern Europe,* which is one of more than 30 titles in my series of guidebooks on European travel. I also produce a public television series, *Rick Steves' Europe,* and a public radio show, *Travel with Rick Steves.* My website, www.ricksteves.com, offers free travel information, a forum for travelers' comments, guidebook updates, my travel blog, an online travel store, and information on European rail passes and our tours of Europe. If you're bringing a mobile device on your trip, you can download free information from Rick Steves Audio Europe, featuring podcasts of my radio shows, free audio tours of major sights in Europe, and travel interviews about Poland (via www.ricksteves.com/audioeurope, iTunes, Google Play, or the Rick Steves Audio Europe free smartphone app). You can also follow me on Facebook and Twitter.

Additional Resources

Tourist Information: www.poland.travel
Passports and Red Tape: www.travel.state.gov
Packing List: www.ricksteves.com/packing
Travel Insurance: www.ricksteves.com/insurance
Cheap Flights: www.kayak.com
Airplane Carry-on Restrictions: www.tsa.gov
Updates for This Book: www.ricksteves.com/update

How Was Your Trip?

If you'd like to share your tips, concerns, and discoveries after using this book, please fill out the survey at www.ricksteves.com/ feedback. Thanks in advance—it helps a lot.

Polish Survival Phrases

Keep in mind a few Polish pronunciation tips: **w** sounds like "v," **ł** sounds like "w," **ch** is a back-of-your-throat "kh" sound (as in the Scottish "loch"), and **rz** sounds like the "zh" sound in "pleasure." The vowels with a tail (**ą** and **ę**) have a slight nasal "n" sound at the end, similar to French.

English	Polish	Pronunciation
Hello. (formal)	Dzień dobry.	jehn **doh**-brih
Hi. / Bye. (informal)	Cześć.	cheshch
Do you speak English? (asked of a man)	Czy Pan mówi po angielsku?	chih pahn **moo**-vee poh ahn-**gyehl**-skoo
Do you speak English? (asked of a woman)	Czy Pani mówi po angielsku?	chih **pah**-nee **moo**-vee poh ahn-**gyehl**-skoo
Yes. / No.	Tak. / Nie.	tahk / nyeh
I (don't) understand.	(Nie) rozumiem.	(nyeh) roh-**zoo**-myehm
Please. / You're welcome. / Can I help you?	Proszę.	proh-sheh
Thank you (very much).	Dziękuję (bardzo).	jehn-**koo**-yeh (**bard**-zoh)
Excuse me. / I'm sorry.	Przepraszam.	psheh-**prah**-shahm
(No) problem.	(Żaden) problem.	(zhah-dehn) proh-blehm
Good.	Dobrze.	**dohb**-zheh
Goodbye.	Do widzenia.	doh veed-**zay**-nyah
one / two	jeden / dwa	**yeh**-dehn / dvah
three / four	trzy / cztery	tzhih / **chteh**-rih
five / six	pięć / sześć	pyench / sheshch
seven / eight	siedem / osiem	**shyeh**-dehm / **oh**-shehm
nine / ten	dziewięć / dziesięć	**jeh**-vyench / **jeh**-shench
hundred / thousand	sto / tysiąc	stoh / **tih**-shants
How much?	Ile?	**ee**-leh
local currency	złoty (zł)	**zwoh**-tih
Write it.	Napisz to.	**nah**-peesh toh
Is it free?	Czy to jest za darmo?	chih toh yehst zah **dar**-moh
Is it included?	Czy jest to wliczone?	chih yehst toh vlee-**choh**-neh
Where can I find / buy...?	Gdzie mogę dostać / kupić...?	guh-**dyeh** moh-geh **doh**-statch / **koo**-peech
I'd like...(said by a man)	Chciałbym...	**khchaw**-beem
I'd like...(said by a woman)	Chciałabym...	**khchah**-wah-beem
We'd like...	Chcielibyśmy...	**khchehl**-ee-bish-mih
...a room.	...pokój.	**poh**-kooey
...a ticket to ___.	...bilet do ___.	**bee**-leht doh ___
Is it possible?	Czy jest to możliwe?	chih yehst toh mohzh-**lee**-veh
Where is...?	Gdzie jest...?	guh-**dyeh** yehst
...the train station	...dworzec kolejowy	**dvoh**-zhehts koh-leh-**yoh**-vih
...the bus station	...dworzec autobusowy	**dvoh**-zhehts ow-toh-boos-**oh**-vih
...the tourist information office	...informacja turystyczna	een-for-**maht**-syah too-ris-**titch**-nah
...the toilet	...toaleta	toh-ah-**leh**-tah
men / women	męska / damska	**mehn**-skah / **dahm**-skah
left / right	lewo / prawo	**leh**-voh / **prah**-voh
straight	prosto	**proh**-stoh
At what time...	O której godzinie...	oh kuh-**too**-ray gohd-**zhee**-nyeh
...does this open / close?	...będzie otwarte / zamknięte?	**bend**-zheh oht-**vahr**-teh / zahm-**knyehn**-teh
Just a moment.	Chwileczkę.	khvee-**letch**-keh
now / soon / later	teraz / niedługo / później	**teh**-rahz / nyed-**woo**-goh / **poozh**-nyey
today / tomorrow	dzisiaj / jutro	**jee**-shigh / **yoo**-troh

In a Polish Restaurant

English	Polish	Pronunciation
I'd like to reserve... (said by a man)	Chciałbym zarezerwować...	**khchaw**-beem zah-reh-zehr-**voh**-vahch
I'd like to reserve... (said by a woman)	Chciałabym zarezerwować...	**khchah**-wah-beem zah-reh-zehr-**voh**-vahch
We'd like to reserve...	Chcielibyśmy zarezerwować...	**khchehl**-ee-bish-mih zah-reh-zehr-**voh**-vahch
...a table for one person / two people.	...stolik na jedną osobę / dwie osoby.	**stoh**-leek nah **yehd**-now oh-**soh**-beh /dvyeh oh-**soh**-bih
Non-smoking.	Niepalący	nyeh-pah-**lohnt**-sih
Is this table free?	Czy ten stolik jest wolny?	chih tehn **stoh**-leek yehst **vohl**-nih
Can I help you?	W czym mogę pomóc?	vchim **moh**-geh **poh**-moots
The menu (in English), please.	Menu (po angielsku), proszę.	**meh**-noo (poh ahn-**gyehl**-skoo) **proh**-sheh
service (not) included	usługa (nie) wliczona	oos-**woo**-gah (nyeh) **vlee**-choh-nah
cover charge	wstęp	vstenp
"to go"	na wynos	nah **vih**-nohs
with / without	z / bez	z / behz
and / or	i / lub	ee / loob
milk bar (cheap cafeteria)	bar mleczny	bar **mletch**-nih
fixed-price meal (of the day)	zestaw (dnia)	**zehs**-tahv (dih-**nyah**)
specialty of the house	specjalność zakładu	speht-**syahl**-nohshch zah-**kwah**-doo
half portion	pół porcji	poow **ports**-yee
daily special	danie dnia	**dah**-nyeh dih-**nyah**
appetizers	przystawki	pshih-**stahv**-kee
bread	chleb	khlehb
cheese	ser	sehr
sandwich	kanapka	kah-**nahp**-kah
soup	zupa	**zoo**-pah
salad	sałatka	sah-**waht**-kah
meat	mięso	**myehn**-soh
poultry	drób	droob
fish	ryba	**rih**-bah
seafood	owoce morza	oh-**voht**-seh **moh**-zhah
fruit	owoce	oh-**voht**-seh
vegetables	warzywa	vah-**zhih**-vah
dessert	deser	**deh**-sehr
(tap) water	woda (z kranu)	**voh**-dah (**skrah**-noo)
mineral water	woda mineralna	**voh**-dah mee-neh-**rahl**-nah
carbonated / not carbonated	gazowana / niegazowana	gah-zoh-**vah**-nah / **nyeh**-gah-zoh-vah-nah
milk	mleko	**mleh**-koh
(orange) juice	sok (pomarańczowy)	sohk (poh-mah-rayn-**choh**-vih)
coffee	kawa	**kah**-vah
tea	herbata	hehr-**bah**-tah
wine	wino	**vee**-noh
red / white	czerwone / białe	chehr-**voh**-neh / bee-**ah**-weh
sweet / dry / semi-dry	słodkie / wytrawne / półwytrawne	**swoht**-kyeh / vih-**trahv**-neh / poow-vih-**trahv**-neh
glass / bottle	szklanka / butelka	**shklahn**-kah / boo-**tehl**-kah
beer	piwo	**pee**-voh
vodka	wódka	**vood**-kah
Cheers!	Na zdrowie!	nah **zdroh**-vyeh
Enjoy your meal.	Smacznego.	smatch-**neh**-goh
More. / Another.	Więcej. / Inny.	**vyehnt**-say / **ee**-nih-nih
The same.	Taki sam.	**tah**-kee sahm
the bill	rachunek	rah-**khoo**-nehk
I'll pay.	Ja płacę.	yah **pwaht**-seh
tip	napiwek	nah-**pee**-vehk
Delicious!	Pyszne!	**pish**-neh

INDEX

Explore Europe

At ricksteves.com you can browse through thousands of articles, videos, photos and radio interviews, plus find a wealth of money-saving travel tips for planning your dream trip. And with our mobile-friendly website, you can easily access all this great travel information anywhere you go.

TV Shows

Preview the places you'll visit by watching entire half-hour episodes of Rick Steves' Europe (choose from all 100 shows) on-demand, for free.

ricksteves.com

your travel dreams into affordable reality

Radio Interviews

Enjoy ready access to Rick's vast library of radio interviews covering travel

tips and cultural insights that relate specifically to your Europe travel plans.

Travel Forums

Learn, ask, share! Our online community of savvy travelers is a great resource for first-time travelers to Europe, as well as seasoned pros. You'll find forums on each country, plus travel tips and restaurant/hotel reviews. You can even ask one of our well-traveled staff to chime in with an opinion.

Travel News

Subscribe to our free Travel News e-newsletter, and get monthly updates from Rick on what's happening in Europe.

Audio Europe™

Pack Light and Right

Rick Steves has

Experience maximum Europe

Save time and energy

This guidebook is your independent-travel toolkit. But for all it delivers, it's still up to you to devote the time and energy it takes to manage the preparation and logistics that are essential for a happy trip. If that's a hassle, there's a solution.

Rick Steves Tours

A Rick Steves tour takes you to Europe's most interesting places with great

with minimum stress

guides and small groups of 28 or less. We follow Rick's favorite itineraries, ride in comfy buses, stay in family-run hotels, and bring you intimately close to the Europe you've traveled so far to see. Most importantly, we take away the logistical headaches so you can focus on the fun.

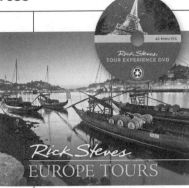

customers—along with us on 40 different itineraries, from Ireland to Italy to Istanbul. Is a Rick Steves tour the right fit for your travel dreams? Find out at ricksteves.com, where you can also get Rick's latest tour catalog and free Tour Experience DVD.

Join the fun

This year we'll take 18,000 free-spirited travelers— nearly half of them repeat

Europe is best experienced with happy travel partners. We hope you can join us.

See our itineraries at ricksteves.com

EUROPE GUIDES

Best of Europe
Eastern Europe
Europe Through the Back Door
Mediterranean Cruise Ports
Northern European Cruise Ports

COUNTRY GUIDES

Croatia & Slovenia
England
France
Germany
Great Britain
Ireland
Italy
Portugal
Scandinavia
Spain
Switzerland

CITY & REGIONAL GUIDES

Amsterdam, Bruges & Brussels
Barcelona
Budapest
Florence & Tuscany
Greece: Athens & the Peloponnese
Istanbul
London
Paris
Prague & the Czech Republic
Provence & the French Riviera
Rome
Venice
Vienna, Salzburg & Tirol

SNAPSHOT GUIDES

Berlin
Bruges & Brussels
Copenhagen & the Best of
    Denmark
Dublin
Dubrovnik
Hill Towns of Central Italy
Italy's Cinque Terre
Krakow, Warsaw & Gdansk
Lisbon
Madrid & Toledo
Milan & the Italian Lakes District
Munich, Bavaria & Salzburg
Naples & the Amalfi Coast
Northern Ireland
Norway
Scotland
Sevilla, Granada & Southern Spain
Stockholm

POCKET GUIDES

Amsterdam
Athens
Barcelona
Florence
London
Paris
Rome
Venice

Rick Steves guidebooks are published by Avalon Travel,
a member of the Perseus Books Group.

NOW AVAILABLE:
eBOOKS, DVD & BLU-RAY

TRAVEL CULTURE

Europe 101
European Christmas
Postcards from Europe
Travel as a Political Act

eBOOKS

Nearly all Rick Steves guides are available as eBooks. Check with your favorite bookseller.

RICK STEVES' EUROPE DVDs

11 New Shows 2013–2014
Austria & the Alps
Eastern Europe
England & Wales
European Christmas
European Travel Skills & Specials
France
Germany, BeNeLux & More
Greece, Turkey & Portugal
Iran
Ireland & Scotland
Italy's Cities
Italy's Countryside
Scandinavia
Spain
Travel Extras

BLU-RAY

Celtic Charms
Eastern Europe Favorites
European Christmas
Italy Through the Back Door
Mediterranean Mosaic
Surprising Cities of Europe

PHRASE BOOKS & DICTIONARIES

French
French, Italian & German
German
Italian
Portuguese
Spanish

JOURNALS

Rick Steves Pocket Travel Journal
Rick Steves Travel Journal

PLANNING MAPS

Britain, Ireland & London
Europe
France & Paris
Germany, Austria & Switzerland
Ireland
Italy
Spain & Portugal

RickSteves.com @RickSteves

Rick Steves books and DVDs are available at bookstores
and through online booksellers.

Photo © Patricia Feaster.

ABOUT THE AUTHORS

RICK STEVES

Since 1973, Rick Steves has spent 100 days every year exploring Europe. Along with writing and researching a bestselling series of guidebooks, Rick produces a public television series *(Rick Steves' Europe)*, a public radio show *(Travel with Rick Steves)*, and an app and podcast *(Rick Steves Audio Europe)*; writes a nationally syndicated newspaper column; organizes guided tours that take over 15,000 travelers to Europe annually; and offers an information-packed website (www.ricksteves.com). With the help of his hardworking staff of 90 at Rick Steves' Europe—in Edmonds, Washington, just north of Seattle—Rick's mission is to make European travel fun, affordable, and culturally enlightening for Americans.

Connect with Rick:

facebook.com/RickSteves twitter: @RickSteves

CAMERON HEWITT

Cameron Hewitt grew up listening to the Polish nursery rhymes of his grandfather, Jan Paweł Dąbrowski. Today he ventures to Eastern Europe often—to simmer in Budapest's thermal baths, twist through the Julian Alps on corkscrew roads, commune with his Polish roots, laugh at a good Czech joke, and set sail on the glimmering Adriatic. Cameron, who also writes and edits other guidebooks for Rick Steves, lives in Seattle with his wife Shawna.

Avalon Travel
a member of the Perseus Books Group
1700 Fourth Street
Berkeley, CA 94710

For the latest on Rick's lectures, guidebooks, tours, public radio show, and public television
series, contact Rick Steves' Europe, 130 Fourth Avenue North, Edmonds, WA 98020,
425/771-8303, fax 425/771-0833, www.ricksteves.com,
rick@ricksteves.com.

ISBN 978-1-61238-999-8

Rick Steves' Europe
Managing Editor: Risa Laib
Editorial & Production Manager: Jennifer Madison Davis
Editors: Glenn Eriksen, Tom Griffin, Suzanne Kotz, Cathy Lu, Carrie Shepherd
Editorial Intern: Kimberly Downing
Maps & Graphics: David C. Hoerlein, Sandra Hundacker, Lauren Mills, Mary Rostad

Avalon Travel
Senior Editor & Series Manager: Madhu Prasher
Editor: Jamie Andrade
Assistant Editor: Maggie Ryan
Copy Editor: Denise Silva
Proofreader: Annette Kohl
Indexer: Stephen Callahan
Production & Typesetting: McGuire Barber Design, Christine DeLorenzo
Cover Design: Kimberly Glyder Design
Maps & Graphics: Kat Bennett, Mike Morgenfeld

Photography: Cameron Hewitt, Rick Steves, David C. Hoerlein, Honza Vihan, Rhonda
Pelikan, Gene Openshaw, Dominic Bonuccelli, Gretchen Strauch, Sandra Hundacker, Debi
Jo Michael
Cover Photo: Kraków Renaissance Sukiennice (Cloth Hall, Drapers' Hall) and St. Mary's
Church © Jan Wlodarczyk / Alamy

Want More Eastern Europe?
Maximize the experience with Rick Steves as your guide

Guidebooks
Prague, Budapest and Croatia guides make side-trips smooth and affordable

Planning Maps
Use the map that's in sync with your guidebook

Rick's DVDs
Preview where you're going with 8 shows on Eastern Europe

Free! Rick's Audio Europe™ App
Hear Eastern Europe travel tips from Rick's radio shows

Small-Group Tours
Rick offers great itineraries through Eastern Europe

For all the details, visit ricksteves.com